THE SACRED PIPE

**Black Elk's
Account of the
Seven Rites of the
Oglala Sioux**

Recorded & Edited by
Joseph Epes Brown

BLACK ELK, HOLY MAN OF THE OGLALA

by Michael F.
Steltenkamp

MJF BOOKS

NEW YORK

Published by MJF Books
Fine Communications
Two Lincoln Square
60 West 66th Street
New York, NY 10023

Library of Congress Catalog Card Number 96-75885
ISBN 1-56731-088-5

The Sacred Pipe Copyright © 1953, 1989 by the University of Oklahoma Press, Norman, Publishing Division of the University.

Black Elk: Holy Man of the Oglala Copyright © 1993 by the University of Oklahoma Press, Norman, Publishing Division of the University.

This edition published by arrangement with the University of Oklahoma Press, Norman

Manufactured in the United States of America

MJF Books and the MJF colophon are trademarks of Fine Creative Media, Inc.

10 9 8 7 6 5 4 3 2 1

THE SACRED PIPE

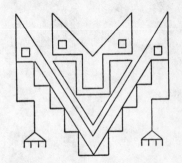

BLACK ELK'S ACCOUNT

OF THE SEVEN RITES OF THE OGLALA SIOUX

RECORDED & EDITED BY

JOSEPH EPES BROWN

Black Elk (*Photograph by J. E. Brown*)

To my people the Sioux

—BLACK ELK

TABLE OF CONTENTS

ILLUSTRATIONS

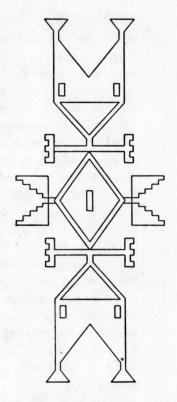

I first learned of the Lakota Sioux sage, Black Elk (Hehaka Sapa), through John Neihardt's *Black Elk Speaks,* a poetic work of great value that first appeared in 1932, published by William Morrow and Company of New York. Because of the war effort at that time, the original copper plates had to be destroyed, and the first edition was out of print soon after publication. During several trips to Europe immediately after the war, I was able to make arrangements through close friends for French, German, and Italian translations, all of which became very popular and have since appeared in many continuing editions.

As a lifelong student of Native American history, traditions, and lifeways, I understood the importance of the Black Elk lore and wished to meet the old man, even though Neihardt had advised me that Black Elk would not speak to me. After much traveling, however, I found Hehaka Sapa in an old canvas wall tent in Nebraska, where his extended family was engaged in digging potatoes. I entered into the tent with great anxiety because of Neihardt's discouraging advice. On my journey west an old Assiniboin had given me a traditional Plains ceremonial pipe, which the old Sage and I smoked in silence. When the ritual smoking was completed, the old man turned to me and asked why I had taken so long in getting there, for he had been expecting my coming. He then invited me to spend the winter with him and his extended family at their home on Wounded Knee Creek, Pine Ridge Reservation. He wished to relate the history and meanings of the seven sacred rites of his people, a project that was completed over several years with much of the translating being done by his son Benjamin Black Elk.

I wish to express great gratitude to all members of the Black Elk extended family and am honored by continuing contacts over the years that affirm that here adoptions into a family are permanent and continuing, never casual, and they involve continuing mutual responsibilities.

JOSEPH EPES BROWN

Stevensville, Montana
January, 1988

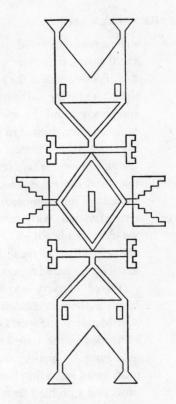

Black Elk first became known to a wide range of readers in 1932 through John G. Neihardt's *Black Elk Speaks: The Life Story of a Holy Man of the Oglala Sioux*. Neihardt's poetic and sympathetic treatment of the old man's life and mission raised the question as to who, in fact, Black Elk really was. For if the account was faithful to only the essential qualities of the man, it was clear that even from a people noted for their large share of great personalities, here was an unusual man of vision; a holy man in the full sense of this term, and a man upon whom destiny, in a time of cultural crisis, had placed a heavy burden of responsibility for the spiritual welfare of his people. Here, also, could be an important message for the larger world.

I went to find Black Elk in the fall of 1947. After I had followed his traces across many of the Western states, we finally met in an old canvas wall tent on a Nebraska farm where his family and other members of their band were employed in harvesting potatoes. During that first encounter we simply sat side by side on a sheepskin, and silently smoked the red stone pipe which I had brought with me as an offering in the traditional manner. Partly crippled, almost completely blind, he seemed a pitiful old man as he sat there hunched over, dressed in poor, cast-off clothing. But the beauty of his face and the reverent quality of his movements as he smoked the pipe revealed that Neihardt had given to us the essence of the man, and the subsequent years spent with Black Elk have confirmed this initial impression. Knowing that Black Elk usually had refused to talk with many other people, it was with relief and wonder that I heard his first words: he had anticipated my coming, and wished me to spend that winter with him, for he had much to tell of the sacred things before they all should pass away.

I lived that very cold winter with Black Elk and his generous family in their little hewn-log house under the pine-covered bluffs near Manderson, South Dakota. Everything the old man told me I recorded in the time available when we were not hunting for wild game, or hauling water from the nearest hand-pump eight miles away, or cutting hardwood in the valley bottom for the iron stove, and I profited from this rigorous life which his family and my many new relatives shared with me.

I am fortunate in having met at least some of those men of the old days who possessed great human and spiritual qualities. But Black Elk had a special quality of power and kindliness and a sense of mission that was unique, and I am sure it was recognized by all who had the opportunity of knowing him.

According to his account, Black Elk was born in 1862. Therefore he had known the times when his people still had the freedom of the plains and hunted the bison; he had fought against the white men at the Little Big Horn and on Wounded Knee Creek. He was a cousin to the famous chief and holy man, Crazy Horse, and had known Sitting Bull, Red Cloud, and American Horse. Although Black Elk spoke no English, he had observed much of the white man's world, having traveled with Buffalo Bill to Italy, France, and England, where he danced for Queen Victoria—

"Grandmother England." But whether hunting, traveling, or fighting, Black Elk was not as other men are. During his youth he had been instructed in the sacred lore of his people by the great men, among whom were Whirlwind Chaser, Black Road, and the sage Elk Head, Keeper of the Sacred Pipe, from whom he learned the history and meanings of his people's spiritual heritage. With this understanding Black Elk prayed and fasted at length, until he himself became one of the wise men, receiving many visions through which he gained special powers to be used for the good of his nation.

This responsibility to "bring to life the flowering tree of his people" haunted Black Elk all his life and caused him much suffering. Although he had been given the power to lead his people in the ways of his grandfathers, he did not understand by what means the vision could be fulfilled. It was certainly due to this pervasive sense of mission that Black Elk wished to make this book, explaining the major rites of the Oglala Sioux, in the hope that in this manner his own people, as well as the white men, would gain a better understanding of the truths of their Indian traditions.

It has now been more than twenty years since Black Elk last spoke, and there have occurred many changes which demand that his message—and, indeed, similar messages of other traditionally oriented peoples—be placed in new perspective and in a new light. At the time when Black Elk was lamenting the broken hoop of his people's nation, it was generally believed, even by the specialists, that it would be only a matter of time—very little time in fact—until the Indians, with their seemingly archaic and anachronistic cultures, would be completely assimilated into a larger American society which was convinced of its superiority and the validity of its goals.

We are still very far from being aware of the dimensions and ramifications of our ethnocentric illusions. Nevertheless, by the very nature of things we are now forced to undergo a process of intense self-examination; to engage in a serious re-evaluation of the premises and orientations of our society. The inescapable reality of the ecological crisis, for example, has shattered for many a kind of dream world, and has forced us not only to seek immediate solutions to the kinds of problems which a highly developed technology has fostered, but also, and above all, to look to our basic values concerning life and the nature and destiny of man. The new generations today may not as yet be sure of the most effective means by which to further this process of re-evaluation, but many are looking with sincerity to the kinds of models which are represented by the American Indians.

In their relationships to this troubled America, Indian groups are seen to be situated across a wide spectrum of positions. On the one hand are the few traditional and conservative groups which, against enormous pressures, have miraculously remained very close to the essence of their ancient and still viable life-ways; and on the other hand are those groups which have been completely assimilated within the larger American society. Yet today, virtually all Indian groups who retain any degree of self-identity are now also re-evaluating, and giving positive valuation to, the fundamental premises of their own traditional cultures. They are also re-examining, through a wide range of means and expressions, their relationships to a larger society which today tends to represent diminishing attractions.

If there is validity to the above statements, it seems clear that it is too early to say that Black Elk's mission to bring his people back to "the good red road" has failed as he thought it had. Rather, it may be succeeding in ways which he could not have anticipated.

As an Oglala Sioux, Black Elk belonged to one of the seven sub-bands of the Western Teton, all of which speak the Lakota dialect of a Siouan language. These Western Teton are one of the seven bands, or "Seven Council Fires," of the Dakota (the "Allied"), which is one of the nations belonging to the large Siouan linguistic family. This linguistic group also includes the Assiniboin, Crow, Hidatsa, Iowa, Kansa, Mandan, Missouri, Omaha, Osage, Oto, Ponca, and Quapaw. According to the early history of the Dakota, they were established in the sixteenth century on the headwaters of the Mississippi, and in the seventeenth century they were driven westward from Minnesota by their enemies the Chippewa. In leaving the forests and lakes the Dakota substituted the horse for the bark canoe with remarkable ease, and in the nineteenth century they were known and feared as one of the most powerful nations of the prairies; indeed, it was these Dakota Sioux who offered perhaps the strongest resistance of all the Indian groups to the westward movement of the whites.

This account of the sacred pipe and the rites of the Sioux, was handed down orally by the former "keeper of the sacred pipe," Elk Head (*Hehaka Pa*), to three men. Of these three, Black Elk was the only one living at the time this history was written. (Black Elk died in August, 1950.) When Elk Head gave this account to Black Elk, he told him that it must be handed down. For as long as it is known, and for as long as the pipe is used, their people will live; but as soon as the pipe is forgotten, the people will be without a center and they will perish.

I wish to acknowledge my gratitude to Benjamin Black Elk, who acted as interpreter for this work and who is the son of Black Elk, to whom we owe this book. It is unusual to have an interpreter who understands both English and Lakota perfectly, and who is also familiar with the wisdom and rites of his people. I wish also to mention Benjamin's wife, Ellen Black Elk, a remarkable person of strong faith and character, who with quiet dignity always saw to it that everyone in her warm home was fed and cared for. Her death in September of 1970 was a loss for all who knew her. Black Elk's close friend Little Warrior assisted us in many ways.

I also acknowledge my gratitude to the Smithsonian Institution for the Barry photograph of Sitting Bull, and to the Illuminated Photo-Ad Service of Sioux Falls, South Dakota, who gave permission for the use of their photograph of the seven Sioux who participated in the battle of the Little Big Horn. These warriors were all close friends of Black Elk.

JOSEPH EPES BROWN

Bloomington, Indiana
February, 1971

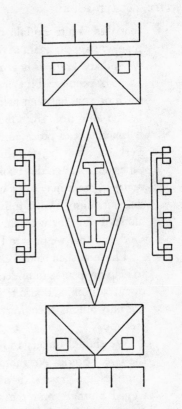

In the great vision which came to me in my youth, when I had known only nine winters, there was something which has seemed to me to be of greater and greater importance as the moons have passed by. It is about our sacred pipe and its importance to our people.

We have been told by the white men, or at least by those who are Christian, that God sent to men His son, who would restore order and peace upon the earth; and we have been told that Jesus the Christ was crucified, but that he shall come again at the Last Judgment, the end of this world or cycle. This I understand and know that it is true, but the white men should know that for the red people too, it was the will of *Wakan-Tanka,* the Great Spirit, that an animal turn itself into a two-legged person in order to bring the most holy pipe to His people; and we too were taught that this White Buffalo Cow Woman who brought our sacred pipe will appear again at the end of this "world," a coming which we Indians know is now not very far off.

Most people call it a "peace pipe," yet now there is no peace on earth or even between neighbors, and I have been told that it has been a long time since there has been peace in the world. There is much talk of peace among the Christians, yet this is just talk. Perhaps it may be, and this is my prayer that, through our sacred pipe, and through this book in which I shall explain what our pipe really is, peace may come to those peoples who can understand, an understanding which must be of the heart and not of the head alone. Then they will realize that we Indians know the One true God, and that we pray to Him continually.

I have wished to make this book through no other desire than to help my people in understanding the greatness and truth of our own tradition, and also to help in bringing peace upon the earth, not only among men, but within men and between the whole of creation.

We should understand well that all things are the works of the Great Spirit. We should know that He is within all things: the trees, the grasses, the rivers, the mountains, and all the four-legged animals, and the winged peoples; and even more important, we should understand that He is also above all these things and peoples. When we do understand all this deeply in our hearts, then we will fear, and love, and know the Great Spirit, and then we will be and act and live as He intends.

BLACK ELK

Manderson, S. D.

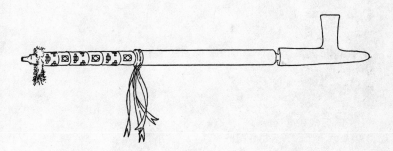

CHAPTER I

THE GIFT OF THE SACRED PIPE

Early one morning, very many winters ago, two Lakota were out hunting with their bows and arrows, and as they were standing on a hill looking for game, they saw in the distance something coming towards them in a very strange and wonderful manner. When this mysterious thing came nearer to them, they saw that it was a very beautiful woman, dressed in white buckskin, and bearing a bundle on her back. Now this woman was so good to look at that one of the Lakota had bad intentions and told his friend of his desire, but this good man said that he must not have such thoughts, for surely this is a *wakan* woman.[1] The mysterious person was now very close to the men, and then putting down her bundle, she asked the one with bad intentions to come over to her. As the

[1] Throughout this work I shall translate the Lakota word *wakan* as "holy" or "sacred," rather than as "power" or "powerful" as used by some

young man approached the mysterious woman, they were both covered by a great cloud, and soon when it lifted the sacred woman was standing there, and at her feet was the man with the bad thoughts who was now nothing but bones, and terrible snakes were eating him.[2]

"Behold what you see!" the strange woman said to the good man. "I am coming to your people and wish to talk with your chief *Hehlokecha Najin* [Standing Hollow Horn]. Return to him, and tell him to prepare a large tipi in which he should gather all his people, and make ready for my coming. I wish to tell you something of great importance!"

The young man then returned to the tipi of his chief, and told him all that had happened: that this *wakan* woman was coming to visit them and that they must all prepare. The chief, Standing Hollow Horn, then had several tipis taken down, and from them a great lodge was made as the sacred woman had instructed.[3] He sent out a crier to tell the people to put on their best buckskin clothes and to gather immediately in the lodge. The people were, of course, all very excited as they waited in the great lodge for the coming of the holy woman, and everybody was wondering where this mysterious woman came from and what it was that she wished to say.

Soon the young men who were watching for the coming of the *wakan* person announced that they saw something in the dis-

-----

ethnologists. This latter term may be a true translation, yet is not really complete, for with the Sioux, and with all traditional peoples in general, the "power" (really the sacredness) of a being or a thing is in proportion to its nearness to its prototype; or better, it is in proportion to the ability of the object or act to reflect most directly the principle or principles which are in *Wakan-Tanka,* the Great Spirit, who is One.

[2] Black Elk emphasized that this should not only be taken as an event in time, but also as an eternal truth. "Any man," he said, "who is attached to the senses and to the things of this world, is one who lives in ignorance and is being consumed by the snakes which represent his own passions."

[3] The Sioux ceremonial lodge is constructed with twenty-eight poles. One of these poles is the "key," holding up all the others, and this pole the holy men say represents *Wakan-Tanka,* who sustains the universe, which is represented by the lodge as a whole.

tance approaching them in a beautiful manner, and then suddenly she entered the lodge, walked around sun-wise,[4] and stood in front of Standing Hollow Horn.[5] She took from her back the bundle, and holding it with both hands in front of the chief, said: "Behold this and always love it! It is *lela wakan* [very sacred], and you must treat it as such. No impure man should ever be allowed to see it, for within this bundle there is a sacred pipe. With this you will, during the winters to come, send your voices to *Wakan-Tanka,* your Father and Grandfather."[6]

After the mysterious woman said this, she took from the bundle a pipe, and also a small round stone which she placed upon the ground. Holding the pipe up with its stem to the heavens, she said: "With this sacred pipe you will walk upon the Earth; for the

[4] The sun-wise or clockwise circumambulation is almost always used by the Sioux; occasionally, however, the counter-clockwise movement is used in a dance or some occasion prior to or after a great catastrophe, for this movement is in imitation of the Thunder-beings who always act in an anti-natural way and who come in a terrifying manner, often bringing destruction.

The reason for the sun-wise circumambulation was once explained by Black Elk in this manner: "Is not the south the source of life, and does not the flowering stick truly come from there? And does not man advance from there toward the setting sun of his life? Then does he not approach the colder north where the white hairs are? And does he not then arrive, if he lives, at the source of light and understanding, which is the east? Then does he not return to where he began, to his second childhood, there to give back his life to all life, and his flesh to the earth whence it came? The more you think about this, the more meaning you will see in it." (*Black Elk Speaks,* recorded by John G. Neihardt).

[5] Standing Hollow Horn, as leader of his people, should be seated at the west, the place of honor; for in sitting at the west of a tipi, one faces the door, or east, from which comes the light, representing wisdom, and this illumination a leader must always possess if he is to guide his people in a sacred manner.

[6] *Wakan-Tanka* as Grandfather is the Great Spirit independent of manifestation, unqualified, unlimited, identical to the Christian Godhead, or to the Hindu *Brahma-Nirguna. Wakan-Tanka* as Father is the Great Spirit considered in relation to His manifestation, either as Creator. Preserver, or Destroyer, identical to the Christian God, or to the Hindu *Brahma-Saguna.*

Earth is your Grandmother and Mother,[7] and She is sacred. Every step that is taken upon Her should be as a prayer. The bowl of this pipe is of red stone; it is the Earth. Carved in the stone and facing the center is this buffalo calf who represents all the four-leggeds[8] who live upon your Mother. The stem of the pipe is of wood, and this represents all that grows upon the Earth. And these twelve feathers which hang here where the stem fits into the bowl are from *Wanbli Galeshka,* the Spotted Eagle,[9] and they represent the eagle and all the wingeds of the air. All these peoples, and all the things of the universe, are joined to you who smoke the pipe—all send their voices to *Wakan-Tanka,* the Great Spirit.

[7] As in the distinction made within *Wakan-Tanka* between Grandfather and Father, so the Earth is considered under two aspects, that of Mother and Grandmother. The former is the earth considered as the producer of all growing forms, in act; whereas Grandmother refers to the ground or substance of all growing things—potentiality. This distinction is the same as that made by the Christian Scholastics between *natura naturans* and *natura naturata.*

[8] The buffalo was to the Sioux the most important of all four-legged animals, for it supplied their food, their clothing, and even their houses, which were made from the tanned hides. Because the buffalo contained all these things within himself, and for many other reasons, he was a natural symbol of the universe, the totality of all manifested forms. Everything is symbolically contained within this animal: the earth and all that grows from her, all animals, and even the two-legged peoples; and each specific part of the beast represents for the Indian, one of these "parts" of creation. Also the buffalo has four legs, and these represent the four ages which are an integral condition of creation.

[9] Since *Wanbli Galeshka* (the Spotted Eagle) flies the highest of all created creatures and sees everything, he is regarded as *Wakan-Tanka* under certain aspects. He is a solar bird, His feathers being regarded as rays of the sun, and when one is carried or worn by the Indian it represents, or rather *is,* the "Real Presence." In wearing the eagle-feathered "war-bonnet," the wearer actually becomes the eagle, which is to say that he identifies himself, his real Self, with *Wakan-Tanka.*

The Spotted Eagle corresponds exactly, in the Hindu tradition, to the *Buddhi,* which is the Intellect, or the formless and transcendant principle of all manifestation; further, the *Buddhi* is often expressed as being a ray directly emanating from the *Atma,* the spiritual sun.

From this it should be clear what is really being expressed in the often misunderstood Ghost Dance song: *"Wanbli galeshka wana ni he o who e,"* "The Spotted Eagle is coming to carry me away."

When you pray with this pipe, you pray for and with everything."

The *wakan* woman then touched the foot of the pipe to the round stone which lay upon the ground, and said: "With this pipe you will be bound to all your relatives: your Grandfather and Father, your Grandmother and Mother. This round rock, which is made of the same red stone as the bowl of the pipe, your Father *Wakan-Tanka* has also given to you. It is the Earth, your Grandmother and Mother, and it is where you will live and increase. This Earth which He has given to you is red, and the two-leggeds who live upon the Earth are red; and the Great Spirit has also given to you a red day, and a red road.[10] All of this is sacred and so do not forget! Every dawn as it comes is a holy event, and every day is holy, for the light comes from your Father *Wakan-Tanka;* and also you must always remember that the two-leggeds and all the other peoples who stand upon this earth are sacred and should be treated as such.

"From this time on, the holy pipe will stand upon this red Earth, and the two-leggeds will take the pipe and will send their voices to *Wakan-Tanka*. These seven circles[11] which you see on the stone have much meaning, for they represent the seven rites in which the pipe will be used. The first large circle represents the first rite which I shall give to you, and the other six circles represent the rites which will in time be revealed to you directly.[12] Stand-

[10] The "red road" is that which runs north and south and is the good or straight way, for to the Sioux the north is purity and the south is the source of life. This "red road" is thus similar to the Christian "straight and narrow way"; it is the vertical of the cross, or the *ec-cirata el-mustaqim* of the Islamic tradition.

On the other hand, there is the "blue" or "black road" of the Sioux, which runs east and west and which is the path of error and destruction. He who travels on this path is, Black Elk has said, "one who is distracted, who is ruled by his senses, and who lives for himself rather than for his people."

[11] The seven circles are arranged in this manner:

[12] According to Black Elk, two of these rites were known to the Sioux prior to the coming of the sacred Woman; these were the purification rites of the sweat lodge, and the *Hanblecheyapi* (crying for a vision); the ritual of the pipe was, however, now added to both of these.

ing Hollow Horn, be good to these gifts and to your people, for they are *wakan!* With this pipe the two-leggeds will increase, and there will come to them all that is good. From above *Wakan-Tanka* has given to you this sacred pipe, so that through it you may have knowledge. For this great gift you should always be grateful! But now before I leave I wish to give to you instructions for the first rite in which your people will use this pipe.

"It should be for you a sacred day when one of your people dies. You must then keep his soul[13] as I shall teach you, and through this you will gain much power; for if this soul is kept, it will increase in you your concern and love for your neighbor. So long as the person, in his soul, is kept with your people, through him you will be able to send your voice to *Wakan-Tanka*.[14]

"It should also be a sacred day when a soul is released and returns to its home, *Wakan-Tanka,* for on this day four women will be made holy, and they will in time bear children who will walk the path of life in a sacred manner, setting an example to your people. Behold Me, for it is I that they will take in their mouths, and it is through this that they will become *wakan.*

"He who keeps the soul of a person must be a good and pure

[13] In translating the Lakota word *wanagi,* I have used the term "soul" in preference to "spirit," which has been used by many ethnologists; I believe this term, understood in its scholastic Christian sense, to be more accurate, for what is kept and purified in this rite is really the totality of the psychic entities of the being, which, although localized within a particular gross form (usually the lock of hair), are really of a subtle nature, intermediate between the gross body and the pure spirit. At the same time it should always be remembered that it is the pure spirit, which is the presence of *Wakan-Tanka,* which is at the "center" of both the subtle and gross entities. The soul is thus kept in the manner to be described so that there may be a prolongation of the individual state and, thus, that the subtle or psychic part of the being may be purified, so that a virtual liberation will be achieved. This corresponds very closely to the Christian state of Purgatory. For further explanation of this important question, see René Guénon, *Man and His Becoming* (London, 1945).

[14] "It is good," Black Elk has said, "to have a reminder of death before us, for it helps us to understand the impermanence of life on this earth, and this understanding may aid us in preparing for our own death. He who is well prepared is he who knows that he is nothing compared with *Wakan-Tanka,* who is everything; then he knows that world which is real."

man, and he should use the pipe so that all the people, with the soul, will together send their voices to *Wakan-Tanka*. The fruit of your Mother the Earth and the fruit of all that bears will be blessed in this manner, and your people will then walk the path of life in a sacred way. Do not forget that *Wakan-Tanka* has given you seven days in which to send your voices to Him. So long as you remember this you will live; the rest you will know from *Wakan-Tanka* directly."

The sacred woman then started to leave the lodge, but turning again to Standing Hollow Horn, she said: "Behold this pipe! Always remember how sacred it is, and treat it as such, for it will take you to the end. Remember, in me there are four ages.[15] I am leaving now, but I shall look back upon your people in every age, and at the end I shall return."

Moving around the lodge in a sun-wise manner, the mysterious woman left, but after walking a short distance she looked back towards the people and sat down. When she rose the people were amazed to see that she had become a young red and brown buffalo calf. Then this calf walked farther, lay down, and rolled, looking back at the people, and when she got up she was a white buffalo. Again the white buffalo walked farther and rolled on the ground, becoming now a black buffalo. This buffalo then walked farther away from the people, stopped, and after bowing to each of the four quarters of the universe, disappeared over the hill.

[15] According to Siouan mythology, it is believed that at the beginning of the cycle a buffalo was placed at the west in order to hold back the waters. Every year this buffalo loses one hair, and every age he loses one leg. When all his hair and all four legs are gone, then the waters rush in once again, and the cycle comes to an end.

A striking parallel to this myth is found in the Hindu tradition, where it is the Bull *Dharma* (the divine law) who has four legs, each of which represents an age of the total cycle. During the course of these four ages (*yugas*) true spirituality becomes increasingly obscured, until the cycle (*manvantara*) closes with a catastrophe, after which the primordial spirituality is restored, and the cycle begins once again.

It is believed by both the American Indian and the Hindu that at the present time the buffalo or bull is on his last leg, and he is very nearly bald. Corresponding beliefs could be cited from many other traditions. See René Guénon, *The Crisis of the Modern World* (London, 1942).

9

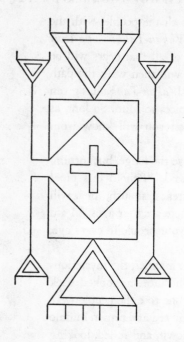

CHAPTER II

THE KEEPING OF THE SOUL

I

It is through this rite that we purify the souls of our dead, and that our love for one another is increased.[1] The four pure women who eat the sacred part of the buffalo,[2] as I shall describe, must always remember that their children will be *wakan* and thus should be raised in a sacred manner. The mother should sacrifice every-

[1] By an extraordinary act of either ignorance or ill will, this rite for the "keeping of the soul" was prohibited by the government in 1890, and it was even required that on a certain day, established by law, all souls kept by the Sioux must be released. For a description of this rite as performed in 1882, see Alice C. Fletcher, "The Shadow or Ghost Lodge," *Annual Report of the Peabody Museum,* Vol. III, Nos. 3, 4 (1884).

[2] The bison, which represents the universe, contains all things; but that part which represents mankind, and especially the holy White Buffalo Woman, is a certain meat from the shoulder of the animal. This meat is regarded by the Sioux in much the same way as is the holy Eucharist by the Christian.

thing for her children, and must develop in herself and in her children a great love for *Wakan-Tanka,* for in time these children will become holy people and leaders of the nation and will have the power to make others *wakan.* At first we kept only the souls of a few of our great leaders, but later we kept the souls of almost all good people.

By keeping a soul according to the proper rites, as given to us by the White Buffalo Cow Woman [known also as White Buffalo Maiden], one so purifies it that it and the Spirit become one, and it is thus able to return to the "place" where it was born—*Wakan-Tanka*—and need not wander about the earth as is the case with the souls of bad people; further, the keeping of a soul helps us to remember death and also *Wakan-Tanka,* who is above all dying.

Whenever a soul is kept, many of the nation go to its tipi to pray, and on the day that the soul is released all the people gather and send their voices to *Wakan-Tanka* through the soul which is to travel upon His sacred path. But now I shall explain to you how this rite was first done by our people.

One of the great-great-grandchildren of Standing Hollow Horn had a child whom the parents loved very much; but it happened that one day this child died, which made the father very sad, and so he went and spoke to the keeper of the sacred pipe, who was at that time High Hollow Horn.

"We have been instructed by the sacred woman in the use of the pipe and in the keeping of the soul of a person who has died. Now I am very sad because I have lost my loved son, but I wish to keep his soul as we have been taught, and, since you are the keeper of the sacred pipe, I wish you to instruct me!"

"*How! Hechetu alo!* It is good!" High Hollow Horn said, and they then went to the place where the child lay, and where the women were crying very bitterly. As they approached, the crying stopped; and going to where the child lay, High Hollow Horn spoke.

"This boy seems to be dead, yet he is not really, for we shall keep his soul among our people, and through this our children and the children of their children will become *wakan.* We shall

11

now do as we were taught by the sacred woman and by the pipe. It is the wish of *Wakan-Tanka* that this be done."

A lock of the child's hair was then taken, and as High Hollow Horn did this he prayed.

"O *Wakan-Tanka* behold us! It is the first time that we do Thy will in this way, as You have taught us through the sacred woman. We will keep the soul of this child so that our Mother the Earth will bear fruit, and so that our children will walk the path of life in a sacred manner."

High Hollow Horn then prepared to purify the child's lock of hair; a glowing coal was brought in, and a pinch of sweet grass was placed upon it.

"O *Wakan-Tanka*," High Hollow Horn prayed, "this smoke from the sweet grass will rise up to You, and will spread throughout the universe; its fragrance will be known by the wingeds, the four-leggeds, and the two-leggeds, for we understand that we are all relatives; may all our brothers be tame and not fear us!"

High Hollow Horn took up the lock of hair, and holding it over the smoke, made a motion with it to Heaven, to Earth, and to the four quarters of the universe; then he spoke to the soul within the hair.

"Behold O soul! Where you dwell upon this earth will be a sacred place; this center will cause the people to be as *wakan* as you are. Our grandchildren will now walk the path of life with pure hearts, and with firm steps!"

After purifying the lock of hair in the smoke, High Hollow Horn turned to the mother and father of the child, saying: "We shall gain great knowledge from this soul which has here been purified. Be good to it and love it, for it is *wakan*. We are now fulfilling the will of *Wakan-Tanka,* as it was made known to us through the sacred woman; for do you not remember as she was leaving how she turned back the second time? This represents the keeping of the soul, which we are now going to do. May this help us to remember that all the fruits of the wingeds, the two-leggeds, and the four-leggeds, are really the gifts of *Wakan-Tanka*. They are all *wakan* and should be treated as such!"

Black Elk, 1947 *(Photograph by J. E. Brown)*

Black Elk. Photograph taken in France when he was about 19 years old and was with the Buffalo Bill Show. *(Photograph from author's collection)*

The lock of hair was wrapped in sacred buckskin, and this bundle was placed at a special place in the tipi. Then High Hollow Horn took up the pipe, and after holding it over the smoke, filled it carefully in a ritual manner; pointing the stem towards heaven, he prayed.

"Our Grandfather, *Wakan-Tanka,* You are everything, and yet above everything! You are first. You have always been. This soul that we are keeping will be at the center of the sacred hoop of this nation; through this center our children will have strong hearts, and they will walk the straight red path in a *wakan* manner.

"O *Wakan-Tanka,* You are the truth. The two-legged peoples who put their mouths to this pipe will become the truth itself; there will be in them nothing impure. Help us to walk the sacred path of life without difficulty, with our minds and hearts continually fixed on You!"

The pipe was then lighted and smoked, and was passed sunwise around the circle. The whole world within the pipe was offered up to *Wakan-Tanka.* When the pipe came back to High Hollow Horn, he rubbed sweet grass over it on the west, north, east, and south sides, in order to purify it lest any unworthy person might have touched it; turning to the people, he then said: "My relatives, this pipe is *wakan.* We all know that it cannot lie. No man who has within him any untruth may touch it to his mouth. Further, my relatives, our Father, *Wakan-Tanka,* has made His will known to us here on earth, and we must always do that which He wishes if we would walk the sacred path. This is the first time that we carry out this sacred rite of keeping the soul, and it will be of great benefit to our children and to their children's children! My relatives, Grandmother and Mother Earth, we are of earth, and belong to You. O Mother Earth from whom we receive our food, You care for our growth as do our own mothers. Every step that we take upon You should be done in a sacred manner; each step should be as a prayer. Remember this my relatives: that the power of this pure soul will be with you as you walk, for it, too, is the fruit of Mother Earth; it is as a seed, planted in your center, which will in time grow in your hearts, and cause our generations to walk in a *wakan* manner."

High Hollow Horn then lifted his hand and sent his voice to *Wakan-Tanka*.[3]

"O Father and Grandfather *Wakan-Tanka,* You are the source and end of everything. My Father *Wakan-Tanka,* You are the One who watches over and sustains all life. O my Grandmother, You are the earthly source of all existence! And Mother Earth, the fruits which You bear are the source of life for the earth peoples. You are always watching over Your fruits as does a mother. May the steps which we take in life upon you be sacred and not weak!

"Help us O *Wakan-Tanka* to walk the red path with firm steps. May we who are Your people stand in a *wakan* manner, pleasing to You! Give to us strength which comes from an understanding of Your powers! Because You have made Your will known to us, we will walk the path of life in holiness, bearing the love and knowledge of You in our hearts! For this and for everything we give thanks!"

A bundle was then made containing the body of the child, and the men took this to a high place away from the camp and placed it upon a scaffold set up in a tree.[4] When they returned, High Hollow Horn went into the tipi with the father of the child, in order to teach him how he must prepare himself for the great duty which he would fulfill and from which he would become a holy man.

"You are now keeping the soul of your own son," High Hollow Horn said, "who is not dead, but is with you. From now on you must live in a sacred manner, for your son will be in this tipi until his soul is released. You should remember that the habits which you establish during this period will remain with you always. You

[3] "We raise our hands (when we pray) because we are wholly dependent on the Great Spirit; it is His liberal hand that supplies all our wants. We strike the ground afterward, because we are miserable beings, worms crawling before His face." (As said by a Blackfoot Sioux to Father De Smet: *Life, Letters, and Travels* [New York, 1905], 253)

[4] It is in this manner that the gross body is given back to the elements from which it came; it is left exposed to the agents of heaven: the four winds, the rains, the wingeds of the air, each of which—and with the Earth —absorbs a part.

must take great care that no bad person enters the lodge where you keep the soul, and that there be no arguments or dissensions; there should always be harmony in your lodge, for all these things have an influence on the soul which is being purified here.

"Your hands are *wakan;* treat them as such! And your eyes are *wakan;* when you see your relatives and all things, see them in a sacred manner![5] Your mouth is *wakan,* and every word you say should reflect this holy state in which you are now living. You should raise your head often, looking up into the heavens. Whenever you eat of the fruit of Mother Earth, feed likewise your son! If you do this and all that I have taught you, *Wakan-Tanka* will be merciful to you. Every day and night your son will be with you; look after his soul all the time, for through this you will always remember *Wakan-Tanka.* From this day on you will be *wakan,* and as I have taught you, so you too will now be able to teach others. The sacred pipe will go a long way, even to the end, and so will the soul of your son! It is indeed so, *Hetchetu welo!*"

11

Before I tell you how the soul is released, I think I should explain several of the other duties which the keeper of a soul should know and should carry out.

He who keeps the soul of a person should never fight, or even use a knife, no matter for what purpose. He must be in prayer all

[5] The sacredness of relationship is one of the most important aspects of Siouan culture; for since the whole of creation is essentially One, all parts within the whole are related. Thus the Sioux refer to each other not by their particular names, but by a term expressing their relationship, which is determined by age levels rather than by blood ties. A young man thus always addresses an older man or woman as *"Ate"* (Father), or *"Ina"* (Mother), or if they are much older by: *"Tunkashila"* (Grandfather), or *"Unchi"* (Grandmother); and in turn the older address the younger as "Son" or "Daughter," "Grandson" or "Granddaughter."

For the Sioux, all relationships on earth are symbolic of the true and great relationship which always exists between man and the Great Spirit, or between man and Earth understood in its principle. In using these terms, the Sioux thus really invoke or recall the principle, and the individual—or really any particular thing—is for them only a dim reflection of this principle.

the time, and he must be an example to his people in everything. The people should love and honor this holy man, frequently bringing food and gifts to him, and the keeper of the soul should in turn offer up his pipe very often to *Wakan-Tanka* for the good of the nation.

When a party of warriors go on a hunt, the holy keeper of the soul should go with them, but while the others hunt, he should sit alone on a hill and with his pipe he should send his voice to the powers above for the good of the hunt and for the good of all the people. Then when a buffalo cow has been killed near the keeper, she belongs to him, and he should go and sit near her; then he should fill his pipe, by first offering pinches of *kinni-kinnik*[6] to the winged powers of the west, north, east, south, Mother Earth, and finally the last he should hold up, offering it to *Wakan-Tanka* in whom are all the powers. When the pipe has been filled in this manner, he should then point its stem towards the nose of the buffalo cow, and he should pray in this manner: "O *Wakan-Tanka*, You have taught us Your will through a four-legged one, so that Your people may walk the sacred path, and that our children, and our children's children, will be blessed. I am offering this pipe to You before all else, for You are always first, and then I offer it to *Tatanka* the buffalo.

"You O *Tatanka* have four ages, and the last time that you looked back upon us we saw that you are the fruit of our Mother Earth from whom we live. You will thus be the first to be placed at the center of our nation's hoop, for you strengthen our bodies and also our spirits when we treat you in a *wakan* manner. You have made known to us the will of *Wakan-Tanka*, so that now there is a holy soul at the center of our hoop. You will be at our center with this soul, and there you will give happiness to your people. Go now forward to the center of the people's hoop!"

[6] *Kinnikinnik*, often called *chanshasha*, is an ingredient of the tobacco of the Sioux; it is the dried inner bark of the red alder or the red dogwood (*Cornus stolonifera*). This is rarely smoked alone because of its bitterness; there is usually added to it an equal part of the Ree twist tobacco and also a small portion of some fragrant root or herb, often the Sweet Ann root. These ingredients are always mixed in a ritual manner.

Men who have been instructed by the keeper of the soul then butcher the *wakan* buffalo cow, saying appropriate prayers for every part. The meat taken from the shoulder represents the two-legged peoples, but especially the holy woman who brought the pipe to us; it is thus *lela wakan,* and is always treated with great respect. The keeper of the soul is not able to do any of the butchering since he can touch neither knife nor blood, as I have already mentioned; but he was able to take this *wakan* meat back to camp on his horse along with the buffalo hide, for this too is *wakan* and will be used for a special purpose. Their arrival at camp is announced by a crier, and the meat is then taken to the tipi of the keeper of the soul. At this moment one of the helpers within the lodge should speak to the soul.

"Grandson, the chosen food will rest at the center of this lodge, your home. It will be of great benefit to the people! *Hetchetu welo!"*

Within the tipi where a soul is kept, there should always be a woman who has been chosen to care for the sacred bundle; the first woman to fulfill this sacred duty was Red Day Woman. This holy person would sun-dry the *wakan* meat, and this would later be made into *wasna,* which is the dried meat (*papa*), pounded together with wild cherries and mixed with tallow taken from the bones of the buffalo. This sacred food is kept in a specially painted buffalo-hide box, and is saved for the day when the soul is released.

On good days the soul-bundle should be taken outside, and should be hung on a tripod, facing the south.[7] On these days the people often come to bring gifts to the soul, and to pray before it, thus gaining much benefit. These gifts also are kept in a specially

[7] The three feet of the tripod are oriented to the west, north, and east; it is thus left open to the south, which is, for the Sioux, the direction towards which the souls of the dead go. The sacred bundle is tied on the south side, just below the place where the three sticks intersect. This central point of intersection represents *Wakan-Tanka* towards whom the soul will soon depart, and from this point there hangs a thong which just touches the ground, representing the way leading from the earth to *Wakan-Tanka.* It is upon this way that the soul is now traveling, and the position of the bundle indicates that the journey has nearly been completed.

painted box, and they are later given away to the poor and needy.

After the buffalo robe has been tanned in a ritual manner, it is painted and is again purified over the smoke of the sweet grass. The keeper of the soul should then point this robe to the four quarters of the universe, and say: "O you soul, my grandson, stand firmly on this earth and look about you; look to the heavens, to the four quarters of the universe, and look upon your Mother the Earth! And you, O buffalo who are really here in this hide, you have come to our people to do them a great service; now you are to unite with this soul. You will both be at the center of the nation's hoop, and will represent the oneness of the people. By placing this robe over you, O soul, I am placing it over all the people as one."

When the sacred bundle is hanging from the tripod outside the lodge, this buffalo robe is placed over it with its hair on the outside, and on top of the tripod there should be placed a war bonnet, made from the feathers of *Wanbli Galeshka,* the Spotted Eagle.

Although the helpers are allowed to handle the equipment, only the holy keeper may touch the sacred bundle. This bundle he always carries against the heart, in the crook of the left arm, for this is the arm that is nearest to the heart, and whenever the bundle is taken back into the tipi it should be offered first to Heaven, then to Earth, and to the four directions of the universe.

Before the rites for the releasing of the soul can be made, many things must be gathered together, and for poor people this may take several years, but the usual length of time for keeping a soul is one year. Should the keeper die before the soul is released, then his wife keeps the soul, and also the soul of her husband; and should the wife die also, then the helpers keep all three souls, and this would of course be a very great and sacred responsibility.

Before the soul of the child is released, all the people gather together, for everybody participates in this great rite, which can best be called The Making of Sacredness. As this time approaches, all the men go hunting for the buffalo, and when many are killed the bones are cracked and boiled, and from this tallow *wasna* is made. The women dry the best part of the meat, which is then called *papa,* and all this is contributed to the rites.

After first consulting with the other holy men of the band, the keeper of the soul—who was for this first rite a relative of Standing Hollow Horn—appoints the special day, and when this times arrives, the helpers make a large ceremonial lodge from several small tipis and cover the earth inside with sacred sage.

The helper of the keeper of the soul then takes a pipe, and holding it up to the heavens, he cries: "Behold, O *Wakan-Tanka!* We are now about to do Thy will. With all the sacred beings of the universe, we offer to You this pipe!"

The helper then takes a pinch of the sacred tobacco *kinni-kinnik,* and holding it and the stem of the pipe towards the west, he cries: "With this *wakan* tobacco, we place You in the pipe, O winged Power of the west. We are about to send our voices to *Wakan-Tanka,* and we wish You to help us!

"This day is *wakan* because a soul is to be released. All over the universe there will be happiness and rejoicing! O You sacred Power of the place where the sun goes down, it is a great thing we are doing in placing You in the pipe. Give to us for our rites one of the two sacred red and blue days which You control!"[8]

This Power of the west, now in the tobacco, is placed in the

[8] The term "red and blue days" is really far more than a wish for good weather, for the Sioux believe that these are the days at the end of the world when the moon will turn red and the sun will turn blue. But since for the traditional man everything in the macrocosm has its counterpart in the microcosm, there may also be an end of the world for the individual here and now, whenever he receives illumination or wisdom from *Wakan-Tanka,* so that his ego or ignorance dies, and he then lives continually in the Spirit.

pipe, and holding another pinch of *kinnikinnik* towards the north, the helper prays.

"O You, Thunder-being, there where *Waziah* has his lodge, who comes with the purifying winds, and who guards the health of the people; O Baldheaded Eagle of the north, Your wings never tire! There is a place for You too in this pipe, which will be offered to *Wakan-Tanka*. Help us, and give to us one of Your two sacred days!"

Then holding another pinch of *kinnikinnik* to the east, the helper continues to pray.

"O You sacred Being of the place where the sun comes up, who controls knowledge! Yours is the path of the rising sun which brings light into the world. Your name is *Huntka,* for You have wisdom and are long-winged. There is a place for You in the pipe; help us in sending our voice to *Wakan-Tanka!* Give to us Your sacred days!"

This Power of the east is placed in the pipe, and then another pinch of *kinnikinnik* is held towards the south, with the prayer: "O You who guard that path leading to the place towards which we always face, and upon which our generations walk, we are placing You in this sacred pipe! You control our life, and the lives of all the peoples of the universe. Everything that moves and all that is will send a voice to *Wakan-Tanka*. We have a place for You in the pipe; help us in sending our voice, and give to us one of Your good days! This we ask of You, O White Swan, there where we always face."

The stem of the pipe and a pinch of *kinnikinnik* are then held towards the earth.

"O You, sacred Earth, from whence we have come, You are humble, nourishing all things; we know that You are *wakan* and that with You we are all as relatives. Grandmother and Mother Earth who bear fruit, for You there is a place in this pipe. O Mother, may Your people walk the path of life, facing the strong winds! May we walk firmly upon You! May our steps not falter! We and all who move upon You are sending our voices to *Wakan-Tanka!* Help us! All together as one we cry: help us!"

When the pipe has thus been filled with all the Powers and with all that there is in the universe,[9] it is given to the keeper of

[9] In filling a pipe, all space (represented by the offerings to the powers of the six directions) and all things (represented by the grains of tobacco) are contracted within a single point (the bowl or heart of the pipe), so that the pipe contains, or really *is,* the universe. But since the pipe is the universe, it is also man, and the one who fills a pipe should identify himself with it, thus not only establishing the center of the universe, but also his own center; he so "expands" that the six directions of space are actually brought within himself. It is by this "expansion" that a man ceases to be a part, a fragment, and becomes whole or holy; he shatters the illusion of separateness.

In order to make clear this identity for the Indian of the body of man with the pipe, I quote the following text of the Osage Indians:

These people had a pipe,
Which they made to be their body.

O *Hon-ga,* I have a pipe that I have made to be my body;
If you also make it to be your body,
You shall have a body that is free from all causes of death.

Behold the joint of the neck, they said,
That I have made to be the joint of my own neck.

Behold the mouth of the pipe,
That I have made to be my mouth.

Behold the right side of the pipe,
That I have made to be the right side of my body.

Behold the spine of the pipe,
That I have made to be my own spine.

Behold the left side of the pipe,
That I have made to be the left side of my own body.

Behold the hollow of the pipe,
That I have made to be the hollow of my own body.

Behold the thong that holds together the pipe and stem;
That I have made to be my windpipe.
. . . use the pipe as an offering in your supplications,
Your prayers shall be readily granted.

(Francis La Flesche, "War Ceremony and Peace Ceremony of the Osage Indians," *Bulletin No. 101 of the Bureau of American Ethnology* [Washington, D. C., 1939], 62, 63)

the soul, who takes it and, crying as he walks, goes to the tipi of the keeper of the most sacred pipe, who was, for this first rite, High Hollow Horn. Entering the tipi, and holding out the pipe with its stem pointing towards the south, he places it in the hands of the keeper of the pipe.

"*Hi Ho! Hi Ho!* Thanks!" the holy man says as he takes the pipe, "this pipe which you have brought to me is really as sacred as the original pipe which was given to us by the White Buffalo Cow Woman. Indeed, to one who understands they are really the same. But this pipe which you have now brought is especially sacred, for I see that there has been placed within it the whole universe. What is it that you wish?"

"We wish you to smoke this pipe and then to lead the rites for releasing the soul of my young son. We wish you to bring with you the original *wakan* pipe which you are keeping."

"*How, hetchetu welo,*" the holy man replied, "I will come!" He then offers the pipe which has been brought to him to the heavens, to the earth, to the four quarters; then he smokes it. When finished, he carefully saves the ashes, for they too are very *wakan*.

The two men return to the lodge where all has been made ready for the great rite. Entering, they walk around sun-wise and sit at the west of the lodge, opposite the door. The wife of the keeper of the soul then goes to her tipi, crying as she walks, picks up the sacred bundle, and returns to the lodge, where she stands in front of the keeper of the sacred pipe, placing the bundle in his two outstretched hands. "Thanks, thanks!" the holy keeper says, and then he speaks to the soul within the bundle:

"You, O soul, were with your people, but soon you will leave. Today is your day, and it is *wakan*. Today your Father, *Wakan-Tanka*, is bending down to see you; all your people have arrived to be with you. All your relatives love you, and have taken good care of you. You and the holy woman of the four ages, who brought to us the sacred pipe, are now together here in this lodge; this robe here, which represents the sacred woman and which has covered you, will cover all your people! The sacred pipe which she brought to us has made the people happy. Behold! This is the sacred day! *Hetchetu welo!*"

A round circle is scraped on the ground to represent a buffalo wallow, and on this the sacred bundle is placed. Another round place is then made from the earth taken from the wallow, upon which a cross is drawn from west to east and from north to south. The pipe is placed upon this cross, with its stem to the west and the bowl at the east. Then the sacred bundle is placed beside the pipe, at the bottom of the good red road, for this is the place to which the soul will soon journey.

One of the helpers then goes to the fire at the center of the tipi and, with a split stick, picks up a glowing coal and places it in front of the keeper of the pipe.[10] The keeper then holds the pipe in his left hand, and, taking up a pinch of a sacred herb in his right hand, he holds it up towards the heavens and lowers it slowly to the coal, stopping four times and praying: "O Grandfather, *Wakan-Tanka,* on this sacred day of Yours, I send to You this fragrance, which will reach to the heavens above. Within this herb, there is the earth, this great island; within it is my Grandmother, my Mother, and all the four-leggeds, the wingeds, and the two-legged peoples, who are all walking in a *wakan* manner. The fragrance of this herb will cover the entire universe. O *Wakan-Tanka,* be merciful to all!"

The bowl of the pipe is placed over the smoke, in such a way that this smoke passes through the pipe, coming out the end of the stem which is held towards the heaven. In this manner, *Wakan-Tanka* is the first to smoke, and by this act the pipe is purified. As he does this, the "keeper of the pipe" prays.

[10] Since, for the Sioux, every tipi is the world in an image, the fire at the center represents *Wakan-Tanka* within the world. To emphasize the sacredness of this central fire, it should be recalled that, when the Sioux were still nomadic, a man was appointed to be the keeper of the fire, and he would usually have his tipi at the center of the camping circle. When camp was moved, this keeper would carry the fire in a small log, and when camp was set up again, each lodge would start its fire from this central source. The fire was extinguished and a new one started, always in a ritual manner, only after there had been some great catastrophe, or when a complete purification was needed for the whole camp.

"O *Wakan-Tanka,* behold the pipe! The smoke from this herb will cover everything upon earth, and will reach even to the heavens. May the way of Thy people be as this smoke. We have offered this pipe to You, and now I place within its bowl the sacred *kinnikinnik.* You have taught us that the round bowl of the pipe is the very center of the universe and the heart of man! O *Wakan-Tanka,* bend down to look upon us today; look upon Thy pipe with which we are about to send a voice, along with the winged peoples, the four-leggeds, and all the fruits of our Mother Earth. All that You have made will join with us in sending this voice!"

As he fills the pipe, the holy keeper makes the ritual offerings of tobacco to the six directions, with the following prayers: "O You, winged Power, there where the sun goes down, You are *wakan!* With You and through You we send a voice to *Wakan-Tanka* before releasing this soul. There is a place for You in this pipe. Help us! Give to our people Your red and blue days, that they may walk the sacred path of life in a *wakan* manner!

"O winged Power of the place where *Waziah* lives [the north]! purifier of the earth, of the two-leggeds, and of all that is unclean, with the soul of a two-legged person we are about to send a voice through You to *Wakan-Tanka.* There is a place for You in the pipe, and so help us in sending this voice! Give to us the two sacred days which You have!

"O You, winged One, of the place from whence the sun comes! You who are long-winged, and who controls knowledge, the Light of the universe, we are about to send a voice to *Wakan-Tanka* with this soul who has been with his people. You also have the two great red and blue days; give these to us, and help us in sending a voice!

"O You, sacred White Swan, of the place towards which we always face, You control the red path leading there where *Waziah* has his lodge. You guide all the four-legged and two-legged people who travel upon this sacred road. We are about to release a soul who is to travel upon Your path; through this soul we are sending a voice to *Wakan-Tanka!* Help us to send this voice, and give to us Your two sacred days!

"O You, Spotted Eagle, who are next to the heavens, close to *Wakan-Tanka!* Your wings are powerful. You are the one who takes care of our nation's sacred hoop and all that is within this circle. May all the people be happy and have many blessings! We are about to release a soul who will go on a long journey, in order that the steps of its generations to come will be *wakan*. There is a place for You in the pipe! Help us to send our voice to *Wakan-Tanka,* and give us the sacred red and blue days which are Yours!

"O *Wakan-Tanka*, we are about to offer to You this pipe. Look down upon us and upon our Grandmother and Mother Earth. Everything is *wakan* that is on our Mother, the earthly source of all life. The steps of our people are upon Her. May they be firm and strong! From You, Grandmother Earth, a soul is to be released. There is a place in this pipe for You, and for all Your sacred things and peoples! All together as one we send our voice to *Wakan-Tanka*. Help us to walk in a *wakan* manner pleasing to You! Give to us the sacred red and blue days which You control!"

In this manner, the whole universe was placed in the pipe, and then, turning to the people, the keeper of the pipe says: "Since we have done all this correctly, the soul should have a good journey, and it will help our people to increase and to walk the sacred path in a manner pleasing to *Wakan-Tanka*."

And then to the soul he says: "O you soul, my grandchild, you are the root of this great rite; from you there will grow much that is *wakan*. Through this rite our people will learn to be generous, to help those in need, and to follow in every way the teachings of *Wakan-Tanka*. O soul, this is your day. The time has now come!

"There will be four virgins who will always carry with them the power of these rites. You, O soul, will cover them over with your sacred buffalo robe. This is your day; it is one of joy, for much Light has come to our people. All that has been with you in the past is here with you today. Your relatives have arrived with food, which will be purified, offered to you, and then given to the four virgins; after this it will be shared with the poor and unfortunate ones. But now the time has come for us to offer up this pipe to *Wakan-Tanka*, and then to smoke it.[11] We offer to Him everything that is in the universe; we send our voices to Him through this pipe. *Hetchetu welo!*

"*Hee-ay-hay-ee-ee!* [four times] *Tunkashila Wakan-Tanka*, Grandfather, Great Spirit, look down upon us! This is the *wakan* day for this soul. May he help the coming generations to walk in a sacred manner! We are offering this pipe to You, O *Wakan-Tanka*, and ask You to help this soul, his relatives, and all the people! Behold the pipe, and bend down to look upon us as we fulfill Thy will! From this earth we are sending a voice to You! Be merciful to us, and to this soul who will be released from the center of his people's hoop! O Grandfather, *Wakan-Tanka*, be merciful to us, that our people may live!"

To this all the people say: "*Hi yee!* Thanks! So be it!" and then the keeper lights the pipe, smokes it for a few puffs, and hands it to the keeper of the soul, who offers it to heaven, earth, and the four directions. After smoking it a little, he passes it around sun-wise, that all the people may smoke. As each man smokes, he asks some blessing, and when the pipe comes back to the keeper of the pipe, it is purified, and the ashes are carefully placed in a special buckskin bag.

After the pipe has been offered up to *Wakan-Tanka*, the keeper begins to cry, and soon all the people are crying.

I should, perhaps, explain to you here, that it is good to cry at this moment, for it shows that we are thinking of the soul and of death, which must come to all created beings and things; and it is also a sign that we are humiliating ourselves before the Great Spirit, for we know that we are as dust before Him, who is everything, and who is all powerful.

[11] It should be noticed that in the complete ritual of the pipe, there are three distinct phases: the *purification* with the smoke of a sacred herb; the "expansion" of the pipe so that it includes the entire universe; and finally, what could be called the "identity," which is the sacrifice of the whole universe in the fire.

These three phases of the rite are common, in one form or another, to all traditional or orthodox methods of prayer, and they always constitute the prerequisite stages for a true spiritual realization. See Frithjof Schuon, *L'Oeil du Coeur* (Paris, 1950); especially the chapter "De la Meditation."

All the food that is to be given to the soul is placed outside the lodge; this food the women pick up and enter the lodge. Within the lodge, on the south side, a willow post will have been set up, as high as a man, and around the top of it a piece of buckskin is tied, upon which a face has been painted. On top of this face there is a war bonnet, and around the post there has been placed a buffalo robe. This figure represents the soul, and leaning against him are his bows and arrows, knives, and all his possessions. As the women enter with the food, they pass around the lodge sun-wise. Stopping at the south, they each hug the "soul post"; then, after leaving their food, they walk out of the lodge.

A small bit of each food that has been brought for the soul is put into a wooden bowl, and this is placed in front of the two holy men who are seated at the west. Four pure virgins then enter and take their places at the north of the lodge, for the Power of this direction is purity. The keeper of the pipe then stands and speaks to the soul.

"You, O soul, are the *hokshichankiya* [spiritual influence, or seed]! You are as the root of the *wakan* tree which is at the center of our nation's hoop. May this tree bloom! May our people and the winged and the four-legged peoples all flourish! O soul, your relatives have brought you this food which you will soon eat, and, by this act, goodness will spread among the people. O soul, *Wakan-Tanka* has given to you four relatives who are sitting there at the north; they represent our true relatives: Grandfather and Father, *Wakan-Tanka*, and Grandmother and Mother, *Maka,* the Earth. Remember these four relatives, who are all really One, and, with Them in mind, look back upon your people as you travel upon the great path!"

A small hole is dug at the foot of the "soul post," and the keeper of the pipe holds the wooden bowl, in which is the purified food, towards the hole, saying to the soul: "You are about to eat this *wakan* food. When it is placed in your mouth its influence will spread, and it will cause the fruits of our Mother, the Earth, to increase and prosper. Your Grandmother is *wakan;* upon Her we stand as we place this food in your mouth. Do not forget us

27

when you go forth to *Wakan-Tanka,* but look back upon us!"

The food is placed in the hole, and on top of it the juice of the wild cherry is poured, for this juice is the water of Life. The hole is then covered over with dirt, for the soul has finished its last meal.

The four virgins then prepare to eat the sacred buffalo meat and to drink the cherry juice; but first the food is purified over the smoke of the sweet grass, and then the keeper of the pipe speaks to the virgins, saying: "Grandchildren, you are now to receive the *hokshichankiya* of the soul; this will cause you and your fruits to be always *wakan.* Grandchildren, remember to share your food—all you have—for in the world there are always the needy, orphans, and old people. But above all, my grandchildren, never forget your four great relatives, who are represented by your relatives here on earth! You are now to eat and drink the sacred fruit of Mother Earth, and through this you and your fruits will be *wakan.* Always remember this my children!"

The keeper of pipe picks up the bowl of food, and each time that he places food in the mouth of a virgin, he says: "I place this food in your mouth. It is sweet and fragrant—*wakan!* The people will see your generations to come!"

The four virgins stoop and drink the juice of the wild cherry which is in the wooden bowl on the ground, and when they have finished eating and drinking, the keeper says to them: "Grandchildren, all that we have done here today is *lela wakan,* for it has all been done according to the instructions given to us by the holy woman, who was also a buffalo, and who brought to us our most holy pipe. She told us that she had four ages; you, too, grandchildren, have these ages. Understand all this deeply, for it is important. It is a great thing we are doing here today. It is so indeed! *Hetchetu welo!*"

The keeper of the pipe then walks around to the south and, picking up the "soul bundle," says to it: "Grandchild, you are about to leave on a great journey. Your father and mother and all your relatives have loved you. Soon they will be happy."

The father of the child then embraces the sacred bundle, by

holding it to each shoulder, and after he has done this, the keeper says to him: "You loved your son, and you have kept him at the center of our people's hoop. As you have been good to this your loved one, so be good to all other people! The sacred influence of your son's soul will be upon the people; it is as a tree that will always bloom."

He then walks around to the north, and as he touches each virgin with the sacred bundle, he says: "The tree which was selected to be at the center of your sacred hoop is this! May it always flourish and bloom in a *wakan* manner!" Then, holding the bundle up towards the heavens, he cries: "Always look back upon your people, that they may walk the sacred path with firm steps!"

This, the keeper cries four times as he walked towards the door of the lodge, and, as he stops the fourth time just outside the door, he cries with a very shrill voice: "Behold your people! Look back upon them!"

The moment the bundle passes out of the lodge,[12] the soul is released; it has departed on the "spirit trail" leading to *Wakan-Tanka*.[13]

Once the soul has left the bundle containing the lock of hair,

---

[12] The significance of this ritual act will be clear if it is recalled that the tipi is the universe, the cosmos; and the space outside the tipi is symbolically the Infinite, or *Wakan-Tanka*.

It is in this same manner that the Plains Indians release the souls which they have taken in the scalps of the enemy.

"The chief . . . looks upward through the opening in the roof, into the blue sky above, then with a quick movement he thrusts the slender poles on which are suspended scalps, through the opening to the sky and pulls them in again, by which act the Spirits of the slain are released." (Francis La Flesche, "War and Peace Ceremony of the Osage Indians," *Bulletin No. 101 of the Bureau of American Ethnology*.)

[13] It is held by the Sioux that the released soul travels southward along the "Spirit Path" (the Milky Way) until it comes to a place where this way divides. Here an old woman, called *Maya owichapaha*, sits; "She who pushes them over the bank," who judges the souls; the worthy ones she allows to travel on the path which goes to the right, but the unworthy she "pushes over the bank," to the left. Those who go to the right attain union with *Wakan-Tanka*, but the ones who go to the left must remain in a conditioned state until they become sufficiently purified.

it is no longer especially *wakan,* but it may be kept by the family, if they wish, as something of a remembrance. The four holy virgins are each given a buffalo robe, and then they leave the lodge immediately after the keeper of the pipe.

With this, the rite is finished, and then the people all over the camp are happy and rejoice, and they rush up to touch the four virgins who are *lela wakan,* and who will always bear with them this great influence, bringing great strength to the people. Gifts are given out to the poor and unfortunate ones, and everywhere there is feasting and rejoicing. It is indeed a good day. *Hetchetu welo!*

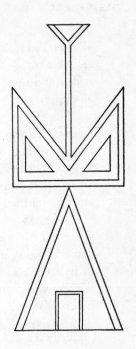

CHAPTER III

Inipi: THE RITE OF PURIFICATION

The rite of the *onikare* (sweat lodge) utilizes all the Powers of the universe: earth, and the things which grow from the earth, water, fire, and air. The water represents the Thunder-beings who come fearfully but bring goodness, for the steam which comes from the rocks, within which is the fire, is frightening, but it purifies us so that we may live as *Wakan-Tanka* wills, and He may even send to us a vision if we become very pure.

When we use the water in the sweat lodge we should think of *Wakan-Tanka* who is always flowing, giving His power and life to everything; we should even be as water which is lower than all things, yet stronger even than the rocks.

The sweat lodge is made from twelve or sixteen young willows, and these, too, have a lesson to teach us, for in the fall their leaves die and return to the earth, but in the spring they come to life again. So, too, men die but live again in the real world of *Wakan-Tanka,* where there is nothing but the spirits of all things; and this true life we may know here on earth if we purify our bodies and minds, thus coming closer to *Wakan-Tanka,* who is all-purity.

The willows which make the frame of the sweat lodge are set up in such a way that they mark the four quarters of the universe; thus, the whole lodge is the universe in an image, and the two-legged, four-legged, and winged peoples, and all things of the world are contained within it, for all these peoples and things too must be purified before they can send a voice to *Wakan-Tanka.*

The rocks which we use represent Grandmother Earth, from whom all fruits come, and they also represent the indestructible and everlasting nature of *Wakan-Tanka.* The fire which is used to heat the rocks represents the great power of *Wakan-Tanka* which gives life to all things; it is as a ray from the sun, for the sun is also *Wakan-Tanka* in a certain aspect.

The round fireplace at the center of the sweat lodge is the center of the universe, in which dwells *Wakan-Tanka,* with His power which is the fire. All these things are *wakan* to us and must be understood deeply if we really wish to purify ourselves, for the power of a thing or an act is in the meaning and the understanding.

The sweat lodge is always constructed with its door to the east, for it is from this direction that the light of wisdom comes. About ten paces from the lodge, at the east, we first construct a sacred fireplace which is called *Peta-owihankeshni,* "fire of no end," or "eternal fire," and this is where the rocks are heated. To make this sacred fireplace, we first place four sticks running east and west, and on top of these we place four sticks running north and south, and then around these we lean sticks as in a tipi, first on the west side, and then on the north, east, and south sides; rocks are then placed at these four directions, and then many more are piled on top. But as we build this fire, we should pray.

"O Grandfather, *Wakan-Tanka,* You are and always were. I am about to do Thy will on this earth as You have taught us. In

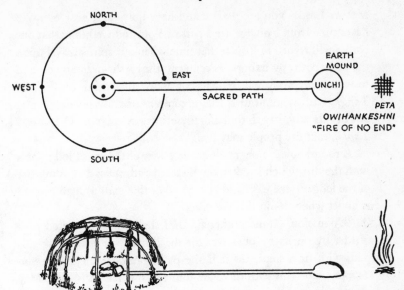

NORTH

EARTH
MOUND

EAST

WEST

UNCHI

SACRED PATH

PETA
OWIHANKESHNI
"FIRE OF NO END"

SOUTH

The *Inipi:* "Purification Lodge"

placing these sacred rocks at the four quarters, we understand that it is You who are at the center. O sacred rocks, you are helping us to do the will of *Wakan-Tanka!*"

And as we light the fire, always on the side facing the east, we pray: "O *Wakan-Tanka,* this is Your eternal fire that has been given to us on this great island! It is Your will that we build this place in a sacred manner. The eternal fire always burns; through it we shall live again by being made pure, and by coming closer to Your powers."

In making the central altar within the sweat lodge, where later the heated rocks will be placed, we first push a stick into the earth at the center of the lodge, and then around this point we draw a circle with a cord of rawhide. While fixing this holy center, we should pray.

"O Grandfather and Father *Wakan-Tanka,* maker of all that is, who always has been, behold me! And You, Grandmother and

33

Mother Earth, You are *wakan* and have holy ears; hear me! We have come from You, we are a part of You, and we know that our bodies will return to You at that time when our spirits travel upon the great path. By fixing this center in the earth, I remember You to whom my body will return, but above all I think of *Wakan-Tanka*, with whom our spirits become as one. By purifying myself in this way, I wish to make myself worthy of You, O *Wakan-Tanka*, that my people may live!"

A round hole is now made at the center of the sweat lodge, and with the dirt which is taken out a sacred path is made leading out of the lodge to the east, and at the end of this path a small mound is built; when doing this we pray.

"Upon You, Grandmother Earth, I shall build the sacred path of life. By purifying ourselves for the people, we shall walk this path with firm steps, for it is the path leading even to *Wakan-Tanka*. Upon this path there are four steps which are sacred. May my people walk this path! May we be pure! May we live again!"

And now, sending a voice directly to *Wakan-Tanka*, we cry: "Grandfather *Wakan-Tanka*, we have learned Thy will, and we know the sacred steps we are to take. With the help of all things and all beings we are about to send our voice to You. Be merciful to us! Help us! I place myself upon this sacred path, and send my voice to You through the four Powers, which we know are but one Power. Help me in all this! O my Grandfather *Wakan-Tanka*, be merciful to us! Help my people and all things to live in a sacred manner pleasing to You! Help us O *Wakan-Tanka* to live again!"

He who leads the purification rite, now enters the lodge alone and with his pipe. He passes around sun-wise and sits at the west and makes an altar of the central hole by placing pinches of tobacco at its four corners. A glowing coal is passed into the lodge and is placed at the center. The leader then burns sweet grass and rubs the smoke all over his body, feet, head, hands, and the pipe too is purified over the smoke; everything is made sacred, and if there is anything in the lodge that is not good it is driven away by the Power of the smoke.

The leader should now offer a pinch of tobacco to the winged

Power of the place where the sun goes down, from which the purifying waters come; this Power is invoked and is asked to help in the rite. After this the sacred tobacco is placed in the pipe, and in the same manner pinches of tobacco are offered to the Powers of the north, whence come the purifying winds; to the east, the place where the sun comes up, and from whence comes wisdom; to the south which is the source and end of all life; above to the heavens, and finally to Mother Earth. As the aid of each Power is invoked and as each pinch of tobacco is placed in the pipe, all those outside the lodge cry "How!" for they are glad and satisfied that this sacred thing has been done.

Now that the pipe has been filled, and everything made *wakan,* the leader leaves the lodge, walks to the east along the sacred path, and then places the pipe on the earth mound, with the bowl on the west side, and with the stem slanting to the east.

All who are to be purified now enter the lodge, the leader first, and as each bows low to enter, he prays.

"*Hi ho! Hi ho! Pila miya* [Thanks]! By bowing low in order to enter this lodge, I am remembering that I am as nothing compared with You, O *Wakan-Tanka,* who are everything. It is You who have placed us upon this island; we are the last to be created by You who are first and who always have been. Help me to become pure, before I send my voice to You! Help us in all that which we are about to do!"

Once within the lodge, the men move around sun-wise and then sit on the sacred sage which had been strewn upon the earth; the leader sits at the east, just beside the door. All remain silent a little while, remembering the goodness of *Wakan-Tanka,* and how it was He who made all things. Then the pipe is handed into the lodge by the helper, who is often a woman, and who remains outside during the rite. The man who sits at the west takes the pipe and places it in front of him, with its stem pointing towards the west.

With a forked stick, the helper now picks up one of the rocks from the sacred fire, *Peta owihankeshni,* and, walking along the sacred path, he hands the rock inside the lodge, where it is placed

35

at the center of the round altar; this first rock is for *Wakan-Tan-ka,* who is always at the center of everything. The man seated at the west touches the foot of the pipe to the rock, and each time that a rock is placed on the altar he touches the pipe to it, and all the men cry: "Hi ye! *Pila miya!* [Thanks]!"

The second rock to be handed into the lodge is placed at the west of the altar, the next at the north, then one for the east, one for the south, one for earth, and finally the hole is filled up with the rest of the rocks, and all these together represent everything that there is in the universe.

The person at the west now offers the pipe to heaven, earth, and the four directions, and then he lights it, and after a few puffs (rubbing the smoke all over his body) he hands the pipe to the one at his left, saying: *"Ho Ate,"* or *"Ho Tunkashila,"* according to their relationship. The one who takes the pipe says in turn: *"How Ate"* or *"How Tunkashila,"* and in this manner the pipe is passed sun-wise around the circle. When the pipe comes back to the man at the west, he purifies it, lest some impure person may have touched it, and carefully empties the ashes, placing them at the edge of the sacred altar. This first use of the pipe within the lodge reminds us of the holy White Buffalo Cow Woman, who long ago entered our lodge in a sacred manner, and then left.

The pipe passes around to the leader sitting at the east, who holds it above the sacred altar, stem pointing to the west, and then moves it along the sacred path to the east, where the helper who is standing just outside the door takes it and, after filling it in a ritual manner, leans it against the sacred earth mound, with the bowl at the east, and the stem slanting towards the west, for the Power of the west is now to be invoked.

The helper closes the door of the sweat lodge, making it completely dark inside, and this darkness represents the darkness of the soul, our ignorance, from which we must now purify ourselves so that we may have the light. During the course of the *Inipi,* the door will be opened four times, letting in the light; this reminds us of the four ages, and how through the goodness of *Wakan-Tanka* we have received the Light in each of these ages.

The man at the west now sends a voice to *Wakan-Tanka* in this manner:

"*Hee-ay-hay-ee-ee!*" (four times)

(This we say whenever we are in need of help, or are in despair, and indeed are we not now in darkness and in need of the Light!)

"I am sending a voice!" (four times) "Hear me!" (Four times) "*Wakan-Tanka,* Grandfather, You are first and always have been. You have brought us to this great island, and here our people wish to live in a sacred manner. Teach us to know and to see all the powers of the universe, and give to us the knowledge to understand that they are all really one Power. May our people always send their voices to You as they walk the sacred path of life!

"O ancient rocks, *Tunkayatakapaka,* you are now here with us; *Wakan-Tanka* has made the Earth, and has placed you next to Her. Upon you the generations will walk, and their steps shall not falter! O Rocks, you have neither eyes, nor mouth, nor limbs; you do not move, but by receiving your sacred breath [the steam], our people will be long-winded as they walk the path of life; your breath is the very breath of life.

"There is a winged One, there where the sun goes down to rest, who controls those waters to which all living beings owe their lives. May we use these waters here in a sacred manner!

"O you people who are always standing, who pierce up through the earth, and who reach even unto the heavens, you tree-people are very many, but one of you has been especially chosen for supporting this sacred purification lodge. You trees are the protectors of the wingeds, for upon you they build their lodges and raise their families; and beneath you there are many people whom you shelter. May all these people and all their generations walk together as relatives!

"To every earthly thing, O *Wakan-Tanka,* You have given a power, and because the fire is the most powerful of Your creations, since it consumes all other things, we place it here at our center, and when we see it and think of it, we really remember

37

You. May this sacred fire always be at our center! Help us in that which we are about to do!"

The leader now sprinkles water on the rocks, once for our Grandfather, *Tunkashila,* once for our Father, *Ate,* once for our Grandmother, *Unchi,* once for our Mother, *Ina,* the Earth, and then once for the sacred pipe; this is done with a sprig of sage or sweet grass, so that the steam will be fragrant, and as it rises and fills the little lodge, the leader cries: "O *Wakan-Tanka,* behold me! I am the people. In offering myself to You, I offer all the people as one, that they may live! We wish to live again! Help us!"

It is now very hot in the lodge, but it is good to feel the purifying qualities of the fire, the air, and the water, and to smell the fragrance of the sacred sage. After these powers have worked well into us, the door of the lodge is thrown open, reminding us of the first age in which we received the Light from *Wakan-Tanka.* Water is now brought in, and the leader at the east passes it around sun-wise, and each man drinks a little, or rubs it over his body. As we do this we think of the place where the sun goes down, and from which comes the water, and the Power of this direction helps us to pray.

The helper outside the lodge then takes the filled pipe from the earth mound, offers it to Heaven and Earth, and walking along the sacred path, hands the pipe—stem first—to the person sitting at the west of the lodge. This man offers the pipe to the six directions, smokes it a little (rubbing the smoke all over his body) after which it is passed around the circle until it has been smoked up. The man at the west then empties the pipe, placing the burned tobacco beside the central altar, and hands the pipe out as before. The helper again fills the pipe, and leans it against the sacred mound, with the stem leaning to the north, for, during the second period of darkness within the lodge, the Power of the winged One of the north will be invoked.

The door of the lodge is closed, and we are in darkness for the second time. It is the person at the north who now prays.

"Behold, O you Baldheaded Eagle, there where the giant *Waziah* has his lodge! *Wakan-Tanka* has placed you there to control this Path; you are there to guard the health of the people, that they may live. Help us with your cleansing wind! May it make us pure so that we may walk the sacred path in a holy manner, pleasing to *Wakan-Tanka.*

"O Grandfather *Wakan-Tanka,* You are above everything! It is You who have placed a sacred rock upon the earth, which is now at the center of our hoop. You have given to us also the fire; and there at the place where the sun goes down, you have given power to *Wakinyan-Tanka* who controls the waters and who guards the most sacred pipe.[1] You have placed a winged One at the place where the sun comes up, who gives to us wisdom; and You have also placed a winged One at the place towards which we always face; He is the source of life, and He leads us on the sacred red path. All these powers, are Your power, and they are really one; they are all now here within this lodge."

[1] The great Thunderbird of the west: *Wakinyan-Tanka,* is one of the most important and profound aspects of Siouan religion. The Indian describes Him as living "in a lodge on the top of a mountain at the edge of the world where the sun goes down. He is many, but they are only as One; He is shapeless, but He has wings with four joints each; He has no feet, yet He has huge talons; He has no head, yet has a huge beak with rows of teeth in it like the teeth of the wolf; His voice is the thunder clap and rolling thunder is caused by the beating of His wings on the clouds; He has an eye, and its glance is lightning. In a great cedar tree beside His lodge He has His nest made of dry bones, and in it is an enormous egg from which His young continually issue. He devours His young and they each become one of His many selves. He flies through all the domain of the sky, hidden in a robe of clouds . . . . His functions are to cleanse the world from filth and to fight the Monsters who defile the Waters. His symbol is a zigzag red line forked at each end." (J. R. Walker, *The Sun Dance and other Ceremonies of the Oglala Division of the Teton Dakota* [Anthropological Papers of the American Museum of Natural History, XVI, Part II] [New York, 1917].)

This Thunderbird is really *Wakan-Tanka* as the giver of Revelation, (symbolized by the lightning); He is the same as the great one-eyed Bird, *Garuda,* of the Hindu tradition, or the Chinese Dragon (the Logos), who rides on the clouds of the storm, and whose voice is the thunder. As giver of Revelation he is identical in function to the Archangel Gabriel of Judaism or Christianity—the *Jibrail* of Islam.

It is fitting that the Thunderbird is for the Indian the protector of the sacred pipe, for the pipe, like the lightning, is the axis joining heaven and earth.

"O *Wakan-Tanka,* Grandfather, above all, it is Thy will that we are doing here. Through that Power which comes from the place where the giant *Waziah* lives, we are now making ourselves as pure and as white as new snow. We know that we are now in darkness, but soon the Light will come. When we leave this lodge may we leave behind all impure thoughts, all ignorance. May we be as children newly born! May we live again, O *Wakan-Tanka!*"

Water is now put on the rocks, four times for the Powers of the four directions, and as the steam rises we sing a song, or even just a chant, for this helps us to understand the mystery of all things.

The door of the lodge is soon opened for the second time, representing the coming of the purifying Power of the north, and also we see the light which destroys darkness, just as wisdom drives away ignorance. Water is passed to the leader at the east, who offers it to the men, mentioning his relationship to each, as I have described before.

The pipe is again handed into the lodge, and is given to the person sitting at the north; he offers it to the six directions, lights it, and after a few puffs (rubbing the smoke all over himself) he passes it around the circle. When all the *kinnikinnik* has been smoked up, the pipe is returned to the north, where it is purified, and the ashes are placed by the central altar. Then the pipe is handed out to the helper who again fills it and leans it upon the mound, this time with the stem pointing to the east, for we shall now invoke the Power of this direction. The door of the lodge is closed, and the man sitting at the east of the lodge now sends his voice in this manner:

"O Great Spirit, *Wakan-Tanka,* I have just seen the day, the Light of life. There where the sun comes up, You have given the power of wisdom to the Morning Star. The winged One who guards this path is long-winded, and with the two sacred days which You, O *Wakan-Tanka,* have given to Him, He has guarded the path of the people. O You who control that path where the sun comes up, look upon us with Your red and blue days, and help us in sending our voices to *Wakan-Tanka!* O You who have

knowledge, give some of it to us, that our hearts may be enlightened, and that we may know all that is sacred!

"O Morning Star, there at the place where the sun comes up;
O You who have the wisdom which we seek, help us in cleansing
ourselves and all the people, that our generations to come will
have Light as they walk the sacred Path. You lead the dawn as it
walks forth, and also the day which follows with its Light which
is knowledge; this You do for us and for all the people of the
world, that they may see clearly in walking the *wakan* path; that
they may know all that is holy, and that they may increase in a
sacred manner!"

Water is again poured on the rocks and we begin to sing a
sacred chant. In a short time, when the heat has worked all through
us, the door is opened for the third time, and the light of the east
comes in upon us. As the pipe is handed in to the man at the east,
all the men cry: *"Hi ho! Hi ho!* [Thanks!]" and the leader holds
the pipe up to heaven and sends his voice:

"Wakan-Tanka, we give thanks for the Light which You have
given to us through the Power of the place where the sun comes up.
Help us, O You Power of the east! Be merciful to us!"

The pipe is then lit and smoked around the circle, and again
when we have finished, the helper takes it and this time leans it
against the mound with its stem slanting to the south. Water is
again passed around sun-wise, and is rubbed all over the body,
especially on top of the head, and then the door is closed for the
last time. It is the man at the south who now sends his voice.

"Grandfather, *Wakan-Tanka,* behold us! You have placed a
great Power there where we always face, and from this direction
many generations have come forth, and have returned. There is a
winged One at this direction who guards the sacred red path, from
which the generations have come forth. The generation which is
here today wishes to cleanse and purify itself, that it may live again!

"We shall burn the sweet grass as an offering to *Wakan-Tanka,*
and the fragrance of this will spread throughout heaven and
earth; it will make the four-leggeds, the wingeds, the star peoples
of the heavens, and all things as relatives. From You, O Grand-

mother earth, who are lowly, and who support us as does a mother, this fragrance will go forth; may its power be felt throughout the universe, and may it purify the feet and hands of the two-leggeds, that they may walk forward upon the sacred earth, raising their heads to *Wakan-Tanka!*"

All that is left of the water is now poured upon the rocks, which are still very hot, and as the steam rises and penetrates everything, we sing or chant a sacred song. Soon the leader of the *Inipi* says: "The helper will soon open the door for the last time, and when it is open we shall see the Light. For it is the wish of *Wakan-Tanka* that the Light enters into the darkness, that we may see not only with our two eyes, but with the one eye which is of the heart [*Chante Ishta*], and with which we see and know all that is true and good.[2] We give thanks to the helper; may his generations be blessed! It is good! It is finished! *Hetchetu alo!*"

As the door of the lodge is opened, all the men cry: *"Hi ho! Hi ho!* Thanks!," and the men are all happy, for they have come forth from the darkness and are now living in the Light.[3] The helper then brings a live coal from the sacred fire, and places it just outside the doorway of the lodge, upon the sacred path. As he burns the sweet grass upon the coal, he says: "This is the fragrance of *Wakan-Tanka.* Through this the two-leggeds, the four-leggeds, the winged ones, and all the peoples of the universe, will be happy, and will rejoice!"

The leader of the rite then says: "This is the fire that will help the generations to come, if they use it in a sacred manner. But if they do not use it well, the fire will have the power to do them great harm."

[2] For a commentary on the "Eye of the Heart," see Frithjof Schuon, *L'Oeil du Coeur.*

[3] Entering into the light after being in the darkness of the purification lodge represents liberation from the universe, the cosmos, or microcosmically the liberation from the ego; both ego and world are "dark" since they have only a relative or illusory reality, for ultimately there is no reality other than *Wakan-Tanka,* who is here represented by the light of day, or by the space around the lodge.

This liberation from the cosmos, or from the individuality, is especially well represented in the purification rite of the Osage Indians: "At the close

The leader purifies his hands and feet over the smoke, and, raising his hands to heaven, he prays: *"Hi ho! Hi ho!"* (four times) *"Wakan-Tanka,* today You have been good to us; for this we give thanks. I now place my feet upon the Earth. With great happiness I walk upon the sacred Earth, our Mother. May the generations to come also walk in this sacred manner!"

Moving around sun-wise, all the men now leave the sweat lodge, and they too purify their hands and feet, and pray to *Wakan-Tanka* as their leader had done.

This most sacred rite has now been finished, and those who have participated are as men born again, and have done much good not only for themselves, but for the whole nation.

I should perhaps mention, that, often, when we are inside the sweat lodge, little children poke their heads inside, and ask the Great Spirit to make their lives pure. We do not chase them away, for we know that little children already have pure hearts.

When we leave the sweat lodge we are as the souls which are kept, as I have described, and which return to *Wakan-Tanka* after they have been purified; for we, too, leave behind in the *Inipi* lodge all that is impure, that we may live as the Great Spirit wishes, and that we may know something of that real world of the Spirit, which is behind this one.

These rites of the *Inipi* are very *wakan* and are used before any great undertaking for which we wish to make ourselves pure or for which we wish to gain strength; and in many winters past our men, and often the women, made the *Inipi* even every day, and sometimes several times in a day, and from this we received much of our power. Now that we have neglected these rites we have lost much of this power; it is not good, and I cry when I think of it. I pray often that the Great Spirit will show to our young people the importance of these rites.

of the ceremony the Chief . . . tells the men that each one must grasp one of the frame poles of the little house, and when they have done so he calls out: 'There is no other way out, my valiant men!' and all the men acting in concert, toss the little house upward, towards the setting sun." (Francis La Flesche, "War and Peace Ceremony of the Osage Indians," *Bulletin No. 101 of the Bureau of American Ethnology.*)

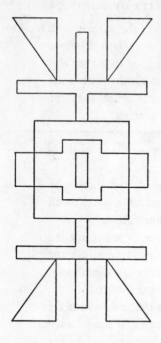

CHAPTER IV

Hanblecheyapi: CRYING FOR A VISION

The "Crying for a Vision" ritual, like the purification rites of the *Inipi,* was used long before the coming of our most sacred pipe. This way of praying is very important, and indeed it is at the center of our religion, for from it we have received many good things, even the four great rites which I shall soon describe.

Every man can cry for a vision, or "lament"; and in the old days we all—men and women—"lamented" all the time. What is received through the "lamenting" is determined in part by the character of the person who does this, for it is only those people who are very qualified who receive the great visions, which are interpreted by our holy man, and which give strength and health to our nation. It is very important for a person who wishes to "lament" to receive aid and advice from a *wichasha wakan* (holy man),[1] so that everything is done correctly, for if things are not done in the right way, something very bad can happen, and even a serpent could come and wrap itself around the "lamenter."

You have all heard of our great chief and priest Crazy Horse, but perhaps you did not know that he received most of his great power through the "lamenting" which he did many times a year, and even in the winter when it is very cold and very difficult. He received visions of the Rock, the Shadow, the Badger, a prancing horse (from which he received his name), the Day, and also of *Wanbli Galeshka,* the Spotted Eagle, and from each of these he received much power and holiness.[2]

There are many reasons for going to a lonely mountaintop to "lament." Some young men receive a vision when they are very young and when they do not expect it,[3] and then they go to "la-

---

[1] Throughout this work I have translated *wichasha wakan* as "holy man" or "priest," rather than "Medicine man," which has been used incorrectly in many books on the Indians. The Lakota term for "medicine man" or "doctor" is really *pejuta wichasa.* In order to clarify these frequently confused terms, I cannot do better than to quote the explanation given by Sword, an Oglala Sioux, to J. R. Walker: *"Wicasa wakan* is the term for a Lakota priest of the old religion; a Lakota medicine man is called *pejuta wacasa.* The white people call our *wicasa wakan,* medicine man, which is a mistake. Again, they say a *wicasa wakan* is making medicine when he is performing ceremonies. This is also a mistake. The Lakota call a thing "medicine" only when it is used to cure the sick or wounded, the proper term (for medicine) being *pejuta."* (*The Sun Dance . . . of the Teton Dakota* [Anthropological Papers of the American Museum of Natural History, XVI, Part II, 152].)

[2] The Indian actually identifies himself with, or becomes, the quality or principle of the being or thing which comes to him in a vision, whether it be a beast, a bird, one of the elements, or really any aspect of creation. In order that this "power" may never leave him, he always carries with him some material form representing the animal or object from which he has received his "power." These objects have often been incorrectly called fetishes, whereas they actually correspond more precisely to what the Christian calls guardian angels, since for the Indian, the animals and birds, and all things, are the "reflections"—in a material form—of the Divine principles. The Indian is only attached to the form for the sake of the principle which is contained within the form.

[3] Black Elk himself received his great vision when he was only nine years old. For a description of this vision, see Neihardt's *Black Elk Speaks,* chap. III.

ment" that they might understand it better. Then we "lament" if we wish to make ourselves brave for a great ordeal such as the Sun Dance or to prepare for going on the warpath. Some people "lament" in order to ask some favor of the Great Spirit, such as curing a sick relative; and then we also "lament" as an act of thanksgiving for some great gift which the Great Spirit may have given to us. But perhaps the most important reason for "lamenting" is that it helps us to realize our oneness with all things, to know that all things are our relatives; and then in behalf of all things we pray to *Wakan-Tanka* that He may give to us knowledge of Him who is the source of all things, yet greater than all things.

Our women also "lament," after first purifying themselves in the *Inipi;* they are helped by other women, but they do not go up on a very high and lonely mountain. They go up on a hill in a valley, for they are women and need protection.

When a person wishes to "lament," he goes with a filled pipe to a holy man; he enters the tipi with the stem of the pipe pointing in front of him, and sits before the old man who is to be his guide. The "lamenter" then places the pipe on the ground with its stem now pointing towards himself, for it is he who wishes to gain knowledge. The holy man raises his hands above to *Wakan-Tanka* and to the four directions, and, taking up the pipe, he asks the man what he wishes.

"I wish to 'lament' and offer my pipe to *Wakan-Tanka*. I need your help and guidance, and wish you to send a voice for me to the Powers above."

To this the old man says: *"How!"* (It is good); and then they leave the tipi, and, walking a short distance, they face the west, the young man standing to the left of the holy man, and they are joined by any others who may happen to be present. All raise their right hands, and the old man prays, holding the stem of the pipe to the heavens.

"Hee-ay-hay-ee-ee! [four times.] Grandfather, *Wakan-Tanka,* You are first and always have been! Everything belongs to You. It is You who have created all things! You are One and alone, and

to You we are sending a voice. This young man here is in difficulty, and wishes to offer the pipe to You. We ask that You give help to him! Within a few days he will offer his body to You. Upon the sacred Earth, our Mother and Grandmother, he will place his feet in a sacred manner.

"All the Powers of the world, the heavens and the star peoples, and the red and blue sacred days; all things that move in the universe, in the rivers, the brooks, the springs, all waters, all trees that stand, all the grasses of our Grandmother, all the sacred peoples of the universe: Listen! A sacred relationship with you all will be asked by this young man, that his generations to come will increase and live in a holy manner.

"O You, winged One, there where the sun goes down, who guards our sacred pipe, help us! Help us to offer this pipe to *Wakan-Tanka,* that He may give a blessing to this young man!"

To this all the people cry "*How!*" and then they sit in a circle upon the ground. The old man offers the pipe to the six directions, lights it, and passes it first to the young man who is to "lament." The "lamenter" offers it up with a prayer, and then it is smoked by everybody in the circle. When the pipe is smoked out, it is handed back to the holy man, who cleans and purifies it and hands it back to the young man, asking him when he wishes to "lament," and a day is then decided upon.

When this chosen day arrives, the young man wears only his buffalo robe, breech cloth, and moccasins, and he goes with his pipe to the tipi of the holy man. Crying as he walks, he enters the lodge and places his right hand on the head of the old man, saying: "*Unshe ma la ye!*" (Be merciful to me!) He then lays the pipe in front of the holy man and asks for his help.

The old man replies: "We all know that the pipe is sacred, and with it you have now come crying. I shall help you, but you must always remember what I am going to tell you; in the winters to come you must walk with the instructions and advice which I give to you. You may "lament" from one to four days, or even longer if you wish; how many days do you choose?"

"I choose two days."

"Good! This, then, is what you must do: First you should build an *Inipi* lodge in which we shall purify ourselves, and for this you must select twelve or sixteen small willows. But before you cut the willows remember to take to them a tobacco offering; and as you stand before them you should say: 'There are many kinds of trees, but it is you whom I have chosen to help me. I shall take you, but in your place there will be others!' Then you should bring these trees back to where we shall make the lodge.

"In a sacred manner you must also gather the rocks and sage, and then you must make a bundle of five long sticks and also five bundles of twelve small sticks, all of which will be used as offerings. These sticks you should lean against the west side of the sweat lodge until we are ready to purify them. We shall also need the Ree twist tobacco, *kinnikinnik,* a tobacco cutting board, buckskin for the tobacco-offering bags, sweet grass, a bag of sacred earth, a knife, and a stone hatchet. These things you must secure yourself, and when you are ready we shall purify ourselves. *Hetchetu welo!"*

When the purification lodge has been built, and all the equipment gathered, the holy man enters the lodge and sits at the west; the "lamenter" enters next and sits at the north, and then a helper enters and sits just to the south of the holy man. A cold rock is brought into the lodge and is placed on the north side of the central altar, where it is purified with a short prayer by the holy man; it is then taken outside by a helper. This is the first rock to be placed on the fire (*peta owihankeshni*) which has been built to the east of the lodge.

Just east of the central altar, within the purification lodge, the helper scrapes a sacred place upon the earth, and upon this he places a hot coal. The holy man now moves around to the east, and, bending over the coal, he holds up a bit of sweet grass and prays in this manner:

"O Grandfather, *Wakan-Tanka,* behold us! Upon the sacred earth I place this Your herb. The smoke that rises from the earth and fire will belong to all that moves in the universe: the four-leggeds, the wingeds, and everything that moves and everything that is. This offering of theirs will now be given to You, O *Wakan-Tanka!* We shall make sacred all that we touch!"

As the sweet grass is put upon the coal, the other two men in the lodge cry, *"Hi ye!"* (Thanks), and as the smoke rises, the holy man rubs his hands in it and then rubs them over his body. In the same manner the "lamenter" and the helper purify themselves with the sacred smoke. The little bag of earth is also purified, and then the three men again take their places at the west, every movement being made, of course, in a sun-wise manner. The purified earth is now very carefully spread all around inside the sacred central hole, and this is done slowly and reverently for this earth represents the whole universe. The helper hands a stick to the holy man, who uses it to mark four places around the hole, the first at the west, and then at the north, east, and south. Next a cross is made by drawing a line on the ground from west to east, then one from the north to the south. All this is very sacred, for it establishes the four great Powers of the universe, and also the center which is the dwelling place of *Wakan-Tanka.* A helper now enters from the outside carrying a hot coal in a split stick; he walks slowly, stopping four times, and the last time the coal is placed upon the center of the cross.

Holding a pinch of sweet grass over the coal, the holy man prays: "My Grandfather, *Wakan-Tanka,* You are everything. And my Father, *Wakan-Tanka,* all things belong to You! I am about to place Your herb on this fire. Its fragrance belongs to You."

The old man then slowly lowers the sweet grass to the fire. The helper now takes up the pipe, and moving with it in a sun-wise direction, hands it to the holy man who prays with it in these words: "O *Wakan-Tanka,* behold Your pipe! I hold it over the smoke of this herb. O *Wakan-Tanka,* behold also this sacred place which we have made. We know that its center is Your dwelling place. Upon this circle the generations will walk. The four-leggeds, the two-leggeds, the wingeds, and the four Powers of the universe, all will behold this, Your place."

The holy man holds the pipe over the smoke, pointing the stem first to the west, and then to the north, the east, the south, and to heaven, then he touches the earth with its foot. He purifies all the sacred equipment: the buffalo robe and all the offering sticks; and then he makes little bags of tobacco which he ties on the ends of the offering sticks.

The old holy man, now seated at the west, takes the tobacco cutting board and begins to chop and mix the *kinnikinnik*. He first judges carefully the size of the pipe, for he must make just enough to fill the pipe bowl and no more. Each time that he shaves off a little piece of the tobacco, he offers it to one of the quarters of the world, taking great care that no piece jumps off the board, for this would make the Thunder-beings very angry. When the mixing has been finished, the old man takes up the pipe with his left hand, and holding up a pinch of the *kinnikinnik* with his right hand, he prays.

"O *Wakan-Tanka,* my Father and Grandfather, You are first, and always have been! Behold this young man here who has a troubled mind. He wishes to travel upon the sacred path; he will offer this pipe to You. Be merciful to him and help him! The four Powers and the whole universe will be placed in the bowl of the pipe, and then this young man will offer it to You, with the help of the wingeds and all things.

"The first to be placed in the pipe is You, O winged Power of the place where the sun goes down. You with Your guards are ancient and sacred. Behold! There is a place for You in the pipe; help us with Your two sacred blue and red days!"

The holy man places this tobacco in the pipe, and then he holds up another pinch towards the place in the north where *Waziah* the Giant lives.

"O You, winged Power, there where the Giant has His lodge, from whence come the strong purifying winds: there is a place for you in the pipe; help us with the two sacred days which you have!"

The Power of this direction is placed in the pipe, and a third pinch of tobacco is held towards the east.

"O You where the sun comes up, who guard the light and who give knowledge, this pipe will be offered to *Wakan-Tanka!* There is a place here for you too; help us with Your sacred days!"

In the same manner the Power of the east is placed in the pipe; and now a pinch of tobacco is held towards the south, the place towards which we always face.

"O You who control the sacred winds, and who live there where we always face, Your breath gives life; and it is from You and to You that our generations come and go. This pipe is about to be offered to *Wakan-Tanka;* there is a place in it for You. Help us with the two sacred days which You have!"

In this manner all the Powers of the four directions have been placed within the bowl of the pipe, and now a pinch of the sacred tobacco is held up towards the heavens, and this is for *Wanbli Galeshka,* the Spotted Eagle, who is higher than all other created beings, and who represents *Wakan-Tanka:*

"O *Wanbli Galeshka,* who circles in the highest heavens, You see all things in the heavens and upon the earth. This young man is about to offer his pipe to *Wakan-Tanka,* in order that he may gain knowledge. Help him, and all those who send their voices to *Wakan-Tanka* through you. There is a place for You in the pipe; give to us Your two sacred red and blue days."

With this prayer the Spotted Eagle is placed in the bowl of the pipe, and now a pinch of the tobacco is held towards Earth, and the old man continues to pray:

"O *Unchi* and *Ina,* our Grandmother and Mother, You are sacred! We know that it is from You that our bodies have come. This young man wishes to become one with all things; he wishes to gain knowledge. For the good of all your peoples, help him! There is a place for you in the pipe; give to us your two sacred red and blue days!"

Thus the Earth, which is now in the tobacco, is placed in the pipe, and in this manner all the six Powers of the universe have here become one. But in order to make sure that all the peoples of the world are included in the pipe, the holy man offers small grains of tobacco for each of the following winged peoples: "O sacred King Bird, who flies on the two sacred days; You who raise families so well, may we increase and live in the same manner. This pipe will soon be offered to *Wakan-Tanka!* There is a place here for You. Help us!" With the same prayer, small grains of tobacco are offered and placed in the pipe, for the meadow lark, the black-bird, the woodpecker, the snowbird, the crow, the magpie, the dove, the hawk, the eagle hawk, the bald eagle, and finally what is left of the tobacco is offered for the two-legged who is about to "lament," offering himself up to *Wakan-Tanka*.

The pipe is then sealed with tallow, for the "lamenter" will take it with him when he goes to the top of the mountain, and there he will offer it to *Wakan-Tanka;* but it will not be smoked until he finishes the "lamenting" and returns to the holy man.

All the offering poles and the equipment which have been purified, are now taken and are placed outside the lodge at the west. The three men leave the lodge and prepare for the *Inipi* by taking off all their clothes except the breech cloth. Any other men who may now be present are permitted to take part in this purification rite.

The "lamenter" enters the *Inipi* first and, moving around sun-wise, sits at the west of the lodge. He takes up his pipe which had been left in the lodge (with its stem pointing to the east) and, turning it around sun-wise, holds it up in front of him; and he remains in this position for the first part of the rite. The holy man enters next and, passing behind the "lamenter," sits at the east, just beside the door. Any other men who wish to take part in the rite then fill in the remaining places; two men remain outside to act as helpers.

One of the helpers fills a pipe in a ritual manner, and this is handed in to the man who sits just at the left of the "lamenter." The rock which had previously been purified is also handed in—on a forked stick, for it is now very hot—and is placed at the center of the sacred hole. A second rock is then placed at the west in the sacred place, and the others are placed at the north, east, and south. As the rocks are put in place, the person who holds the pipe to be smoked in the rite touches its foot to each rock, and as he does this all the men cry: *"Hi ye! Hi ye!"* The pipe is then lit, offered to Heaven, Earth, and the four directions, and is smoked around the circle. As it passes around, each man mentions his relationship to the person next to him, and after everybody has smoked they all say together: *"mitakuye oyasin!"* (We are all relatives!). The one who lit the pipe now empties it, placing the ashes upon the center altar, and after purifying it he hands it to the left, and it is passed out of the lodge. The helper again fills the pipe and leans it on the sacred mound with the stem pointing to the west. The door of the lodge is closed, and the holy man at the east begins to pray in the darkness: "Behold! All that moves in the universe is here!" This is repeated by everybody in the lodge, and at the end they all say: *"How!"*

"*Hee-ay-hay-ee-ee!* [four times] I am sending a voice! Hear me! [four times] *Wakan-Tanka,* Grandfather, behold us! O *Wakan-Tanka,* Father, behold us! On this great island there is a two-legged who says that he will offer a pipe to You. On this day his promise will be fulfilled. To whom could one send a voice except to You, *Wakan-Tanka,* our Grandfather and Father. O *Wakan-Tanka,* this young man asks You to be merciful to him. He says that his mind is troubled and that he needs Your help. In offering this pipe to You, he will offer his whole mind and body. The time has now come; he will soon go to a high place, and there he will cry for Your aid. Be merciful to him!

"O You four Powers of the universe, you wingeds of the air, and all the peoples who move in the universe—you have all been placed in the pipe. Help this young man with the knowledge which has been given to all of you by *Wakan-Tanka.* Be merciful to him! O *Wakan-Tanka,* grant that this young man may have relatives; that he may be one with the four winds, the four Powers of the world, and with the light of the dawn. May he understand his relationship with all the winged peoples of the air. He will place his feet upon the sacred earth of a mountaintop; may he receive understanding there; may his generations to come be holy! All things give thanks to You, O *Wakan-Tanka,* who are merciful, and who help us all. We ask all this of You because we know that You are the only One, and that You have power over all things!"

As a little water is poured on the red hot rocks, all the men sing:

Grandfather, I am sending a voice!
To the Heavens of the universe, I am sending a voice;
That my people may live!

As the men sing this, and as the hot steam rises, the "lamenter" cries, for he is humbling himself, remembering his nothingness in the presence of the Great Spirit.[4]

After a short time the door of the lodge is opened by the helper, and the "lamenter" now embraces his pipe, holding it first to one shoulder and then to the other, and crying all the time to the Great Spirit: "Be merciful to me! Help me!" This pipe is then passed around the circle, and all the other men embrace it and cry in the same manner. It is then passed out of the lodge to the helpers, who also embrace it and then lean it on the little mound, with its stem to the east; for this direction is the source of light and understanding.

The second pipe which is being used for the purification rite, and which had been leaning on the sacred mound with its stem to the west, is now handed into the lodge, and is given to the person sitting just to the left of the "lamenter." This pipe is lit, and after it has been smoked by everybody in the circle, it is passed out of the lodge. After this, water is passed around, and the "lamenter" is now allowed to drink all that he wishes, but he must be careful not to spill any or to put any on his body, for this would anger the Thunder-beings who guard the sacred waters, and then they might visit him every night that he "laments." The holy man tells the "lamenter" to rub his body with the sage, and then the door is closed once more. A prayer is said by the next holiest man in the lodge, one who has had a vision.

"On this sacred earth, the Thunder-beings have been merci-

---

[4] This humiliation in which the Indian makes himself "lower than even the smallest ant," as Black Elk once expressed it, is the same attitude as that which, in Christianity, is called the "spiritual poverty"; this poverty is the *faqr* of the Islamic tradition or the *balya* of Hinduism and is the condition of those who realize that in relation to the Divine principle their own individuality is as nothing.

54

ful to me, and have given to me a power from where the Giant
Waziah lives. It was an eagle who came to me. He will see you too
when you go to cry for a vision. Then from the place where the
sun comes up, they sent to me a Baldheaded Eagle; he too will
see you. From the place towards which we always face, they sent
to me a winged one. They were very merciful to me. In the depths
of the heavens there is a winged being who is next to *Wakan-
Tanka;* He is the Spotted Eagle, and He too will behold you. You
will be seen by all the Powers and by the sacred earth upon which
you stand. They have given to me a good road to follow upon this
earth; may you too know this way! Set your mind upon the meanings of these things, and you will see! All this is so; do not forget!
Hechetu welo!"

This old man then sings:

> *They are sending a voice to me.*
> *From the place where the sun goes down,*
> *Our Grandfather is sending a voice to me.*
> *From where the sun goes down,*
> *They are talking to me as they come.*
> *Our Grandfather's voice is calling to me.*
> *That winged One there where the Giant lives,*
> *Is sending a voice to me. He is calling me.*
> *Our Grandfather is calling me!"*

As the old man chants this song, water is put on the rocks, and
after the men have been in the hot fragrant steam and darkness
for a short time, the door is opened, and the fresh air and light fill
the little lodge. Once again the pipe is taken from the sacred mound
and is handed in to the man at the north of the lodge. After it has
been smoked it is placed again on the mound with its stem pointing to the east. The door is closed, and this time it is the holy man
at the east who prays.

"O *Wakan-Tanka,* behold all that we do and ask here! O You,
Power, there where the sun goes down, who control the waters:
with the breath of your waters this young man is purifying himself. And you too, O very aged rocks who are helping us here,

55

listen! You are firmly fixed upon this earth; we know that the winds cannot shake you. This young man is about to send his voice, crying for a vision. You are helping us by giving to him some of your power; through your breath he is being made pure.

"O eternal fire there where the sun comes up, from you this young man is gaining strength and light. O you standing trees, *Wakan-Tanka* has given you the power to stand upright. May this young man always have you as an example; may he hold firmly to you! It is good. *Hechetu welo!*"

All the men now chant again, and after a little while the door is opened, and the pipe is sent to the holy man at the east, who lights it, and after smoking for a few puffs, hands it around the circle. When the tobacco has been smoked up, the helper again takes the pipe and places it on the earth mound, with the stem leaning to the south. The door of the *Inipi* is closed for the last time, and now the holy man addresses his prayer to the rocks.

"O you ancient rocks who are sacred, you have neither ears nor eyes, yet you hear and see all things. Through your powers this young man has become pure, that he may be worthy to go to receive some message from *Wakan-Tanka*. The men who guard the door of this sacred lodge will soon open it for the fourth time, and we shall see the light of the world. Be merciful to the men who guard the door! May their generations be blessed!"

Water is placed on the rocks, which are still very hot, and after the steam has penetrated throughout the lodge for a short time, the door is opened, and all the men cry: *"Hi ho! Hi ho!* Thanks!"

The "lamenter" leaves the lodge first, and goes and sits upon the sacred path, facing the little mound, and crying all the while. One of the helpers then takes up the buffalo robe, which had been purified, and places it over the shoulders of the "lamenter"; and another helper takes the pipe which has been leaning all this time on the mound, and hands it to the "lamenter," who is now ready to go up to the high mountain, there to cry for a vision.

Three horses are brought, and upon two of these the bundles of offering sticks and some sacred sage are loaded; the "lamenter" rides on the third horse, and all this time he is crying most pitifully and is holding his pipe in front of him. When they arrive at the foot of the chosen mountain, the two helpers go on ahead with all the equipment in order to prepare the sacred place on the mountaintop. When they arrive they enter the chosen place by walking in a direction always away from their camping circle, and they go directly to the spot which they have chosen to be the center and place all the equipment here. At this center they first make a hole, in which they place some *kinnikinnik,* and then in this hole they set up a long pole with the offerings tied at the top. One of the helpers now goes about ten stride to the west, and in the same manner he sets up a pole here, tying offerings to it. He then goes to the center where he picks up another pole, and this he fixes at the north again returning to the center. In the same manner he sets up poles at the east and at the south. All this time the other

helper has been making a bed of sage at the center, so that when the "lamenter" is tired he may lie with his head against the center pole, and his feet stretching towards the east. When everything has been finished the helpers leave the sacred place by the north path, and then return to the "lamenter" at the foot of the mountain.

The "lamenter" now takes off his moccasins and even his breech cloth—for if we really wish to "lament" we must be poor in the things of this world—and he walks alone up to the top of the mountain, holding his pipe in front of him, and carrying his buffalo robe which he will use at night. As he walks he cries continually: *"Wakan-Tanka onshimala ye oyate wani wachin cha!"* (O Great Spirit, be merciful to me that my people may live!)

Entering the sacred place, the "lamenter" goes directly to the center pole, where he faces the west, and holding up his pipe with both hands he continues to cry: "O *Wakan-Tanka,* have pity on me, that my people may live!" Then walking very slowly he goes to the pole at the west, where he offers up the same prayer, and then returns to the center. In the same manner he goes to the poles at the north, east, and south, always returning to the center each time. After completing one of these rounds, he raises his pipe to

57

the heavens asking the wingeds and all things to help him, and then pointing the pipe stem to the Earth, he asks aid from all that grows upon our Mother.

All this takes very little time to tell, yet the "lamenter" should do it all so slowly and in such a sacred manner that often he may take an hour or even two to make one of these rounds. The "lamenter" can move in no other manner than this, which is in the form of a cross, although he may linger at any one place as long as he wishes; but all day long this is what he does, praying constantly, either out loud or silently to himself, for the Great Spirit is everywhere; he hears whatever is in our minds and hearts, and it is not necessary to speak to Him in a loud voice. The "lamenter" need not always use this prayer that I have given, for he may remain silent with his whole attention directed to the Great Spirit or to one of His Powers. He must always be careful lest distracting thoughts come to him, yet he must be alert to recognize any messenger which the Great Spirit may send to him, for these people often come in the form of an animal, even one as small and as seemingly insignificant as a little ant. Perhaps a Spotted Eagle may come to him from the west, or a Black Eagle from the north, or the Bald Eagle from the east, or even the Red-headed Woodpecker may come to him from the south. And even though none of these may speak to him at first, they are important and should be observed. The "lamenter" should also notice if one of the little birds should come, or even perhaps a squirrel. At first the animals or winged peoples may be wild, but soon they become tame, and the birds will sit on the poles, or even little ants or worms may crawl on the pipe. All these people are important, for in their own way they are wise and they can teach us two-leggeds much if we make ourselves humble before them. The most important of all the creatures are the wingeds, for they are nearest to the heavens, and are not bound to the earth as are the four-leggeds, or the little crawling people.

It may be good to mention here that it is not without reason that we humans are two-legged along with the wingeds; for you see the birds leave the earth with their wings, and we humans may also leave this world, not with wings, but in the spirit. This will help you to understand in part how it is that we regard all created beings as sacred and important, for everything has a *wochangi* or influence which can be given to us, through which we may gain a little more understanding if we are attentive.

All day long the "lamenter" sends his voice to *Wakan-Tanka* for aid, and he walks as we have described upon the sacred paths which form a cross. This form has much power in it, for whenever we return to the center, we know that it is as if we are returning to *Wakan-Tanka,* who is the center of everything; and although we may think that we are going away from Him, sooner or later we and all things must return to Him.

In the evening the "lamenter" is very tired, for you should remember that he may neither eat nor drink during the days that he cries for a vision. He may sleep on the bed of sage which had been prepared for him, and must lean his head against the center pole, for even though he sleeps he is close to *Wakan-Tanka,* and it is very often during sleep that the most powerful visions come to us; they are not merely dreams, for they are much more real and powerful and do not come from ourselves, but from *Wakan-Tanka.* It may be that we shall receive no vision or message from the Great Spirit the first time that we "lament," yet we may try many times, for we should remember that *Wakan-Tanka* is always anxious to aid those who seek Him with a pure heart. But of course much depends on the nature of the person who cries for a vision, and upon the degree to which he has purified and prepared himself.

In the evenings the Thunder-beings may come, and although they are very terrifying, they bring much good, and they test our strength and endurance. Then too they help us to realize how really very small and insignificant we are compared to the great powers of *Wakan-Tanka.*

I remember one time when I "lamented," and a great storm came from the place where the sun goes down, and I talked with the Thunder-beings who came with hail and thunder and lightning and much rain, and the next morning I saw that there was hail all piled up on the ground around the sacred place, yet inside it was perfectly dry. I think that they were trying to test me. And then, on one of the nights the bad spirits came and started tearing the offerings off the poles; and I heard their voices under the ground, and one of them said: "Go and see if he is crying." And I heard rattles, but all the time they were outside the sacred place and could not get in, for I had resolved not to be afraid, and did not stop sending my voice to *Wakan-Tanka* for aid. Then later, one of the bad spirits said from somewhere under the ground: "Yes, he is surely crying," and the next morning I saw that the poles and offerings were still there. I was well prepared, you see, and did not weaken, and so nothing bad could happen.

The "lamenter" should get up in the middle of the night, and he should again go to the four quarters, returning to the center each time, and all the while he should be sending his voice. He should always be up with the morning star, and he should walk towards the east, and, pointing his pipe stem towards this sacred star, he should ask it for wisdom; this he should pray silently in his heart, and not out loud. All this the "lamenter" should do for the three or four days.

At the end of this period the helpers come with their horses and take the "lamenter" with his pipe back to the camp, and there he immediately enters the *Inipi* which has already been made ready for him. He should sit at the west, holding his pipe in front of him all the time. The holy man—the spiritual guide of the "lamenter"—enters next and, passing behind the "lamenter," sits at the east, and all the other men fill the remaining places.

The first sacred rock, which has already been heated, is brought into the lodge and is placed at the center of the altar, and then all the other rocks are brought in, as I have described before. All this is done very solemnly but more rapidly than before, for all the men are anxious to hear what the "lamenter" has to tell and to know what great things may have come to him up there on the mountain. When all has been made ready, the holy man says to the "lamenter":

"Ho! You have now sent a voice with your pipe to *Wakan-*

Black Elk with his wife, about 1883. *(Photograph from author's collection)*

Black Elk (left) and Yellow Hand (right), when they were with the Buffalo Bill Show. *(Photograph from author's collection)*

Tanka. That pipe is now very sacred, for the whole universe has seen it. You have offered this pipe to all the four sacred Powers; they have seen it! And each word that you said up there was heard, even by our Grandmother and Mother Earth. The coming generations will hear you! These five ancient rocks here will hear you! The winged Power of the place where the sun goes down, who controls the waters, will hear you! The standing trees who are present here will hear you! And also the most sacred pipe which was given to the people will hear you; so tell us the truth, and be sure that you make up nothing! Even the tiny ants and the crawling worms may have come to see you up there when you were crying for a vision; tell us everything! You have brought back to us the pipe which you offered; it is finished! And since you are about to put this pipe to your mouth, you should tell us nothing but the truth. The pipe is *wakan* and knows all things; you cannot fool it. If you lie, *Wakinyan-Tanka,* who guards the pipe, will punish you! *Hechetu welo!*"

The holy man rises from his position at the east and, moving around the lodge sun-wise, sits just at the right of the "lamenter." Dried buffalo chips are placed in front of the "lamenter," and upon these the pipe is placed with its stem pointing towards the heavens. The holy man now takes the tallow seal off the bowl of the pipe and places it upon the buffalo chips. He lights the pipe with a coal from the fire and, after offering it up to the Powers of the six directions, points the stem towards the "lamenter," who just touches it with his mouth. The holy man then makes a circle in the air with the stem of the pipe, smokes it a little himself, and again touches it to the mouth of the "lamenter." Then he again waves the pipe stem in a circle and again smokes it a little himself. This is done four times, and then the pipe is passed around the circle for all the men to smoke. When it returns to the holy man, with four motions he empties it upon the top of the tallow seal and the buffalo chips and then purifies it. Holding the pipe up in front of himself, the holy man says to the "lamenter": "Young man, you left here three days ago with your two helpers, who have set up for you the five posts upon the sacred place. Tell us everything that happened to you up there after these helpers left! Do not omit anything! We have prayed much to *Wakan-Tanka* for you and have asked the pipe to be merciful. Tell us now what happened!"

The "lamenter" replies, and after each time he says something of importance all the men in the lodge cry "*Hi ye!*"

"I went up on the mountain, and, after entering the sacred place, I walked continually to each of the four directions, always returning to the center as you had instructed me. During the first day, as I was facing the place where the sun goes down, I saw an eagle flying towards me, and when it came nearer I saw that it was a sacred Spotted Eagle. He rested on a tree near me but said nothing; and then he flew away to the place where the Giant *Waziah* lives."

To this all the men cry: "*Hi ye!*"

"I returned to the center, and then I went to the north, and as I stood there I saw an eagle circling above, and as he lighted near me I noticed that he was a young eagle, but it, too, said nothing to me, and soon he circled and soared off towards the place towards which we always face.

"I went back to the center where I cried and sent my voice, and then I went towards the place where the sun comes up. There I saw something flying towards me, and soon I saw that it was a baldheaded eagle, but he too said nothing to me.

"Crying, I returned to the center, and then when I went towards the place which we always face, I saw a red-breasted woodpecker standing on the offering pole. I believe he may have given to me something of his *wochangi*, for I heard him say to me very faintly yet distinctly: 'Be attentive! [*wachin ksapa yo!*] and have no fear; but pay no attention to any bad thing that may come and talk to you!' "

All the men now say more loudly: "*Hi ye!*"; for this message which the bird gave is very important.

The "lamenter" continues: "Although I was crying and sending my voice continually, this was all that I heard and saw that first day. Then night fell, and I lay down with my head at the center and went to sleep; and in my sleep I heard and saw my people, and I noticed that they were all very happy.

"I arose in the middle of the night, and again walked to each of the four directions, returning to the center each time, continually sending my voice. Just before the morning star came up, I again visited the four quarters, and just as I reached the place where the sun rises, I saw the Morning Star, and I noticed that at first it was all red, and then it changed to blue, and then into yellow, and finally I saw that it was white, and in these four colors I saw the four ages. Although this star did not really speak to me, yet it taught me very much.

"I stood there waiting for the sun to rise, and just at dawn I saw the world full of little winged people, and they were all rejoicing. Finally the sun came up, bringing its light into the world, and then I began to cry and returned to the center where I lay down, leaning my pipe against the center offering-pole.

"As I lay there at the center I could hear all sorts of little wingeds who were sitting on the poles, but none of them spoke to me. I looked at my pipe and there I saw two ants walking on the stem. Perhaps they wished to speak to me, but soon they left.

"Often during the day as I was crying and sending my voice, birds and butterflies would come to me, and once a white butterfly came and sat on the end of the pipe stem, working his beautiful wings up and down. During this day I saw no large four-leggeds, just the little peoples. Then just before the sun went down to rest, I saw that clouds were gathering, and the Thunder-beings were coming. The lightning was all over the sky, and the thunder was terrifying, and I think that perhaps I was a little afraid. But I held my pipe up and continued to send my voice to *Wakan-Tanka;* and soon I heard another voice saying: *'Hee-ay-hay-ee-ee! Hee-ay-hay-ee-ee!'* Four times they said this, and then all the fear left me, for I remembered what the little bird had told me, and I felt very brave. I heard other voices, also, which I could not understand. I stood there with my eyes closed—I do not know how long —and when I opened them everything was very bright, brighter even than the day; and I saw many people on horseback coming towards me, all riding horses of different colors. One of the riders even spoke to me saying: 'Young man, you are offering the pipe to *Wakan-Tanka;* we are all very happy that you are doing this!' This is all that they said, and then they disappeared.

"The next day, just before the sun came up, as I was visiting the four quarters, I saw the same little red-breasted bird; he was sitting on the pole there where we always face, and he said almost the same thing to me as before: 'Friend, be attentive as you walk!' That was all. Soon after this the two helpers came to bring me back. This is all that I know; I have told the truth and have made nothing up!"

Thus the "lamenter" finishes his account. Now the holy man gives to him his pipe, which he embraces, and it is then passed around the circle, and a helper takes it and leans it, with its stem to the west, against the sacred mound at the east of the lodge. More hot rocks are handed into the lodge; the door is closed; and the *Inipi* begins.

The holy man prays, giving thanks to *Wakan-Tanka:* "Hee-ey-hay-ee-ee! [four times] O Grandfather, *Wakan-Tanka,* today You have helped us. You have been merciful to this young man by giving him knowledge and a path which he may follow. You have made his people happy, and all the beings who move in the universe are rejoicing!

"Grandfather, this young man who has offered the pipe to You, has heard a voice which said to him, 'be attentive as you walk!' He wants to know what this message means; it must now be explained to him. It means that he should always remember You, O *Wakan-Tanka,* as he walks the sacred path of life; and he must be attentive to all the signs that You have given to us. If he does this always, he will become wise and a leader of his people. O *Wakan-Tanka,* help us all to be always attentive!⁵

[5] This message—"Be attentive!"—well expresses a spirit which is central to the Indian peoples; it implies that in every act, in every thing, and in every instant, the Great Spirit is present, and that one should be continually and intensely "attentive" to this Divine presence.

This presence of *Wakan-Tanka,* and one's consciousness of it, is that which the Christian saints have termed "living in the moment," the "eter-

"This young man also saw four ages in that star there where the sun comes up. These are the ages through which all creatures must pass in their journey from birth to death.

"O *Wakan-Tanka,* when this young man saw the dawn of the day, he saw Your light coming into the universe; this is the light of wisdom. All these things You have revealed to us, for it is Your will that the peoples of the world do not live in the darkness of ignorance.

"O *Wakan-Tanka,* You have established a relationship with this young man; and through this relationship he will bring strength to his people. We who are now sitting here represent all the people, and thus we all give thanks to You, O *Wakan-Tanka.* We all raise our hands to You and say: '*Wakan-Tanka,* we thank you for this understanding and relationship which you have given to us.' Be merciful to us always! May this relationship exist until the very end!"

All the men now sing this sacred chant.

> *Grandfather, behold me!*
> *Grandfather, behold me!*
> *I held my pipe and offered it to You,*
> *That my people may live!*

---

nal now," or what in the Islamic tradition is termed the *Waqt.* In Lakota this presence is called *Taku Skanskan,* or simply *Skan* in the sacred language of the holy men. The following conversation between the Lakota priest Finger and J. R. Walker well explains this:

"'What causes the stars to fall?' '*Taku Skanskan....* He causes everything that falls to fall, and He causes everything to move that moves.' 'When you move, what is it that causes you to move?' '*Skan.*' 'If an arrow is shot from a bow what causes it to move through the air?' '*Skan....* *Taku Skanskan* gives the spirit to the bow, and He causes it to send the arrow from it.' 'What causes smoke to go upward?' '*Taku Skanskan.*' 'What causes water to flow in a river?' '*Skan.*' 'What causes the clouds to move over the world?' '*Skan.*' 'Lakota have told me that *Skan* is the sky. Is that so?' 'Yes. *Skan* is a Spirit and all that mankind can see of Him is the blue of the sky; but He is everywhere!' 'Is *Skan Wakan-Tanka?*' 'Yes!'" (*The Sun Dance ... of the Teton Dakota* [Anthropological Papers of the American Museum of Natural History, XVI, Part II].)

> *Grandfather, behold me!*
> *Grandfather, behold me!*
> *I give to You all these offerings,*
> *That my people may live!*
>
> *Grandfather, behold me!*
> *Grandfather, behold me!*
> *We who represent all the people,*
> *Offer ourselves to You,*
> *That we may live!*

After this chant, water is put on the rocks, and the *Inipi* is continued in the same manner that I have described before. This young man who has cried for a vision for the first time, may perhaps become *wakan;* if he walks with his mind and heart attentive to *Wakan-Tanka* and His Powers, as he has been instructed, he will certainly travel upon the red path which leads to goodness and holiness. But he must cry for a vision a second time, and this time the bad spirits may tempt him; but if he is really a chosen one, he will stand firmly and will conquer all distracting thoughts and will become purified from all that is not good. Then he may receive some great vision that will bring strength to the nation. But should the young man still be in doubt after his second "lamenting," he may try a third and even a fourth time; and if he is always sincere, and truly humiliates himself before all things, he shall certainly be aided, for *Wakan-Tanka* always helps those who cry to Him with a pure heart.

Wiwanyag Wachipi: THE SUN DANCE

The *wiwanyag wachipi* (dance looking at the sun) is one of our greatest rites and was first held many, many winters after our people received the sacred pipe from the White Buffalo Cow Woman. It is held each year during the Moon of Fattening (June) or the Moon of Cherries Blackening (July), always at the time when the moon is full, for the growing and dying of the moon reminds us of our ignorance which comes and goes; but when the moon is full it is as if the eternal light of the Great Spirit were upon the whole world. But now I will tell you how this holy rite first came to our people and how it was first made.

Our people were once camped in a good place, in a circle, of course, and the old men were sitting having a council, when they noticed that one of our men, Kablaya (Spread), had dropped his robe down around his waist, and was dancing there all alone with

67

his hand raised towards heaven. The old men thought that per-haps he was crazy, so they sent someone to find out what was the matter; but this man who was sent suddenly dropped his robe down around his waist, too, and started dancing with Kablaya. The old men thought this very strange, and so they all went over to see what could be the matter. Kablaya then explained to them:

"Long ago *Wakan-Tanka* told us how to pray with the sacred pipe, but we have now become lax in our prayers, and our people are losing their strength. But I have just been shown, in a vision, a new way of prayer; in this manner *Wakan-Tanka* has sent aid to us."

When they heard this the old men all said, *"How!"* and seemed very pleased. They then had a conference and sent two men to the keeper of the sacred pipe, for he should give advice on all matters of this sort. The keeper told the men that this was certainly a very good thing, for "we were told that we would have seven ways of praying to *Wakan-Tanka,* and this must certainly be one of them, for Kablaya has been taught in a vision, and we were told in the beginning that we should receive our rites in this manner."

The two messengers brought this news back to the old men, who then asked Kablaya to instruct them in what they must do. Kablaya then spoke to the men, saying: "This is to be the sun dance; we cannot make it immediately but must wait four days, and during this time we shall prepare, as I have been instructed in my vision. This dance will be an offering of our bodies and souls to *Wakan-Tanka* and will be very *wakan*. All our old and holy men should gather; a large tipi should be built and sage should be placed all around inside it. You must have a good pipe, and also all the following equipment:

Ree twist tobacco	a tanned buffalo calf hide
bark of the red willow	rabbit skins
Sweet grass	eagle plumes
a bone knife	red earth paint
a flint axe	blue paint
buffalo tallow	rawhide

a buffalo skull

a rawhide bag

eagle tail feathers

whistles from the wing bones
of the Spotted Eagle.

After the people had secured all these sacred things, Kablaya
then asked all those who could sing to come to him that evening
so that he could teach them the holy songs; he said that they should
bring with them a large drum made from a buffalo hide, and they
should have very stout drum sticks, covered at the end with buffalo
hide, the hair side out.

Since the drum is often the only instrument used in our sacred
rites, I should perhaps tell you here why it is especially sacred and
important to us. It is because the round form of the drum represents the whole universe, and its steady strong beat is the pulse,
the heart, throbbing at the center of the universe. It is as the voice
of *Wakan-Tanka,* and this sound stirs us and helps us to understand the mystery and power of all things.

That evening the singers, four men and a woman, came to
Kablaya, who spoke to them in this manner: "O you, my relatives,
for a very long time we have been sending our voices to *Wakan-
Tanka.* This He has taught us to do. We have many ways of praying to Him, and through this sacred manner of living our generations have learned to walk the red path with firm steps. The sacred
pipe is always at the center of the hoop of our nation, and with it
the people have walked and will continue to walk in a holy manner.

"In this new rite which I have just received, one of the standing
peoples has been chosen to be at our center; he is the *wagachun*
(the rustling tree, or cottonwood); he will be our center and also
the people, for the tree represents the way of the people. Does it
not stretch from the earth here to heaven there?[1] This new way of
sending our voices to *Wakan-Tanka* will be very powerful; its use
will spread, and, at this time of year, every year, many people will

[1] In the *Atharva Veda Samhita* of the Hindu scriptures, we find a description of the significance of their World Tree, which is quite identical
to the symbolism of the tree for the Lakota: "The World Tree in which
the trunk, which is also the sun pillar, sacrificial post, and *axis mundi,*

pray to the Great Spirit. Before I teach you the holy songs, let us first offer the pipe to our Father and Grandfather, *Wakan-Tanka*."

"O Grandfather, Father, *Wakan-Tanka*, we are about to fulfill Thy will as You have taught us to do in my vision. This we know will be a very sacred way of sending our voices to You; through this, may our people receive wisdom; may it help us to walk the sacred path with all the Powers of the universe! Our prayer will really be the prayer of all things, for all are really one; all this I have seen in my vision. May the four Powers of the universe help us to do this rite correctly; O Great Spirit, have mercy upon us!"

The pipe was smoked by all, and then Kablaya began to teach the songs to the five people. Many other people had gathered around the singers, and to these Kablaya said that while they listen they should frequently cry "O Grandfather, *Wakan-Tanka*, I offer the pipe to You that my people may live!"

There were no words to the first song that Kablaya taught the singers; it was simply a chant, repeated four times, and the fast beat on the drum was used. The words to the second song were:

> *Wakan-Tanka, have mercy on us,*
> *That our people may live!*

And the third song was:

> *They say a herd of buffalo is coming;*
> *It is here now!*
> *Their blessing will come to us.*
> *It is with us now!*

The fourth song was a chant and had no words.

----

rising from the altar at the navel of the earth, penetrates the world door and branches out above the roof of the world (A. V. X. 7. 3.); as the 'nonexistent (unmanifested) branch that yonder kindreds know as the Supernal' (A. V. X. 7. 21)." (Translated by A. K. Coomaraswamy, Svayamatrna: Janua Coeli," *Zalmoxis*.)

For a full explanation of the symbolism of the tree, see René Guénon, *Le Symbolisme de la Croix*, Les Editions Vega (Paris, 1931); especially Chap. IX, "L'Arbre du Milieu."

Then Kablaya taught the men who had brought their eagle-bone whistles how they should be used, and he also told the men what equipment they should prepare and explained the meaning of each ritual object.

"You should prepare a necklace of otter skin, and from it there should hang a circle with a cross in the center. At the four places where the cross meets the circle there should hang eagle feathers which represent the four Powers of the universe and the four ages. At the center of the circle you should tie a plume taken from the breast of the eagle, for this is the place which is nearest to the heart and center of the sacred bird. This plume will be for *Wakan-Tanka,* who dwells at the depths of the heavens, and who is the center of all things.

"You all have the eagle-bone whistles, and to the ends of each of these an eagle plume should be tied. When you blow the whistle always remember that it is the voice of the Spotted Eagle; our Grandfather, *Wakan-Tanka,* always hears this, for you see it is really His own voice.

"A *hanhepi wi* [night sun, or moon] should be cut from raw-hide in the shape of a crescent, for the moon represents a person and, also, all things, for everything created waxes and wanes, lives and dies. You should also understand that the night represents ignorance, but it is the moon and the stars which bring the Light of *Wakan-Tanka* into this darkness. As you know the moon comes and goes, but *anpetu wi,* the sun, lives on forever; it is the source of light, and because of this it is like *Wakan-Tanka.*

"A five-pointed star should be cut from rawhide. This will be the sacred Morning Star who stands between the darkness and the light, and who represents knowledge.

"A round rawhide circle should be made to represent the sun, and this should be painted red; but at the center there should be a round circle of blue, for this innermost center represents *Wakan-Tanka* as our Grandfather. The light of this sun enlightens the entire universe; and as the flames of the sun come to us in the morning, so comes the grace of *Wakan-Tanka,* by which all creatures are enlightened. It is because of this that the four-leggeds and the wingeds always rejoice at the coming of the light. We can all see in the day, and this seeing is sacred for it represents the sight of that real world which we may have through the eye of the heart. When you wear this sacred sign in the dance, you should remember that you are bringing Light into the universe, and if you concentrate on these meanings you will gain great benefit.

"A round circle should be cut and painted red, and this will represent Earth. She is sacred, for upon Her we place our feet, and from Her we send our voices to *Wakan-Tanka*. She is a relative of ours, and this we should always remember when we call Her "Grandmother" or "Mother." When we pray we raise our hand to the heavens, and afterwards we touch the earth, for is not our Spirit from *Wakan-Tanka,* and are not our bodies from the earth? We are related to all things: the earth and the stars, everything, and with all these together we raise our hand to *Wakan-Tanka* and pray to Him alone.

"You should also cut from rawhide another round circle, and this should be painted blue for the heavens. When you dance you should raise your head and hand up to these heavens, looking at them, for if you do this your Grandfather will see you. It is He who owns everything; there is nothing which does not belong to Him, and thus it is to Him alone that you should pray.

"Finally, you should cut from rawhide the form of *tatanka,* the buffalo. He represents the people and the universe and should always be treated with respect, for was he not here before the two-legged peoples, and is he not generous in that he gives us our homes and our food? The buffalo is wise in many things, and, thus, we should learn from him and should always be as a relative with him.

"Each man should wear one of these sacred symbols on his chest, and he should realize their meanings as I have explained to you here. In this great rite you are to offer your body as a sacrifice in behalf of all the people, and through you the people will gain understanding and strength. Always be conscious of these things which I have told you today; it is all *wakan!*"

The next day it was necessary to locate the sacred rustling tree which was to stand at the center of the great lodge, and so Kablaya told his helper of the type of tree which he should find and mark with sage, that the war party will be able to locate it and bring it back to camp. Kablaya also instructed the helpers how they must mark out the ground where the sacred sun-dance lodge will be set up, around the holy tree, and how they should mark the doorway at the east with green branches.

The following day the scouts, who had been chosen by the spiritual leaders, went out and pretended to scout for the tree. When it was found they returned immediately to camp, and after circling sun-wise around the place where the lodge was to be, they all charged for the doorway, trying to strike a coup on it. These scouts then took up a pipe, and, after offering it to the six directions, they swore that they would tell the truth. When this had been done, Kablaya spoke to the men in this manner:

"You have taken up the holy pipe, and so you must now tell us with truth all that you have seen. You know that running through the stem of the pipe there is a little hole leading straight to the center and heart of the pipe; let your minds be as straight as this Way. May your tongues not be forked. You have been sent out to find a tree that will be of great benefit to the people, so now tell us truthfully what you have found."

Kablaya then turned the pipe around four times, and pointed the stem towards the scout who was to give the report.

"I went over a hill, and there I saw many of the sacred standing peoples."

"In which direction were you facing, and what did you see beyond the first hill?"

"I was facing the west," the scout replied, "and then I went further and looked over a second hill and saw many more of the sacred standing people living there."

In this manner the scout was questioned four times, for as you know with our people all good things are done in fours; and then this is the manner in which we always question our scouts when we are on the warpath, for you see we are here regarding the tree as an enemy who is to be killed.

When the scouts had given their report, they all dressed as if they were going on the warpath; and then they left the camp as if to attack the enemy. Many other people followed behind the scouts. When they came to the chosen tree, they all gathered around it; then, last of all, Kablaya arrived with his pipe, which he held with its stem pointing towards the tree; he spoke in this manner:

"Of all the many standing peoples, you O rustling cottonwood have been chosen in a sacred manner; you are about to go to the center of the people's sacred hoop, and there you will represent the people and will help us to fulfill the will of *Wakan-Tanka*. You are a kind and good-looking tree; upon you the winged peoples have raised their families; from the tip of your lofty branches down to your roots, the winged and four-legged peoples have made their homes. When you stand at the center of the sacred hoop you will be the people, and you will be as the pipe, stretching from heaven to earth. The weak will lean upon you, and for all the people you will be a support. With the tips of your branches you hold the sacred red and blue days. You will stand where the four sacred paths cross—there you will be the center of the great Powers of the universe. May we two-leggeds always follow your sacred example, for we see that you are always looking upwards into the heavens. Soon, and with all the peoples of the world, you will stand at the center; for all beings and all things you will bring that which is good. *Hechetu welo!*"

Kablaya then offered his pipe to Heaven and Earth, and then with the stem he touched the tree on the west, north, east, and south sides; after this he lit and smoked the pipe.

I think it would be good to explain to you here why we consider the cottonwood tree to be so very sacred. I might mention first, that long ago it was the cottonwood who taught us how to make our tipis, for the leaf of the tree is an exact pattern of the tipi, and this we learned when some of our old men were watching little children making play houses from these leaves. This too is a good example of how much grown men may learn from very little children, for the hearts of little children are pure, and, therefore, the Great Spirit may show to them many things which older people miss. Another reason why we choose the cottonwood tree to be at the center of our lodge is that the Great Spirit has shown to us that, if you cut an upper limb of this tree crosswise, there you will see in the grain a perfect five pointed star, which, to us, represents the presence of the Great Spirit. Also perhaps you have noticed that even in the very lightest breeze you can hear the voice of the cottonwood tree; this we understand is its prayer to the Great Spirit,[2] for not only men, but all things and all beings pray to Him continually in differing ways.

The chiefs then did a little victory dance there around the tree, singing their chief's songs, and as they sang and danced they selected the man who was to have the honor of counting coup on the tree; he must always be a man of good character, who has shown himself brave and self-sacrificing on the warpath. Three other men were also chosen by the chiefs, and then each of these four men stood at one of the four sides of the tree—the leader at the west. This leader then told of his great deeds in war, and when he had finished the men cheered and the women gave the tremulo. The brave man then motioned with his axe three times towards the tree, and the fourth time he struck it. Then the other three men in turn told of their exploits in war, and when they finished they also struck the tree in the same manner, and at each blow all the people shouted *"hi! hey!"* When the tree was nearly ready to fall, the chiefs went around and selected a person with a quiet and holy nature, and this person gave the last blow to the tree; as it fell there was much cheering, and all the women gave the tremulo. Great care was taken that the tree did not touch the ground when it fell, and no one was permitted to step over it.

The tree was then carried by six men towards the camp, but before they reached camp they stopped four times, and after the

[2] An interesting parallel to this attitude towards trees is found in an Islamic source: "[Holy] men dance and wheel on the [spiritual] battle-field: From within them musicians strike the tambourine: at their ecstacy the seas burst into foam. You see it not, but for *their* ears the leaves too on the boughs are clapping hands. . . . one must have the spiritual ear, not the ear of the body." (Jalaluddin Rumi, *The Mathnawi* [R. A. Nicholson translation, 8 vols., Cambridge University Press, Cambridge, 1926], III 9.)

last stop they all howled like coyotes—as do the warriors when returning from the war path; then they all charged into camp and placed the sacred tree up upon poles—for it must not touch the ground—and pointed its base towards the hole which had already been prepared, and its tip faced towards the west. The lodge around the tree had not yet been set up, but all the poles had been prepared, and all the equipment for constructing the *Inipi* had been gathered.

The chief priest, Kablaya, and all those who were to take part in the dance, then went into a large tipi where they were to prepare themselves and receive instructions. The lodge was shut up very tightly, and leaves were even placed all around the base.

Kablaya, who was seated at the west, scraped a bare place on the ground in front of him, and here a coal was placed; as Kablaya burned sweet grass upon the coal, he said: "We burn this sacred herb for *Wakan-Tanka*, so that all the two-legged and winged peoples of the universe will be relatives and close to each other. Through this there shall be much happiness."

A small image of a drying rack was then made from two forked sticks and one straight one, and all were painted blue, for the drying rack represents heaven, and it is our prayer that the racks always be as full as heaven. The pipe was then taken up, and after being purified over the smoke, it was leaned against the rack, for in this way it represents our prayers and is the path leading from earth to heaven.

All the sacred things to be used in the dance were then purified over the smoke of the sweet grass: the hide figures; the sacred paints; the calf skin; and the buckskin bags; and the dancers, also, purified themselves. When this had been done, Kablaya took up his pipe, and, raising it to heaven, he prayed.

"O Grandfather, *Wakan-Tanka*, You are the maker of everything. You have always been and always will be. You have been kind to your people, for You have taught us a way of prayer with the pipe which You have given us; and now through a vision You have shown to me a sacred dance which I must teach to my people. Today we will do Thy will."

"As I stand upon this sacred earth, upon which generations of our people have stood, I send a voice to You by offering this pipe. Behold me, O *Wakan-Tanka,* for I represent all the people. Within this pipe I shall place the four Powers and all the wingeds of the universe; together with all these, who shall become one, I send a voice to You. Behold me! Enlighten my mind with Your never fading Light!"

"I offer this pipe to *Wakan-Tanka,* first through You O winged Power of the place where the sun goes down; there is a place for You in this pipe. Help us with those red and blue days which make the people holy!"

Kablaya then held up a pinch of tobacco, and after motioning with it to Heaven, Earth, and the four Powers, he placed it in the bowl of the pipe. Then after the following prayers, he placed pinches of tobacco in the pipe for each of the other directions.

"O winged Power of the place where *Waziah* lives, I am about to offer this pipe to *Wakan-Tanka;* help me. with the two good red and blue days which You have—days which are purifying to the people and to the universe. There is a place for You in the pipe, and so help us!"

"O You, Power there where the sun comes up; You who give knowledge and who guard the dawn of the day, help us with Your two red and blue days which give understanding and Light to the people. There is a place for You in this pipe which I am about to offer to *Wakan-Tanka;* help us!"

"O You, most sacred Power at the place where we always face; You who are the source of life, and who guard the people and the coming generations, help us with Your two red and blue days! There is a place for You in the pipe.

"O You, Spotted Eagle of the heavens! we know that You have sharp eyes with which you see even the smallest object that moves on Grandmother Earth. O You, who are in the depths of the heavens, and who know everything, I am offering this pipe to *Wakan-Tanka!* Help us with Your two good red and blue days!

"O You, Grandmother Earth, who lie outstretched, supporting all things! upon You a two-legged is standing, offering a pipe to the Great Spirit. You are at the center of the two good red and blue days. There will be a place for You in the pipe and so help us!"

Kablaya then placed a small grain of tobacco in the pipe for each of the following birds: the kingbird; the robin; the lark, who sings during the two good days; the woodpecker; the hawk, who makes life so difficult for the other winged peoples; the eagle hawk; the magpie, who knows everything; the blackbird; and many other wingeds. Now all objects of creation and the six directions of space have been placed within the bowl of the pipe. The pipe was sealed with tallow and was leaned against the little blue drying rack.

Kablaya then took up another pipe, filled it, and went to where the sacred tree was resting. A live coal was brought, and the tree and the hole were purified with the smoke from sweet grass.

"O *Wakan-Tanka*," Kablaya prayed as he held his pipe up with one hand, "behold this holy tree-person who will soon be placed in this hole. He will stand with the sacred pipe. I touch him with the sacred red earth paint from our Grandmother and also with the fat from the four-legged buffalo. By touching this tree-person with the red earth, we remember that the generations of all that move come from our Mother the Earth. With your help, O tree, I shall soon offer my body and soul to *Wakan-Tanka*, and in me I offer all my people and all the generations to come."

Kablaya then took the red paint, offered it to the six directions, and again spoke to the sacred tree: "O tree, you are about to stand up; be merciful to my people, that they may flourish under you."

Kablaya painted stripes of red on the west, north, east, and south sides of the tree, and then he touched a very little paint to the tip of the tree for the Great Spirit, and he also put some at the base of the tree for Mother Earth. Then Kablaya took up the skin of a buffalo calf, saying: "It is from this buffalo person that our people live; he gives to us our homes, our clothing, our food, everything we need. O buffalo calf, I now give to you a sacred place upon the tip of the tree. This tree will hold you in his hand and will raise you up to *Wakan-Tanka*. Behold what I am about to do! Through this, all things that move and fly upon the earth and in the heavens will be happy!"

Kablaya next held up a small cherry tree, and continued to pray: "Behold this, O *Wakan-Tanka,* for it is the tree of the people, which we pray will bear much fruit."

This little tree was then tied upon the sacred cottonwood, just below the buffalo hide, and with it there was tied a buckskin bag in which there was some fat.

Kablaya then took up the hide images of a buffalo and a man, and, offering them to the six directions, he prayed: "Behold this buffalo, O Grandfather, which You have given to us; he is the chief of all the four-leggeds upon our sacred Mother; from him the people live, and with him they walk the sacred path. Behold, too, this two-legged, who represents all the people. These are the two chiefs upon this great island; bestow upon them all the favours that they ask for, O *Wakan-Tanka!*"

These two images were then tied upon the tree, just underneath the place where the tree forks; after this Kablaya held up a bag of fat to be placed underneath the base of the tree, and he prayed in this manner:

"O Grandfather, *Wakan-Tanka,* behold this sacred fat, upon which this tree-person will stand; may the earth always be as fat and fruitful as this. O tree, this is a sacred day for you and for all our people; the earth within this hoop belongs to you, O tree, and it is here underneath you that I shall offer up my body and soul for the sake of the people. Here I shall stand, sending my voice to You, O *Wakan-Tanka,* as I offer the sacred pipe. All this may be difficult to do, yet for the good of the people it must be done. Help me, O Grandfather, and give to me courage and strength to stand the sufferings which I am about to undergo! O tree, you are now admitted to the sacred lodge!"

With much cheering and many shrill tremulos, the tree was raised, very slowly, for the men stopped four times before it was straight and dropped into the hole prepared for it. Now all the people—the two-leggeds, four-leggeds, and the wingeds of the air —were rejoicing, for they would all flourish under the protection of the tree. It helps us all to walk the sacred path; we can lean upon it, and it will always guide us and give us strength.

A little dance was held around the base of the tree, and then the surrounding lodge was made by putting upright, in a large circle, twenty-eight forked sticks, and from the fork of each stick a pole was placed which reached to the holy tree at the center.

I should explain to you here that in setting up the sun dance lodge, we are really making the universe in a likeness; for, you see, each of the posts around the lodge represents some particular object of creation, so that the whole circle is the entire creation, and the one tree at the center, upon which the twenty-eight poles rest, is *Wakan-Tanka,* who is the center of everything. Everything comes from Him, and sooner or later everything returns to Him. And I should also tell you why it is that we use twenty-eight poles. I have already explained why the numbers four and seven are sacred; then if you add four sevens you get twenty-eight. Also the moon lives twenty-eight days, and this is our month; each of these days of the month represents something sacred to us: two of the days represent the Great Spirit; two are for Mother Earth; four are for the four winds; one is for the Spotted Eagle; one for the sun; and one for the moon; one is for the Morning Star; and four for the four ages; seven are for our seven great rites; one is for the buffalo; one for the fire; one for the water; one for the rock; and finally one is for the two-legged people. If you add all these days up you will see that they come to twenty-eight. You should also know that the buffalo has twenty-eight ribs, and that in our war bonnets we usually use twenty-eight feathers. You see, there is a significance for everything, and these are the things that are good for men to know, and to remember. But now we must return to the sun dance.

The warriors all dressed and painted themselves, and after entering the sacred lodge they danced around the center tree, for in this way the ground was purified and made smooth by the dancing feet. The chiefs then gathered and selected braves, one of which was to be the leader of the dancers. These chosen men then danced first towards the west, and then back to the center, then to the

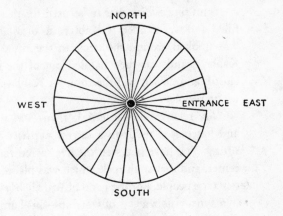

NORTH

WEST — ENTRANCE EAST

SOUTH

A Sun Dance Lodge

north and to the center, to the east and to the center, and finally to the south and then back to the center, and in this way they made a path in the shape of a cross.

Kablaya then entered the *Inipi* lodge, carrying the sacred pipe which had already been filled, and he sat at the west; all the other men who were to take part in the dance also entered, taking care not to pass in front of Kablaya, and then one woman entered last, taking her seat next to the door.

All the buffalo robes to be used in the dance were placed on top of the *Inipi* lodge, for in this way they are purified. The five hot rocks for the five directions were brought in and put in their proper places at the sacred altar, and then a sixth rock was placed upon the sacred path.

81

Kablaya held that pipe which was to be used in the dance, but a second pipe which was to be used for the rites of the *Inipi* was filled and was handed to Kablaya to bless and to light. This pipe was smoked around the circle in the ritual manner, purified by Kablaya, and was then handed out of the lodge. The door was closed, and now it was the time for Kablaya to explain his vision to the people.

"My relatives all—listen! *Wakan-Tanka* has been kind to us, and has placed us upon a sacred Earth; upon Her we are now sitting. You have just seen the five sacred rocks placed here at the center, and that sixth rock which was placed upon the path represents the people. For the good of you all *Wakan-Tanka* has taught to me in a vision, a way of worship—this I am now teaching to you.

"The heavens are sacred, for it is there that our Grandfather, the Great Spirit, lives; these heavens are as a cloak for the universe—this robe is now upon me as I stand here. O *Wakan-Tanka,* I show to You the sacred hoop of our nation, which is this circle within which there is a cross; this circle one of us wears upon his breast. And I show to You the earth which You have made, and which You are always making; it is represented by this round red circle which we wear. The never-ending Light which turns the night into day, we also wear, that the Light may be amongst our people, that they may see. I show to You also the Morning Star which gives knowledge to us. The four-legged buffalo whom You have placed here before the two-legged people is also here with us. And here is also the sacred woman who came to us in such a holy manner. All these holy peoples and holy things are now hearing what I say!

"Very soon I shall suffer and endure great pain with my relatives here, in behalf of my people. In tears and suffering I shall hold my pipe and raise my voice to You, O *Wakan-Tanka*. I shall offer up my body and soul that my people may live. In sending my voice to You, *Wakan-Tanka,* I shall use that which connects the four Powers, Heaven, and Earth, to You. All that which moves on the universe—the four-leggeds, the insects, and the wingeds— all rejoice and help me and all my people!"

Kablaya then sang his sacred song:

> *The Sun, the Light of the world,*
> *I hear Him coming.*
> *I see His face as He comes.*
> *He makes the beings on earth happy,*
> *And they rejoice.*
> *O* Wakan-Tanka, *I offer to You this world of Light.*

The pipe to be used in the sacred dance was then wrapped in sage and was taken out of the lodge by the woman; she carried it along the sacred path to the east and placed it upon the buffalo skull, being careful to have its stem point towards the east. This woman then remained outside the little lodge and assisted in opening and closing the door. The *Inipi* then began as I have described before, but after the second time the door was closed, Kablaya made a special prayer in this manner:

"Grandfather, *Wakan-Tanka,* behold us! The sacred pipe which You have given to us, and with which we have raised our children, will soon go to the center of the universe, along with the buffalo, who has helped to make strong the bodies of the people. The sacred woman who once before came to the center of our hoop will again come to our center, and a two-legged who will suffer for his people will also go to the center. O *Wakan-Tanka,* when we are all at the center, may we have only You in our minds and hearts!"

Kablaya then sang another of the sacred songs which he had received in his vision.

> *I hear Him coming; I see His face.*
> *Your day is sacred! I offer it to You.*
> *I hear Him coming; I see His face.*
> *This sacred day You made the buffalo roam.*
> *You have made a happy day for the world;*
> *I offer all to You.*

Water was then put on the rocks as Kablaya prayed: "O *Wak-*

an-Tanka, we are now purifying ourselves, that we may be worthy to raise our hands to You."

Then raising their right hands, all the men sang.

> *Grandfather, I send my voice to You.*
> *Grandfather, I send my voice to You.*
> *With all the universe I send my voice to You,*
> *That I may live.*

When the door was opened the third time, the men were all allowed to drink a little water, but this was the only time during the whole rite that this was permitted. As the men received the water, Kablaya said to them: "I give you water, but remember the One in the west who guards the waters and the sanctity of all things. You are about to drink the water, which is life, and so you should not spill any of it. When you finish you should raise your hands in thanks to the Power of the place where the sun goes down; he will help you to bear the difficulties which you are about to undergo."

The door was closed for the last time, and again all the men sang as the heat and steam purified them. And when the door was finally opened, they all came out, led by Kablaya, and they raised their hands to the six directions, saying: *"Hi ho! Hi ho! Pila-miya!"* (thanks).

Each dancer had a helper, who took a purified buffalo robe from the top of the *Inipi* lodge and put it around the dancer. Kablaya then took his pipe which had been resting on the buffalo skull, and, with all the men, he entered a sacred tipi and placed his pipe against the little drying rack, which had been painted blue to represent the heavens. Sweet grass was put on a coal, and Kablaya and all the men purified themselves in the sacred smoke. After this, the drum and drumsticks were blessed and purified, and as he did this Kablaya said: "This drum is the buffalo and will go to the center. By using these sticks upon the drum, we shall certainly defeat our enemies."

All the clothing and equipment to be used in the dance were then purified; the four buffalo skulls were also purified, for one of the men would soon fasten these to his skin, bearing them in this way until they break loose.

Kablaya then explained to the men that their bodies had been purified and, thus were now sacred and should not even be touched by their own hands. The men must carry little sticks in their hair with which to scratch themselves, should it be necessary, and even when they paint themselves with the red earth paint they must use sticks instead of their hands.

Kablaya put around his neck the round blue hide circle representing the heavens, and each of the other men wore the different symbols: the circle with the cross; the red earth circle; the sun; the moon; and the Morning Star. The seventh man wore the buffalo, and the woman carried the pipe, for she represents the White Buffalo Cow Woman. The men also put rabbit skins on their arms and legs, for the rabbit represents humility, because he is quiet and soft and not self-asserting—a quality which we must all possess when we go to the center of the world. The men also put feathers in their hair, and, after these preparations, Kablaya instructed them in what they must do when they enter the sacred dance lodge.

"When we go to the center of the hoop we shall all cry, for we should know that anything born into this world which you see about you must suffer and bear difficulties. We are now going to suffer at the center of the sacred hoop, and by doing this may we take upon ourselves much of the suffering of our people."

Each of the men then declared which of the sacrifices he would undergo, and Kablaya made his vow first: "I will attach my body to the thongs of the Great Spirit which come down to earth—this shall be my offering."

(I think I should explain to you here, that the flesh represents ignorance, and, thus, as we dance and break the thong loose, it is as if we were being freed from the bonds of the flesh. It is much the same as when you break a young colt; at first a halter is necessary, but later when he has become broken, the rope is no longer necessary. We too are young colts when we start to dance, but soon we become broken and submit to the Great Spirit.)

85

The second dancer said: "I will tie myself to the four Powers of the world which *Wakan-Tanka* has established."

Here the dancer actually is the center—for standing at the center of four posts, rawhide thongs from these posts are tied into the flesh of his shoulders, his breast, and his back, and in this manner he dances until these thongs have broken out from his flesh.

The third dancer made his vow: "I will bear four of my closest relatives, the ancient buffalo."

By this the dancer means that four thongs will be tied into his back, to which will be attached four buffalo skulls, and these four bonds represent the pull of ignorance which should always be behind us as we face the light of truth which is before us.

The fourth dancer said: "I will leave twelve pieces of my flesh at the foot of the sacred tree. One shall be for *Wakan-Tanka,* our Grandfather, one for *Wakan-Tanka,* our Father, one for the Earth, our Grandmother, and one for the Earth, our Mother. I will leave four pieces of flesh for the Powers of the four directions, and then I will leave one for the Spotted Eagle, one for the Morning Star, one for the moon, and one for the sun."

The fifth dancer said: "I will make an offering of eight pieces of my flesh; two shall be for *Wakan-Tanka,* two for the Earth, and four for the Powers of the four directions."

The sixth dancer said: "I will leave at the sacred tree four pieces of my flesh; one shall be for *Wakan-Tanka,* one for the Earth upon whom we walk, one for the people that they may walk with firm steps, and one for the wingeds of the universe."

The seventh dancer made his vow: "I will leave one piece of my flesh for *Wakan-Tanka* and one for the Earth."

Then the eighth dancer, who was the woman, made her vow: "I will offer one piece of my flesh to *Wakan-Tanka* and for all moving things of the universe, that they may give their powers to the people, that they with their children may walk the red path of life."

When all had finished making their vows, Kablaya told them to purify themselves by rubbing sage on their faces and all over their bodies, "for we are now about to approach a sacred place where the tree stands, as the pipe, stretching from Heaven to Earth. We must be worthy to go to this center!"

All the people of the band had gathered around the outside of the sacred lodge, and within the lodge at the south were the singers, with the women who were their helpers, and all were wearing wreaths around their foreheads and holding little sprigs of some sacred plant.

Then the dancers arrived, being led by the woman, who carried the sacred pipe, and followed by Kablaya, carrying the buffalo skull, and at the end of the line were the helpers who carried all the equipment. They all walked slowly around the outside of the lodge, in a sun-wise direction, and all the time they were crying most pitifully: "O *Wakan-Tanka*, be merciful to me, that my people may live! It is for this that I am sacrificing myself."

And as the dancers chanted this, all the other people cried, for they were the people—the nation—for whom the dancers were to suffer. The dancers entered the lodge at the east and, after moving around the lodge sun-wise, took their places at the west. Then Kablaya placed the buffalo skull between the dancers and the sacred tree, with the nose of the skull facing the east; and just in front of him, he set up the three blue forked sticks, and upon this rack the woman rested the sacred pipe.

The singers then sang one of the sacred songs:

> Wakan-Tanka *be merciful to me. We want to live!*
> *That is why we are doing this.*
> *They say that a herd of buffalo is coming;*
> *Now they are here.*
> *The power of the buffalo is coming upon us;*
> *It is now here!"*

After the chanting of this song the people all cried, and then, for the rest of the day and all that night, they danced. This dance, during the first night, represents the people in the darkness of ignorance; they were not yet worthy to meet the Light of the Great Spirit which would shine upon them with the coming of the next

87

day; first they must suffer and purify themselves before they could be worthy to be with *Wakan-Tanka*.

Just before dawn, the dance stopped, and at this time the dancers, or their relatives, placed offerings outside the sacred lodge at each of the four quarters.

At dawn the dancers again entered the lodge, and with them there was the keeper of the sacred pipe; this holy man had been asked by Kablaya to make the sacred altar, but he had replied, "this is your vision Kablaya, and you should make the altar; but I will be present beside you, and when you have finished I will offer up the prayer."

Thus, it was Kablaya who made the sacred place; he first scraped a round circle in the ground in front of him, and then within this circle he placed a hot coal.[3] Then taking up some sweet grass and holding it above him, he prayed.

"O Grandfather, *Wakan-Tanka*, this is Your sacred grass which I place on the fire; its smoke will spread throughout the world, reaching even to the heavens. The four-leggeds, the wingeds, and all things will know this smoke and will rejoice. May this offering help to make all things and all beings as relatives to us; may they all give to us their powers, so that we may endure the difficulties ahead of us. Behold, O *Wakan-Tanka,* I place this sweet grass on the fire, and the smoke will rise to You."

As Kablaya placed the sacred grass on the fire, he sang this song:

> *I am making sacred smoke;*
> *In this manner I make the smoke;*
> *May all the peoples behold it!*
> *I am making sacred smoke;*

[3] This coal was taken from a fire which had been kept burning all through the previous night, and which will burn every night during the dance. It is located to the east, outside the lodge, and, according to Black Elk, it is kept in order to remind the people of the eternal presence of *Wakan-Tanka*. During the day this fire is not necessary because the sun is then present as a reminder.

May all be attentive and behold!
May the wingeds, and the four-leggeds
  be attentive and behold it!
In this manner I make the smoke;
All over the universe there will be rejoicing!

The knife which was to be used for piercing the breasts of the dancers was purified over the smoke, as was also a small stone hatchet and a small quantity of earth. Kablaya was then ready to make the sacred altar; but first he prayed.

"O Grandfather, *Wakan-Tanka,* I shall now make this Your sacred place. In making this altar, all the birds of the air and all creatures of the earth will rejoice, and they will come from all directions to behold it! All the generations of my people will rejoice! This place will be the center of the paths of the four great Powers. The dawn of the day will see this holy place! When Your Light approaches, O *Wakan-Tanka,* all that moves in the universe will rejoice!"

A pinch of the purified earth was offered above and to the ground and was then placed at the center of the sacred place. Another pinch of earth was offered to the west, north, east, and south and was placed at the west of the circle. In the same manner, earth was placed at the other three directions, and then it was spread evenly all around within the circle. This earth represents the two-leggeds, the four-leggeds, the wingeds, and really all that moves, and all that is in the universe. Upon this sacred place Kablaya then began to construct the altar. He first took up a stick, pointed it to the six directions, and then, bringing it down, he made a small circle at the center; and this we understand to be the home of *Wakan-Tanka.* Again, after pointing the stick to the six directions, Kablaya made a mark starting from the west and leading to the edge of the circle. In the same manner he drew a line from the east to the edge of the circle, from the north to the circle, and from the south to the circle. By constructing the altar in this manner, we see that everything leads into, or returns to, the center;

and this center which is here, but which we know is really every-where, is *Wakan-Tanka*.

Kablaya then took up a small bundle of sage, and, offering it up to *Wakan-Tanka*, he prayed.

"O *Wakan-Tanka*, behold us! Next to the two-leggeds, the chief of all the four-leggeds is *tatanka*, the buffalo. Behold his dried skull here; by this we know that we, too, shall become skull and bones, and, thus, together we shall all walk the sacred path back to *Wakan-Tanka*. When we arrive at the end of our days, be merciful to us, O *Wakan-Tanka*. Here on earth we live together with the buffalo, and we are grateful to him, for it is he who gives us our food, and who makes the people happy. For this reason I now give grass to our relative the buffalo."

Kablaya then made a little bed of sage to the east of the sacred altar, and, taking up the buffalo skull by the horns, and facing the east, he sang:

> *I give grass to the buffalo;*
> *May the people behold it,*
> *That they may live.*

Then turning, and holding the skull to the west, Kablaya sang:

> *Tobacco I give to the buffalo;*
> *May the people behold it,*
> *That they may live.*

Then turning to the north, Kablaya sang:

> *A robe I give to the buffalo;*
> *May the people behold it,*
> *That they may live.*

And turning to the south he sang:

> *Paint I give to the buffalo;*
> *May the people behold it,*
> *That they may live.*

Then standing over the sage, Kablaya sang:

> *Water I will give to the buffalo;*
> *May the people behold it,*
> *That they may live.*

The buffalo skull was then placed on the bed of sage, facing east, and Kablaya placed little balls of sage in its eyes and tied a little bag of tobacco on the horn which was facing south, and he also tied a piece of deerhide on the horn at the north, for this hide represents the robe for the buffalo. Then Kablaya painted a red line around the head of the buffalo and drew, also, a red line from the forehead to the tip of the nose. As he did this Kablaya said: "You, O buffalo, are the earth! May we understand this, and all that I have done here. *Hechetu welo!* It is good!"

When the offerings to the buffalo had been completed, the dancers walked around the lodge and stood at the doorway facing east, in order to greet the rising sun.

"Behold these men, O *Wakan-Tanka,*" Kablaya prayed as he raised his right hand. "The face of the dawn will meet their faces; the coming day will suffer with them. It will be a sacred day, for You, O *Wakan-Tanka,* are present here!"

Then, just as the day-sun peeped over the horizon, the dancers all chanted in a sacred manner, and Kablaya sang one of his *wakan* songs.

> *The light of* Wakan-Tanka *is upon my people;*
> *It is making the whole earth bright.*
> *My people are now happy!*
> *All beings that move are rejoicing!*

As the men chanted, and as Kablaya sang the sacred song, they all danced, and as they danced they moved so that they were facing the south, then the west, the north, and then they stood again at the east; but this time they faced towards the sacred tree at the center.

The singing and drumming stopped, and the dancers sat at the west of the lodge, upon beds of sage which had been prepared for them. With sage the helpers rubbed all the paint off the men, and then upon their heads they placed wreaths of sage and plumes from the eagle, and the women also wore eagle feathers in their hair.

In every sun dance we wear wreaths of sage upon our heads, for it is a sign that our minds and hearts are close to *Wakan-Tanka* and His Powers, for the wreath represents the things of the heavens —the stars and planets, which are very mysterious and *wakan*.

Kablaya then told the dancers how they must paint themselves: the bodies were to be painted red from the waist up; the face, too, must be painted red, for red represents all that is sacred, especially the earth, for we should remember that it is from the earth that our bodies come, and it is to her that they return. A black circle should be painted around the face, for the circle helps us to remember *Wakan-Tanka,* who, like the circle, has no end. There is much power in the circle, as I have often said; the birds know this for they fly in a circle, and build their homes in the form of a circle; this the coyotes know also, for they live in round holes in the ground. Then a black line should be drawn from the forehead to a point between the eyes; and a line should be drawn on each cheek and on the chin, for these four lines represent the Powers of the four directions. Black stripes were painted around the wrists, the elbow, the upper part of the arm, and around the ankles. Black, you see, is the color of ignorance,[4] and, thus, these stripes are as the bonds which tie us to the earth. You should also notice that these stripes start from the earth and go up only as far as the breasts, for this is the place where the thongs fasten into the body, and these thongs are as rays of light from *Wakan-Tanka*. Thus, when we tear ourselves away from the thongs, it is as if the spirit were liberated from our dark bodies. At this first dance all the

[4] The Sioux also paint their faces black for the dance which is held when they return from the warpath, for, as Black Elk has said, "By going on the warpath, we know that we have done something bad, and we wish to hide our faces from *Wakan-Tanka*."

Sitting Bull, 1885 *(Bureau of American Ethnology)*

Little Warrior, close friend of Black Elk, 1947 *(Photograph by J. E. Brown)*

men were painted in this manner; it is only in recent times that each dancer is painted with a different design, according to some vision which he may have had.

After all the dancers were painted, they purified themselves in the smoke of sweet grass and put on the various symbols which I have described before. The dancer who had vowed to drag the four buffalo skulls wore the form of the buffalo on his chest, and on his head he wore horns made from sage.

When all the preparations were finished, the dancers stood at the foot of the sacred tree, at the west, and, gazing up at the top of the tree, they raised their right hands and blew upon the eagle-bone whistles. As they did this, Kablaya prayed.

"O Grandfather, *Wakan-Tanka,* bend down and look upon me as I raise my hand to You. You see here the faces of my people. You see the four Powers of the universe, and You have now seen us at each of these four directions. You have beheld the sacred place and the sacred center which we have fixed, and where we shall suffer. I offer all my suffering to You in behalf of the people.

"A good day has been set upon my forehead as I stand before You, and this brings me closer to You, O *Wakan-Tanka.* It is Your light which comes with the dawn of the day, and which passes through the heavens. I am standing with my feet upon Your sacred Earth. Be merciful to me, O Great Spirit, that my people may live!"

Then all the singers chanted together:

> O Wakan-Tanka, *be merciful to me!*
> *I am doing this that my people may live!*

The dancers all moved around to the east, looking towards the top of the sacred tree at the west, and, raising up their hands, they sang:

> Our Grandfather, Wakan-Tanka,
> *has given to me a path which is sacred!*

Moving now to the south, and looking towards the north, the dancers blew upon their eagle-bone whistles, as the singers chanted:

A buffalo is coming they say.
He is here now.
The Power of the buffalo is coming;
It is upon us now!

As the singers chanted this, the dancers moved around to the west, and faced the east, and all the time they blew upon their shrill eagle-bone whistles. Then they went to the north and faced the south, and, finally, they again went to the west and faced towards the east.

Then the dancers all began to cry, and Kablaya was given a long thong and two wooden pegs, and with these he went to the center, and grasping the sacred tree he cried: "O *Wakan-Tanka,* be merciful to me. I do this that my people may live."

Crying in this manner continually, Kablaya went to the north of the lodge, and from there he walked around the circle of the lodge, stopping at each of the twenty-eight lodge poles, and then returned to the north. Carrying their thongs and pegs, all the dancers then did as Kablaya had done. When they all returned to the north and faced the south, Kablaya once again went to the center and grasped the sacred tree with both hands.

As the singers and drummers increased the speed of their chanting and drumming, the helpers rushed up and, grasping Kablaya roughly, threw him on the ground. The helper then pulled up the skin of Kablaya's left breast, and through this loose skin a sharp stick was thrust; and in the same manner the right breast was pierced. The long rawhide rope had been tied at its middle, around the sacred tree, towards its top, and then the two ends of the rope were tied to the pegs in Kablaya's chest. The helpers stood Kablaya up roughly, and he blew upon his eagle-bone whistle, and, leaning back upon his thongs, he danced, and continued to dance in this manner until the thongs broke loose from his flesh.

I should explain here why we use two thongs, which are really one long thong, for it is tied to the tree at its center, and also it was made from a single buffalo hide, cut in a spiral. This is to help us remember that although there seem to be two thongs, the two are really only one; it is only the ignorant person who sees many where there is really only one. This truth of the oneness of all things we understand a little better by participating in this rite, and by offering ourselves as a sacrifice.

The second dancer then went to the center, and, grasping the sacred tree, he too cried as Kablaya had done. The helpers again rushed up and, after throwing him roughly on the ground, pierced both his breasts and both sides of his back; wooden pegs were thrust through the flesh, and to these pegs four short thongs were attached. This brave dancer was then tied at the center of four poles, so tightly that he could not move in any direction. At first he cried, not as a child from the pain, but because he knew that he was suffering for his people, and he was understanding the sacredness of having the four directions meet in his body, so that he himself was really the center. Raising his hands to heaven, and blowing upon his eagle whistle, this man danced until his thongs broke loose.

The third dancer who was to bear the four buffalo skulls then went to the center, and, after grasping the sacred tree, he was thrown on his face by the helpers, and four sticks were thrust through the flesh of his back. To these were tied the four buffalo skulls. The helpers pulled on the skulls to see that they were firmly attached, and then they gave to the dancer his eagle whistle, and upon this he blew continually as he danced. I think that you can understand that all this was very painful for him, for every time he moved the sharp horns of the skulls cut into his skin, but our men were brave in those days and did not show any signs of suffering; they were really glad to suffer if it was for the good of the people.

Friends or relatives would sometimes go to the dancers and dance beside them, giving encouragement; sometimes a young woman who liked one of the dancers would put a herb which she had been chewing into the mouth of the dancer in order to give him strength and to ease his thirst. And all this time the drum-

95

ming, singing, and dancing never stopped, and above it all you could hear the shrill call of the eagle-bone whistles.

The fourth man, who had vowed to give twelve pieces of his flesh, then went and sat at the foot of the tree, holding on to it with both hands; the helpers took a bone awl and, raising up little pieces of flesh on the shoulders, cut off six small pieces from each. This flesh was left as an offering at the foot of the tree, and the man then stood up and continued dancing with the others.

In the same manner, the fifth dancer sacrificed eight pieces of his flesh; the sixth dancer gave four pieces of his flesh; and the seventh dancer sacrificed two pieces. Then, finally, the woman grasped the sacred tree, crying as she sat down, and said: "Father, *Wakan-Tanka*, in this one piece of flesh I offer myself to You and to Your heavens and to the sun, the moon, the Morning Star, the four Powers, and to everything."

They all continued to dance, and the people cheered Kablaya, telling him to pull harder upon the thongs, which he did until finally one thong broke loose, and then all the people cried *"hi ye!"* Kablaya fell, but the people helped him up, and he continued to dance until the other thong broke loose. Again he fell, but, rising, he raised both hands to heaven, and all the people cheered loudly. They then helped him to the foot of the sacred tree, where he rested on a bed of sage, and, pulling the loose flesh from his breast, where the bonds had broken loose, he placed twelve pieces of it at the foot of the tree. The medicine men put a healing herb on his wounds, and they carried him to a place in the shade where he rested for a few moments. Then, getting up, he continued to dance with the others.

Finally, the man who had been dancing for a long time with the four skulls lost two of them, and Kablaya gave the order that his skin should be cut so that the other two should break loose. But even though he was free from the four skulls, this brave man still continued to dance.

Then the man who had been dancing at the center of the four posts broke loose from two of his bonds, and Kablaya said that he, too, had had enough, and with a knife the skin was cut, so that he broke loose from the other two bonds. These two men each offered twelve pieces of their flesh to the sacred tree, and then all the men and many of the people continued to dance until the sun was nearly down.

Just before sundown, a pipe was taken to the singers and drummers as an indication that their work had been finished and that they may now smoke. Then the dancers and the keeper of the most sacred pipe sat at the west of the lodge, and the holy woman took up in her two hands the pipe which had been resting in front of her; holding the stem of the pipe up, she walked around the buffalo skull, and, standing in front of the keeper of the pipe, she prayed.

"O holy Father, have pity on me! I offer my pipe to *Wakan-Tanka*. O Grandfather, *Wakan-Tanka,* help me! I do this that my people may live, and that they may increase in a sacred manner."

The woman then offered the pipe to the keeper three times, and the fourth time she gave it to him. *"How!"* the keeper said as he received the pipe; and then he went and stood under the north side of the sacred tree and prayed.

"Hee-ay-hay-ee-ee! [four times] Grandfather, *Wakan-Tanka,* You are closer to us than anything. You have seen everything this day. It is now finished; our work has ended. Today a two-legged person has made a very sacred rite, which You have appointed him to do. These eight people here have offered their bodies and souls to You. In suffering they have sent their voices to You; they have even offered to You a part of their flesh, which is now here at the foot of this sacred tree. The favor that they ask of You is that their people may walk the holy path of life and that they may increase in a sacred manner.

"Behold this pipe which we—with the Earth, the four Powers, and with all things—have offered to You. We know that we are related and are one with all things of the heavens and the earth, and we know that all the things that move are a people as we. We all wish to live and increase in a holy manner. The Morning Star and the dawn which comes with it, the moon of the night, and the stars of the heavens are all brought together here. You have taught us our relationship with all these things and beings, and for this we give thanks, now and always. May we be continually aware of this relationship which exists between the four-leggeds, the two-leggeds, and the wingeds. May we all rejoice and live in peace!

"Behold this pipe which is the one that the four-legged brought to the people; through it we have carried out Thy will. O *Wakan-Tanka,* You have put Your people upon a sacred path; may they walk upon it with firm and sure steps, hand in hand with their children, and may their children's children, too, walk in this sacred manner!

"Have mercy, O *Wakan-Tanka,* on the souls that have roamed the earth and have departed. May these souls be worthy to walk upon that great white path which You have established! We are about to light and smoke the sacred pipe, and we know that this offering is very *wakan.* The smoke that rises will spread throughout the universe, and all beings will rejoice."

The dancers then sat at the west side of the lodge, and the keeper took the tallow from the top of the bowl of the pipe and placed it upon a purified buffalo chip. The pipe was then lit from a coal, and, after offering it to the six directions, and after taking a few puffs himself, the keeper handed it to Kablaya, who cried as he offered the pipe and, after smoking it a little, handed it to the person next to him. After each man had offered and smoked the pipe, he handed it back to Kablaya, who then handed it on to the next man. When all had smoked in this manner, Kabalaya slowly and carefully placed the ashes upon the very middle of the sacred altar and then prayed.

"O *Wakan-Tanka,* this sacred place is Yours. Upon it all has been finished. We rejoice!"

Two helpers then placed upon the altar the ashes from the sacred fire at the east of the lodge; the purified earth was also placed upon the altar, and then all the wreaths, furs, feathers, and symbols which had been used in the dance were all piled up in the center of the sacred place. This was done because these things were too sacred to be kept and should be returned to the earth. Only the buffalo robes and the eagle-bone whistles were kept, and these things will always be regarded as especially sacred, for they were used in this first great rite of the sun dance. On top of the pile of sacred things the buffalo skull was placed, for this skull reminds us of death and also helps us to remember that a cycle has here been completed.

The people all rejoiced, and the little children were allowed to play tricks on the old people, at this time, but nobody cared; and they were not punished, for everybody was very happy.

The dancers, however, had not yet finished, for they now took their buffalo robes and returned to the preparation tipi. Here they took off their clothes, except for the breech cloth, and they all entered the *Inipi* lodge, except the woman who guarded the door for the men. The five rocks were brought in, and the pipe was smoked around the circle; but, as each man took the pipe, he first touched one of the rocks with it. The door of the lodge was closed, and Kablaya spoke.

"My relatives, I wish to say something. Listen closely! This day you have done a sacred thing, for you have given your bodies to the Great Spirit. When you return to your people always remember that through this act you have been made holy. In the future you will be the leaders of your people, and you should be worthy of this sacred duty. Be merciful to your people, be good to them and love them! But always remember this, that your closest relative is your Grandfather and your Father, *Wakan-Tanka,* and next to Him is your Grandmother and your Mother, the Earth."

Water was put on the hot rocks, and, after a short time, when the little lodge was filled with steam and was very hot, the door was opened and water was handed in. Sweet grass was put in the water and was then touched to the mouths of the dancers, but this was all the water that was allowed at this time. The pipe was passed around; the door was closed; and again Kablaya spoke to the men.

"By your actions today you have strengthened the sacred hoop of our nation. You have made a sacred center which will always be with you, and you have created a closer relationship with all things of the universe."

Water was again put on the rocks, and as the steam rose the men chanted a sacred song. When the door was opened this third time the men were allowed to drink one mouthful of water; after this the pipe was passed around as before. Again the door was closed, and as the steam rose from the rocks, all the men sang.

> *I am sending a voice to my Grandfather!*
> *I am sending a voice to my Grandfather!*
> *Hear me!*
> *Together with all things of the universe,*
> *I am sending a voice to* Wakan-Tanka.

Then Kablaya said: "The four paths of the four Powers are your close relatives. The dawn and the sun of the day are your relatives. The Morning Star and all the stars of the sacred heavens are your relatives; always remember this!"

The door was then opened for the fourth and last time, and the men drank all the water they wished; and when they had finished drinking and had smoked, Kablaya said to them: "You have now seen the Light of *Wakan-Tanka* four times. This Light will be with you always. Remember that it is four steps to the end of the sacred path.[5] But you shall get there. It is good! It is finished! *Hechetu welo!*"

The men then went back to the sacred tipi, where much food was brought to them, and all the people were happy and rejoicing, for a great thing had been done, and in the winters to come much strength would be given to the life of the nation through this great rite.

[5] The four steps represent, to the Sioux, the four ages or phases of a cycle: the rock age, the bow age, the fire age, and the pipe age. The rock, bow, fire, or pipe constitutes the main ritual support for each age. The four ages may also refer, microcosmically, to the four phases of a man's life, from birth to death.

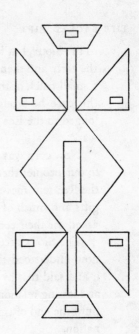

CHAPTER VI

Hunkapi: THE MAKING OF RELATIVES

In this rite we establish a relationship on earth, which is a reflection of that real relationship which always exists between man and *Wakan-Tanka*. As we always love *Wakan-Tanka* first, and before all else, so we should also love and establish closer relationships with our fellow men, even if they should be of another nation than ours. In establishing and participating in this rite which I shall describe, we are carrying out the will of the Great Spirit, for this is one of the seven rites which in the beginning the White Buffalo Cow Woman promised us.

Other nations claim that they were the originators of this rite, but this is not so, for it was the Lakota Matohoshila (Bear Boy), a very holy man, who received this rite in a vision from *Wakan-Tanka*.

You should know that the sacred plant, the corn, is not native to the Sioux, but long ago Matohoshila had his great vision about the corn, and then later, when traveling to the southeast, he found a small patch of the corn, exactly as he had seen in his vision; and this corn he brought back to his people, not knowing that it belonged to the Ree nation, with whom the Sioux had long been at war.[1]

Now corn was as important and sacred to the Ree as is the pipe to our people; therefore, shortly after their corn had disappeared, the Ree sent messengers to the camp of the Sioux, bearing many gifts and much of their twist tobacco which we prize highly, and asked for their corn back again.

The Sioux accepted the peace offering, and Matohoshila, who now understood the significance of his vision, told his people of it and said that by holding this rite now we shall establish a close and lasting relationship with the Ree nation—one that will endure until the end of time, and one that will be an example to all other nations.

All the people gladly accepted this and gave to Matohoshila the authority and power to establish the peace through the *hunkapi* rite. Matohoshila then explained that, whenever this rite is carried out, the one who wishes another to be his relative is regarded as a Ree, and it is he who must sing over the other. Matohoshila then told the visiting Ree to set up a sacred tipi and that they should choose one of their men to represent their whole Ree nation, and he should be the one to sing over Matohoshila, who in turn should represent the whole Sioux nation.

A little later, Matohoshila filled his pipe and went to the Ree who had been chosen to represent his people. Offering the pipe to him, Matohoshila said: "I wish you to help me in establishing a rite which, for the benefit of all our people, has been given to me in a vision by the Great Spirit. It is His will that we do this. He, who is our Grandfather and Father, has established a relationship with my people the Sioux; it is our duty to make a rite which should extend this relationship to the different people of different

[1] The Ree or Arikara are of the Caddo family and thus are closely related to the Pawnee.

nations. May that which we do here be an example to others!

"You represent the Ree people as a whole, and I represent the Sioux nation. You have come here in order to make peace, and we have accepted your offer; but, as you see, we are going to establish here something deeper than that for which you have asked. In asking for peace you have brought to us your tobacco which we cherish very much, and, likewise, we shall give to you the sacred corn which you cherish more than anything. They both are sacred, for they are from the Great Spirit; they have been made by Him for our use!"

Matohoshila then instructed the Ree how to make the offering which would later be brought to the Sioux and told him what equipment was necessary for the rite:

a pipe	dried buffalo meat
tobacco	red and dark blue paint
four stalks of corn with ears	eagle plumes
one cornstalk without ears	a knife
a buffalo skull	sweet grass
three sticks for a rack	dried buffalo bladder

When this equipment had been gathered, Matohoshila took a knife and made a clean place upon the earth inside the tipi. Upon this sacred place four live coals were placed, and upon them Matohoshila placed some sweet grass, and prayed.

"O Grandfather, *Wakan-Tanka,* behold us! Here we shall make relatives and peace; it is Your will that this be done. With this sweet grass which is Yours, I am now making smoke, which will rise to You. In everything that we do, You are first, and this our sacred Mother Earth is second, and next to Her are the four quarters. By making this rite we shall carry out Thy will upon this earth, and we shall make a peace that will last to the end of time. The smoke from this sweet grass will be upon everything in the universe. It is good!"

All the equipment was purified over the smoke; the three sticks were set up as a drying rack; and the pipe was rested against it. Matohoshila then put the buffalo bladder in front of him, and, holding up a piece of the tobacco to the west, he prayed.

"O You who guard the path where the sun goes down, and who control the waters! we are about to establish a relationship and a sacred peace. You have two sacred days—may the people have these, and may they walk the path of life with firm steps! You are to be included in this relationship and peace which we are about to establish; help us! We are making here on earth the same relationship which *Wakan-Tanka* always has with his people."

This tobacco which was identified with the Power of the west was then placed in the bladder.

I should perhaps tell you that the buffalo bladder is, for many peoples, as sacred as our pipe, for it also may contain the whole universe.

A pinch of tobacco was next offered to the north, with this prayer:

"O You where the giant Waziah lives, who control the purifying winds, You are to be placed in this sacred bag, and so help us with Your two holy days, and assist us in walking upon the straight path of life."

The Power of the north, now in the tobacco, was placed in the bag; and then Matohoshila offered a pinch of tobacco to the Power of the east.

"O You who control the path where the sun comes up, and who give knowledge, You are included in this offering, and so help us with Your two sacred days!"

After placing this Power of the east in the bag, a pinch of tobacco was offered, with a prayer, to the place where we always face.

"O You, White Swan, who control the path upon which the generations walk, there is a place for You in this sacred bag, and so help us with Your two red and blue days!"

After placing this Power of the south in the bag, Matohoshila offered a pinch of tobacco to the heavens.

"Grandfather, *Wakan-Tanka*, of the sacred heavens, Father, *Wakan-Tanka*, Grandmother Earth, and Mother Earth, may we know this our four-fold relationship with You; may we use this knowledge in making peace with another nation. By making relatives here on earth, we know that we do Thy will. O *Wakan-Tanka,* You are above everything, but You are here with us today."

This tobacco for the Great Spirit was then put into the bag, and, holding a pinch of tobacco to the ground, Matohoshila prayed.

"Grandmother Earth, hear me! Upon You we are making a relationship with a people, just as You have made a relationship with us, by bringing to us our sacred pipe. The two-leggeds, the four-leggeds, the wingeds, and all that move upon You are Your children. With all beings and all things we shall be as relatives; just as we are related to You, O Mother, so we shall make peace with another people and shall be related to them. May we walk with love and mercy upon that path which is holy! O Grandmother and Mother, we are placing You in this bag. Help us in making relatives and a lasting peace here!"

The Earth was then put in the bag, the mouth of which was tied, and the hair of a buffalo and some sweet grass were placed on top of it.

Matohoshila then said to the Ree: "You must now take care of this bag, which is very *wakan,* for it is really the same as the sacred pipe which was brought to us Sioux, and it, too, will make peace and relatives among many peoples. But you should always remember this, that our closest relatives are our Grandfather and Father, *Wakan-Tanka,* and our Grandmother and Mother, the Earth. With this sacred bag you should go to the leaders of the Sioux, and with it the relationship will be made."

The bag was then rolled up in a buckskin and tied at both ends with a rawhide rope in such a way that it could be carried easily. With this the first day of the rite was concluded.

The following day, just as the sun came up, Matohoshila took his pipe and went to the tipi of the Ree. After offering the pipe to the six directions, then smoking it a little, Matohoshila passed it to the Ree, who said, *"Hi ho! Hi ho!"* and embraced the pipe. After smoking for a few puffs, he passed it to the others in the tipi.

After the pipe had been passed among everybody, it was returned to Matohoshila, who then purified it and returned it to its bag. Then Matohoshila left for his own tipi, where he and the other Sioux chiefs and wise men were to wait for the Ree who was to come bearing the offering which he had been instructed to make the previous day.

When the Sioux saw the Ree approaching, they all cried "*Hi ho! Ho ho!*" and four of the Sioux went to meet him and led him into the tipi. The Ree walked around the lodge sun-wise, stood before Matohoshila, who was seated at the west, and placed before him the sacred offering bundle. A hot coal was placed before Matohoshila, who burned some sweet grass and held the sacred bundle over the smoke. Then after crying "*Hi ho! Hi ho!*" and embracing the bundle, he prayed.

"Grandfather, *Wakan-Tanka,* Father, *Wakan-Tanka,* behold us! Upon this earth we are fulfilling Thy will. By giving to us the sacred pipe, You have established a relationship with us, and this relationship we are now extending by making this peace with another nation with whom we were once at war. We know that we are now fulfilling one of the seven sacred rites which in the beginning were promised to us. Through this rite may these two peoples always live in peace, and set an example to other nations. With this offering my people will rejoice. This is a sacred day! It is good! Now we shall open this holy bundle, and through this offering we shall be bound to You and to all Your Powers. *Wakan-Tanka,* behold what we are doing!"

Matohoshila then slowly undid the *wakan* bundle, and when he and the people saw the buffalo bladder, they all cried "*Hi ye!*" for, of course, everybody knew why this bladder was so sacred. Matohoshila then held the bladder over the smoke of the sweet grass and embraced it, saying all the time, "*Hi ye!*" and then he prayed.

"Be merciful to me! Now that You have come to us, the people will walk the sacred path with their children in hand. I am the people, and I love You, shall cherish You, and shall always care for You. The people from whom You came [the Ree] will also always cherish You and will always know You to be *wakan.*"

Matohoshila then offered the bladder to the six directions, and, as he embraced it and kissed the opening of the bag, all the people cried *"Hi ho!"* Then, turning to the Ree, Matohoshila said: "To our people this offering means that you wish peace, and that you wish to establish a relationship with us. Is it for this reason that you have brought such a sacred offering?"

"Yes!" the Ree replied, "we wish to have a relationship with you which is as close as the relationship which exists between your people and *Wakan-Tanka.*"

The Sioux were pleased at this reply, and the sacred bladder was then sent out of the lodge and was passed around among all the people, who embraced it and kissed its mouth, in the same manner that Matohoshila had done. In order now to show that the peace offering of the Ree had been accepted, and in order to place the bundle at the very most sacred place, it was tied at the top of the twenty-eighth lodge pole. As I have explained before, this twenty-eighth pole represents *Wakan-Tanka,* for it is this key pole which holds up all the twenty-seven other poles of the tipi. In this manner the bringing of the offering was finished, and then the Ree returned to their lodges in order to prepare for the next day; Matohoshila, too, prepared a special tipi for the rites which were to come. This special lodge had, at either side of the entrance, hides which formed a pathway some ten strides long and about four feet high, and this makes the road of life leading into the tipi; thus, you see that one who enters upon this path cannot turn either to the right or left because of this screen of hides; he must walk straight to the center.

The following day four Ree were chosen to represent the whole nation, and bearing with them the equipment needed for the rites of the day, they went to the lodge which Matohoshila had prepared. Within the lodge Matohoshila was seated at the west and was preparing to make the sacred altar, but first he spoke, saying: "The corn that we Sioux now have really belongs to the Ree, for they cherish it and regard it as sacred, in the same manner that we regard our pipe; for they, too, have received their corn through a vision from the Great Spirit. It is the will of *Wakan-Tanka* that they have their corn. Thus, we shall not only return to them their lost corn but we shall also at this time establish a rite in which we shall create not only peace but also a real relationship which will be a reflection of that relationship which exists between us and *Wakan-Tanka*.

"I will now make a fragrant smoke which will reach to the sacred heavens and to the morning star, which divides the day into darkness and light, and it will reach, also, to the four Powers which guard the universe. This smoke is now going forth from our Grandmother and Mother Earth."

Matohoshila then put sweet grass upon the coals, and over the smoke he purified the sacred pipe, the corn, the hatchet, and all the equipment; he was now ready to make the sacred altar.

Taking up the hatchet, Matohoshila pointed it to the six directions and then struck the ground at the west. Again pointing the hatchet to the six directions, he struck the ground at the north, and in the same manner the other two directions were established. Then holding the hatchet to the heavens, he struck the ground twice at the center for the Earth and then again twice at the center for the Great Spirit. He scraped the ground level, and with a stick which had been purified, and which was first offered to the six directions, he drew a line from the west to the center, and then from the east to the center, from the north to the center, from the south to the center, and then, offering the stick to the heavens, he touched the center, and offering the stick to the earth, he again touched the center. In this manner the altar was made, and, as I have said before, it is very sacred, for we have here established the center of the Earth, and this center, which in reality is everywhere, is the home, the dwelling place of *Wakan-Tanka*.

Matohoshila took up an ear of corn, and at one end of it he pushed in a stick, and at the other end of the ear he tied the plume of an eagle.

"This corn really belongs to the Ree," Matohoshila said, "and so it will be returned to them, because they cherish it as we do our pipe. The ear of the corn which you see here has twelve important meanings connected with it, for there are twelve rows of kernels, which it receives from the various powers of the universe. As we think of the different things the corn can teach us, we should, above all, never forget the peace and the relationship which it is establishing here. But always, above everything else, we should remember that our closest relatives are our Grandfather and Father, *Wakan-Tanka,* our Grandmother and Mother, the Earth, the four Powers of the universe, the red and blue days, the two divisions of the day [light and darkness], the morning star, the Spotted Eagle, who guards all that is sacred about the corn; and also our pipe, which is as a relative, for he guards the people; and it is through him that we pray to *Wakan-Tanka.*

"The tassel which grows upon the top of the ear of corn, and which we have represented here by the eagle plume, represents the presence of the Great Spirit, for, as the pollen from the tassel spreads all over, giving life, so it is with *Wakan-Tanka,* who gives life to all things. This plume, which is always on top of the plant, is the first to see the light of the dawn as it comes, and it sees also the night and the moon and all the stars. For all these reasons it is very *wakan.* And this stick which I have stuck into the ear of corn is the tree of life, reaching from Earth to Heaven, and the fruit, which is the ear with all its kernels, represents the people and all things of the universe. It is good to remember these things if we are to understand the rites which are to come."

Matohoshila then rested the ear of corn against the rack which had been set up near the sacred altar; this rack was an image of the rack upon which the buffalo meat was dried, and it was now a drying rack for corn, for, you see, the corn was as important to the Ree as was the buffalo to the Sioux.

Matohoshila took off an ear of corn from its stalk, and giving it to the Ree, said: "It is the will of *Wakan-Tanka* that this corn return to you. In this way we shall make peace and establish a relationship which shall be an example to all nations. We have often spoken of the twelve Powers of the universe; we shall bind these twelve Powers, with the Sioux and the Ree, into one. In doing this, the Ree must sing over the Sioux. I shall represent my people; your chief shall represent your nation; and, by our becoming related, these two nations will be as one and shall live in peace. In the past, the two-leggeds which *Wakan-Tanka* placed upon this island have been enemies, but through this rite there will be peace, and, in the future, through this rite other nations of this island will become as relatives.

"You Ree should now pretend that you are on the warpath with us; you should go out and scout for the enemy, singing your war songs."

Holding ears of the corn in their right hands and cornstalks in their left hands, the Ree then pretended that they were scouting for the enemy—the Sioux. As they chanted their war songs, they waved the cornstalks back and forth. The swinging of the cornstalks in this manner is very *wakan*, for it represents the corn when the breath of the Great Spirit is upon it, since, when the wind blows, the pollen drops from the tassel upon the silk surrounding the ear, through which the fruit becomes mature and fertile.

You thus see that this relationship illustrated by the example of the corn is the same as that which we are establishing between these two peoples.

As the Ree pretended to be scouting for their enemy, the Sioux, all the people gathered about to watch them, and everybody was really very happy, for they understood that which was being done here. Soon the Ree stood in front of the tipi within which were the four Sioux; the Ree chief addressed his braves.

"Which of you has been the first to make a coup on the warpath? It is for you now to count coup on this lodge and then to go in and capture Matohoshila; and afterwards we shall capture the rest. But first you must tell us of your great deeds done on the warpath."

The chosen Ree then began to tell of his brave deeds, and, after each sentence, the people all cried *"Hi ho! Hi ho!"* and the women gave the tremulo. When he had finished, the Ree rushed at the tipi, counting coup; and then they entered and brought out Matohoshila. The other Ree captured and brought out the other four Sioux. The Ree continued to chant their war songs, and all the people—Ree and Sioux—were very happy and gave each other gifts of food, clothing, and even horses.

Then a procession was formed, led by the Ree who were still swinging the cornstalks, and after them came the five captured Sioux, among whom there was a Lakota woman and a small boy and a girl, for in all these people the whole nation was represented. The children were carried on the shoulders of the Ree, and at the end of the procession came the singers, drummers, and all the people of both nations who were watching. The procession stopped four times, and each time they stopped they howled as do the coyotes, for this is what is always done by a returning war party. Soon they came to the sacred lodge which had been prepared at the center of the camping circle, and the captured Sioux were led to beds at the west of the lodge, upon which were piled many gifts which the Ree were really giving to the Sioux.

The Ree helpers then took buffalo robes and held them up in front of the five Sioux and the Ree chief, and this is called "the hiding of the *hunkas.*" A Ree warrior and a Ree woman then went behind the curtain and began to paint the faces of the Sioux. The woman painted the faces of the Sioux woman and the Sioux girl red, and the Ree warrior painted the faces of the Lakota men and the boy red, with a blue circle around the face, and a blue line on the forehead, on both cheek bones, and on the chin. And all the time that the people were being painted, the Ree were still swinging the cornstalks, and were chanting their sacred song. The eagle plumes were then taken off the ears of corn and were put in the hair of the Sioux. While all this was being done, a buffalo skull was painted red, and the four Powers were represented by four lines upon it; sage was stuffed in the eyes and nose of the skull, and it was then placed—facing east—on a mound of earth which had been scraped from the sacred place.

The buffalo robes were then taken aside so that all could see the Sioux who had been painted. I should perhaps explain here what this represents. By being painted, the people have been changed; they have undergone a new birth, and with this they have new responsibilities, new obligations, and a new relationship. This transformation is so sacred that it must be undergone in darkness; it must be hidden from the view of the people. But when the curtain is taken aside, they come forth pure, free from ignorance, and must now have forgotten all troubles of the past. They are now one with the Ree; the relationship has been made.

Swinging their cornstalks, the Rees then chanted.

> *All these are related* [hunka].
> *All these are relatives.*

Then turning to each of the four directions, they chanted:

> *O You, Power, there where the sun goes down:*
> *You are a relative.*
> *O You, Power, where the Giant lives:*
> *You are a relative.*
> *O You, where the sun comes from:*
> *You are a relative.*
> *O You, Power, there where we always face:*
> *You are a relative.*

And then looking towards the Heaven, they chanted:

> *That relative!*

And bending over the Earth, and also over the buffalo, they chanted:

> *The Earth is our relative.*

And finally, waving the corn over the five Sioux, they chanted:

> *These four are our relatives;*
> *We are all related;*
> *We are all one!*

Matohoshila then rose, and, taking the pipe from the rack, he stood in the middle of the tipi, and, raising his right hand, and holding up the pipe in his left hand, he prayed.

"O *Wakan-Tanka,* I raise my hand to You. This day You are standing close to us. I offer You my pipe. To You also, O winged Power where the sun goes down, we offer this pipe. On this holy day, we have united into one all that is sacred in the universe. On this day a true relationship has been established. On this day a great peace has been made. O Grandfather, *Wakan-Tanka,* Your will which You have taught us has been done here on this earth. May this peace and relationship always be, and may no person or circumstance ever destroy it. It is now about to be completed; there will be peace, and these peoples will walk together that one path which is red and sacred."

Turning then to the people, Matohoshila said: "Now it is nearly finished, for we are bound together; we are one! O you Ree, that corn which you cherished, but lost, will be given back to you!"

At this all the people cheered loudly, and the women gave the tremulo. Once again the chanting began, and the two Ree with the cornstalks danced towards the door at the east, and then five times they rushed towards the five Sioux, and after this the swinging and dancing ceased.

Much food was brought into the tipi, and, purifying pieces of dried buffalo meat over the smoke of sweet grass, the Ree chief said: "O *Wakan-Tanka,* behold me and be merciful to me! This meat is the *hoksi chan ki ya* [root or seed]; it is to be placed in Your mouth, and it will become Your body and soul, which the Great Spirit has given to You with all His goodness. As He is merciful to You, so You too must be merciful to others!"

This the Ree chief said, as he put the sacred meat in the mouth of each of the four Sioux; and then he and Matohoshila moved and sat opposite each other at the center of the tipi. In front of Matohoshila was the buffalo skull and the pipe, and in front of the Ree chief there was the ear of corn and the four cornstalks. The Ree chief then took up a piece of the buffalo meat, and, after purifying it in the smoke of sweet grass, he held it in front of Matohoshila.

"*Ho,* son! I am to be your father. On this day which belongs to *Wakan-Tanka* He has seen our faces; the dawn of this day has seen us, and our Grandmother, the Earth, has listened to us. We are here at the center, and the four Powers of the universe join in us. This meat I shall put in your mouth, and from this day forth you shall never fear my home, for my home is your home, and you are my son!"

The chief then put the meat in Matohoshila's mouth, and at this all the Ree people rejoiced and gave thanks, for by this act the two people had been made one. Then Matohoshila, in turn, took up a piece of meat, purified it over the smoke, and, holding it in front of the Ree chief, said:

"*Ho,* Father! This day we have done the will of the Great Spirit, and through this we have established a relationship and peace, not only among ourselves, but within ourselves and with all the Powers of the universe. The dawn of the day has surely seen us, and with us today there has been the buffalo, who is our source of life here on earth, and who guards the people; and there has been with us our sacred pipe, which gives to our people the food for their souls; and also we have had with us your corn, which is so sacred to you, and with which we have made peace and have created a relationship. This food I shall place in your mouth, so you will never fear my home, for it is your home. In doing this, may *Wakan-Tanka* be merciful to us."

Matohoshila then placed the meat in the mouth of the Ree chief, and for this act all the Sioux cheered and gave thanks. Then, taking up his pipe and lighting it, Matohoshila offered it to the six directions and, after puffing on it four times, handed it to the Ree, saying: "*Ho,* father! Take this and smoke it with nothing but the truth in your heart."

The Ree took the sacred pipe, offered it to the six directions, and, after puffing on it four times, handed it around among the people. All the Ree and Sioux then took turns smoking it, and even after the fire had gone out, they put it to their mouths and embraced it. As the pipe was being passed among the people, the Ree chief said to Matohoshila:

"*Ho,* son! You have given back to us the corn which *Wakan-Tanka* had given to us, but which you took from us because of a vision which you had. Since we wanted our corn back, we came to you offering peace; but you have given to us more than this by making this relationship here today. In order now to bind us even more closely together, I give back to you a part of the corn and the freedom to use it in your rites. You, too, may now regard it as sacred as we do."

All the people were very happy that this great thing had been done, and they then held a feast which lasted throughout the night.

I wish to mention here, that through these rites a three-fold peace was established. The first peace, which is the most important, is that which comes within the souls of men when they realize their relationship, their oneness, with the universe and all its Powers, and when they realize that at the center of the universe dwells *Wakan-Tanka,* and that this center is really everywhere, it is within each of us. This is the real Peace, and the others are but reflections of this. The second peace is that which is made between two individuals, and the third is that which is made between two nations. But above all you should understand that there can never be peace between nations until there is first known that true peace which, as I have often said, is within the souls of men.

Ishna Ta Awi Cha Lowan:
PREPARING A GIRL FOR WOMANHOOD

These rites are performed after the first menstrual period of a woman. They are important because it is at this time that a young girl becomes a woman, and she must understand the meaning of this change and must be instructed in the duties which she is now to fulfill. She should realize that the change which has taken place in her is a sacred thing, for now she will be as Mother Earth and will be able to bear children, which should also be brought up in a sacred manner. She should know, further, that each month when her period arrives she bears an influence with which she must be careful, for the presence of a woman in this condition may take away the power of a holy man. Thus, she should observe carefully the rites of purification which we shall describe here, for these rites were given to us by *Wakan-Tanka* through a vision.

Ishna Ta Awi Cha Lowan: PREPARING FOR WOMANHOOD

Before we received these rites[1] it was customary that during each menstrual period the woman or young girl should go to a small tipi apart from the camping circle; food was brought to her, and no one else could go near the tipi. During the first period of a young girl, she was instructed by an older woman in the things a woman should know, even in the making of moccasins and clothes. This older woman who helped the girl should have been a good and holy person, for at this time her virtues and habits passed into the young girl whom she was purifying. Before she was permitted to return to her family and to her people the young girl had to be further purified in the *Inipi* lodge. But now I shall tell you how we received the new rites for preparing our young girls for womanhood.

A Lakota by the name of Slow Buffalo (*Tatanka Hunkeshne*) once had a vision of a buffalo calf who was being cleansed by her mother, and through the power of this vision Slow Buffalo became a holy man (*wichasha wakan*) and understood that he had been given rites which should be used for the benefit of the young women of his nation.

A few moons after Slow Buffalo received his vision, a young girl of fourteen called "White Buffalo Cow Woman Appears," had her first period, and of course her father, Feather on Head, thought immediately of Slow Buffalo's vision, so he took a filled pipe and offered it to Slow Buffalo, who accepted it, saying: *"Hi ho! Hi ho!* For what reason do you bring this sacred pipe?"

"I have a girl who is about to pass through her first period," Feather on Head replied, "and I want you to purify her and prepare her for womanhood, for I know that you have had a very powerful vision through which you have learned how this should be done in a better and more *wakan* manner than that which we have followed."

"Certainly, I shall do as you wish," Slow Buffalo replied. "The buffalo people, who have been taught by *Wakan-Tanka,* and who have given us this rite, are next to the two-leggeds, and are our source of life in many ways. For it was the White Buffalo Cow

[1] *Ishna Ta Awi Cha Lowan* is literally "Her alone they sing over."

Woman who, in the beginning, brought to us our most sacred pipe, and from that time we have been relatives with the four-leggeds and all that moves. *Tatanka,* the buffalo, is the closest four-legged relative that we have, and they live as a people, as we do. It is the will of our Grandfather, *Wakan-Tanka,* that this be so; it is His will that this rite be done here on earth by the two-leggeds. We shall now establish a sacred rite that will be of great benefit to all the people. It is true that all the four-leggeds and all the peoples who move on the universe have this rite of purification, and especially our relative the buffalo, for, as I have seen, they too purify their children and prepare them for bearing fruit. It will be a sacred day when we do this, and it will please *Wakan-Tanka* and all the peoples who move. All these peoples, and all the Powers of the universe, you must first place in the pipe, so that with them we may send a voice to the Great Spirit!

"I shall make a sacred place for your daughter, who is pure, and who is about to become a woman. The dawn of the day, which is the Light of *Wakan-Tanka,* will be upon this place, and all will be sacred.

"Tomorrow you must build a tipi just outside of the camping circle, and it must be built with a sheltered way leading to it, as is done in the *hunkapi* rite, and then you must gather together the following things:

a buffalo skull	a pipe
a wooden cup	some Ree tobacco
some cherries	*kinnikinnik*
water	a knife
sweet grass	a stone hatchet
sage	some red and blue paint

Feather on Head then gave to Slow Buffalo offerings of horses, and other gifts, and then he left to prepare for the next day.

The following day everything had been made ready in the sacred tipi, and all the people gathered around it, except those women who were preparing the feast which would come after the rites. Slow Buffalo was seated at the west of the tipi, and in front of him a place had been scraped in the earth, where a hot coal was placed. Holding sweet grass above the coal, Slow Buffalo prayed.

"Grandfather, *Wakan-Tanka,* Father, *Wakan-Tanka,* I offer to You Your sacred herb. O Grandmother Earth, from whence we come, and Mother Earth, who bears much fruit, listen! I am going to make smoke which will penetrate the heavens, reaching even to our Grandfather, *Wakan-Tanka;* it will spread over the whole universe, touching all things!"

After placing the sweet grass on the coal, Slow Buffalo purified first the pipe and then all the equipment which was to be used in the rite.

"All that will be done today," Slow Buffalo said, "will be accomplished with the aid of the Powers of the universe. May they help us to purify and to make sacred this girl who is about to become a woman. I now fill this sacred pipe, and in doing this I am placing within it all the Powers, who are helping us here today!"

Slow Buffalo first purified himself over the smoke, and then, holding the pipe in his left hand, he took a pinch of tobacco and prayed.

"Grandfather, *Wakan-Tanka,* we are about to send a voice through our pipe to You. This is a special day, for we are about to purify this young girl, White Buffalo Cow Woman Appears. There is a place for all the Powers of the universe in this pipe, and so have mercy upon us and accept our offering!

"O You where the sun goes down, who guard the pipe, and who come so terribly in order to purify the world and its people, we are about to offer this pipe to *Wakan-Tanka* and need Your help today, especially with your cleansing waters, for we are about to purify and make sacred not only a young girl, but also a whole generation. Help us with your two good red and blue days! There is a place for you in the pipe!"

Slow Buffalo put this tobacco in the pipe, and then, holding some tobacco to the place from which come the purifying winds (the north), he prayed.

"O You, giant *Waziah,* Power of the north, who guard the

health of the people with your winds, and who purify the earth by making it white, you are the one who watches that path upon which our people walk. Help us especially today with your purifying influence, for we are about to make sacred a virgin, White Buffalo Cow Woman Appears, from whom will come the generations of our people. There is a place for you in this pipe, help us with your two good days!"

The power of the north was put in the pipe, and then, holding a pinch of tobacco to the direction from which the light comes, Slow Buffalo continued to pray.

"O You, *Huntka,* the being and power of that place from whence comes the dawn of the day and the light of *Wakan-Tanka;* O You who are long-winded, and who give knowledge to the people, give of Your wisdom today to this virgin, White Buffalo Cow Woman Appears, who is about to be purified. Help us with Your two red and blue days. There is a place for You in the pipe."

Slow Buffalo then put into the pipe this Power of the place from whence comes the light, and then, holding tobacco to the place towards which we always face (the south), he prayed.

"O You, White Swan, Power of the place where we always face, who control the path of the generations and of all that moves, we are about to purify a virgin, that her generations to come may walk in a sacred manner upon that path which You control. There is a place for You in the pipe! Help us with Your two red and blue days!"

The Power of the south was then put in the pipe, and, holding now a pinch of tobacco up to the heavens, Slow Buffalo continued.

"O *Wakan-Tanka,* Grandfather, behold us! We are about to offer the pipe to You!" [Then holding the tobacco to the earth]:

"O You, Grandmother, upon whom the generations of the people have walked, may White Buffalo Cow Woman Appears and her generations walk upon you in a sacred manner in the winters to come. O Mother Earth, who gives forth fruit, and who is as a mother to the generations, this young virgin who is here today will be purified and made sacred; may she be like You, and may her children and her children's children walk the sacred path in a holy manner. Help us, O Grandmother and Mother, with Your red and blue days!"

The Earth, as Grandmother and Mother, was now in the tobacco, and was placed in the pipe, and again Slow Buffalo held tobacco towards the heavens and prayed.

"O *Wakan-Tanka,* behold us! We are about to offer this pipe to You." [Then pointing the same tobacco to the buffalo skull]: "O you, our four-legged relative, and who of all the four-legged peoples are the nearest to the two-leggeds, you too are to be placed in the pipe, for you have taught us how you cleanse your young, and it is this your way that we shall use in purifying White Buffalo Cow Woman Appears. I give to you as an offering, O four-legged, water, paint, cherry juice, and also grass. There is a place for you in the pipe—help us!"

Thus all the four-legged buffalo people were placed in the pipe, and now for the last time Slow Buffalo held tobacco up to *Wakan-Tanka* and prayed.

"O *Wakan-Tanka* and all the winged Powers of the universe, behold us! This tobacco I offer especially to You, the Chief of all the Powers, who is represented by the Spotted Eagle who lives in the depths of the heavens, and who guards all that is there! We are about to purify a young girl, who is soon to be a woman. May You guard those generations which will come forth from her! There is a place for You in the pipe—help us with the red and blue days!"

The pipe, containing now the whole universe, was leaned against the little drying rack, with its "foot" on the earth, and its "mouth" pointing towards the heavens. Then Slow Buffalo prepared to make the sacred place, and only the close relatives of White Buffalo Cow Woman Appears were allowed within the tipi, for the rites which were to follow are too sacred to be seen by all the people.

"*Wakan-Tanka* has given to the people a fourfold relationship—with their Grandfather, Father, Grandmother, and Mother," Slow Buffalo said. "These are always our closest relatives. Since all that is good is done in fours, the two-leggeds will walk through four ages, being relatives with all things. Our closest relative among the four-leggeds is *tatanka,* the buffalo, and I wish to tell you that they have established a relationship with me. I am about to make a sacred place for this virgin, White Buffalo Cow Woman Appears, and I have been given the power to do this from the buffalo. All things and all beings have been gathered together here today to witness this and to help us. It is so! *Hechetu welo!"*

Smoke was then made from the sweet grass, and, standing over it, Slow Buffalo again purified his whole body. When this was finished it was necessary before making the sacred place that Slow Buffalo demonstrate to all the people that he had truly received a power from the buffalo; so he began to chant his holy song which the buffalo had taught him.

> *This they are coming to see!*
> *I am going to make a place which is sacred.*
> *That they are coming to see.*
> *White Buffalo Cow Woman Appears*
> *Is sitting in a* wakan *manner.*
> *They are all coming to see her!*

Just then, as Slow Buffalo finished this song, he let out a loud *Huh!* like the bellow of a buffalo. As he did this a red dust came out of his mouth, just as a buffalo cow is able to do when she has a calf. This Slow Buffalo did six times, blowing the red smoke on the girl, and on the sacred place; everywhere within the tipi there was nothing but this red smoke, and if there were any children peeping in the door of the tipi, they were frightened and ran quickly away, for it was indeed a very terrible sight.

Slow Buffalo then took up his stone hatchet, and after purifying it over the smoke of the sweet grass, he struck the ground near the center of the tipi and then began to dig out a hollow in the shape of a buffalo wallow, piling the loose earth in a little mound just to the east of this sacred place. He then took a pinch of tobacco and, after holding it up to the heavens, placed it at the center of this place; then with tobacco he made a line from the west to the east and another line from the north to the south, thus making a cross. The whole universe was now within this holy place. Then taking some of the blue paint, and after holding it up to the heavens, Slow Buffalo touched the center of the sacred place. With more paint he drew blue lines on top of the tobacco, first from the west to the east, and then from the north to the south.

The use of this blue paint is very important and very sacred, if you understand the meaning, for, as I have often said, the power of a thing or an act is in the understanding of its meaning. Blue is the color of the heavens, and by placing the blue upon the tobacco, which represents the earth, we have united heaven and earth, and all has been made one.

Slow Buffalo then placed a buffalo skull upon the earth mound, with its face towards the east; then he painted a red line around its head and a straight red line between the horns, running down the forehead. Next he put balls of sage in the eyes of the skull, and then placed a wooden bowl of water in front of the buffalo's mouth. Cherries were placed in the water, for these represent the fruits of the earth, which are the same as the fruits of the two-leggeds. The cherry tree you see is the universe, and it stretches from Earth to Heaven; the fruits which the tree bears, and which are red as are we two-leggeds, are as all the fruits of our Mother, the Earth; for this and for more reasons than I could tell, this tree is very sacred to us.

Slow Buffalo next made a little bundle with sweet grass, the bark of the cherry tree, and the hair of a live buffalo. This hair is very *wakan* because it has been taken off a living tree, for you see the buffalo people, too, have a religion, and this is their offering which they have made to the tree.

White Buffalo Cow Woman Appears was then told to stand, and, holding this bundle of sacred things over her head, Slow Buffalo said:

"This which is over your head is like *Wakan-Tanka,* for when you stand you reach from Earth to Heaven; thus, anything above your head is like the Great Spirit. You are the tree of life. You will now be pure and holy, and may your generations to come be fruitful! Wherever your feet touch will be a sacred place, for now you will always carry with you a very great influence. May the four Powers of the universe help to purify you, for, as I mention the name of each power, I shall rub this bundle down that side of you. May the cleansing waters from where the sun goes down purify you! May you be as the purifying snow which comes from the place where *Waziah* lives. When the dawn of the day comes upon you, may you receive knowledge from the morning star. May you be made pure by the Power of the place towards which we always face, and may those peoples who have walked this straight and good path help to purify you. May you be as the White Swan who lives at this place there where you face, and may your children be as pure as the children of the Swan!"

The young girl sat down, and Slow Buffalo began to explain to the people how he had received his power from the buffalo, in a vision.

"I saw a great people who were breaking camp in preparation for a journey. I went towards them, and then suddenly they all gathered in a circle, and I was there with them. Then they brought a child into the center, and they told me that this child was to be purified according to the custom of their people. They then made a sacred place, a buffalo wallow as we have made here, and upon it they placed the child and asked me to breathe upon her, that she might be purified. I breathed upon her, but soon they said to me that they would show me their way which is better, and immediately they all turned into buffalo, and then a large bull came and blew a red powder upon the little calf in the center. As the calf lay there all the buffalo came and licked her, and each time they licked her they snorted and a sacred red smoke came out of their noses and mouths. They told me that this was the way that they purified their children. Now that the little buffalo calf had been purified, she would go forth and would bear fruit in a sacred manner, and in going forth she would travel to the end of the four ages; she would walk the sacred path as a leader of her people, and she would teach her children, too, to walk the path of life in a sacred manner. After showing me this they then established a

Seven Sioux Warriors who participated in the battle of the Little Big Horn: left to right, *top row:* Iron Hail, age 90; High Eagle, age 88; Iron Hawk, age 99; Little Warrior, age 80; *bottom row:* Comes Again, age 86; Pemmican, age 85; John Sitting Bull, age 80 (*Illuminated Foto-Ad Service, Sioux Falls, S.D.*)

Black Elk and J. E. Brown 1947 *(Photograph from author's collection)*

relationship with me, for they showed me a large buffalo bull and said that He would be my Grandfather, and then showing me a younger buffalo they said that He would be my Father; then they pointed to a buffalo cow and said that She was my Grandmother, and finally showing me a younger cow they said that She would be my Mother. They said that, with this fourfold relationship, I should return to my people and that I should teach them what I had been taught there. This is what I saw, and this is what I am doing here in purifying one of my own people in this manner; for this virgin, White Buffalo Cow Woman Appears, is that little calf which I saw. I shall now take her to drink of the sacred water, and this water is Life."

Slow Buffalo then began to sing another of his holy songs.

> *These peoples are sacred;*
> *From all over the universe they are coming to see it.*
> *White Buffalo Cow Woman Appears is sitting here in*
> *a sacred manner;*
> *They are all coming to see her.*

Slow Buffalo then picked up the buffalo skull by the horns, and, as he chanted his holy song, red smoke came out of the nose of the buffalo skull. Acting as a buffalo would, he began to push the young girl with the skull, shoving her towards the bowl of water, at which she then knelt and drank four sips; and when all the people saw all this it made them very happy.

A piece of buffalo meat was then given to Slow Buffalo; after purifying it over the smoke of the sweet grass, and after offering it to the six directions, he held it in front of the girl and said:

"White Buffalo Cow Woman Appears, you have prayed to *Wakan-Tanka;* you will now go forth among your people in a holy manner, and you will be an example to them. You will cherish those things which are most sacred in the universe; you will be as Mother Earth—humble and fruitful. May your steps, and those of your children, be firm and sacred! As *Wakan-Tanka* has been merciful to you, so you, too, must be merciful to others, especially to those children who are without parents. If such a child should ever come to your lodge, and if you should have but one piece of meat which you have already placed in your mouth, you should take it out and give it to her. You should be as generous as this! As I now place this meat in your mouth, we should all remember how merciful *Wakan-Tanka* is in providing for our wants. In the same manner you must provide for your children!"

Slow Buffalo placed the meat in the mouth of the girl, and then the bowl of water with the cherries was passed around among all the people, and each took a sip from it. Then Slow Buffalo took up the pipe from its rack, and, holding the stem up, he prayed.

"*Hee-ay-hay-ee-ee!* [four times] Grandfather, *Wakan-Tanka,* behold them! These people and all the generations to come are Yours. Look upon this virgin, White Buffalo Cow Woman Appears, who has been purified and honored this good day. May Your Light which never fails be upon her always and upon all her relatives! Grandmother, and great Mother Earth, upon You the people will walk; may they follow the sacred path with Light, not with the darkness of ignorance. May they always remember their relatives at the four quarters, and may they know that they are related to all that moves upon the universe, and especially the buffalo, who is the chief of the four-leggeds, and who helps to raise the people. O *Wakan-Tanka,* help us and be merciful to us, that we may live in a happy and sacred manner. Be merciful to us, *Wakan-Tanka,* that we may live!"

All the people then said "*Hi ho! Hi ho!*" and everybody was rejoicing and happy because of the great thing which had been done that day. White Buffalo Cow Woman Appears was brought out of the tipi, and all the people rushed up to her and placed their hands upon her, for now she was a woman, and, because of the rites which had been performed for her, there was much holiness in her. There was then a great feast, and a "give away," and those who were poor received much. It was in this manner that the rites for preparing a young girl for womanhood were first begun, and they have been the source of much holiness, not only for our women, but for the whole nation.

CHAPTER VIII

Tapa Wanka Yap: THE THROWING OF THE BALL

There was, until recently, a game among our people which was played with a ball, four teams and four goals which were set up at the four quarters. But there are only a few of us today who still understand why the game is sacred, or what the game originally was long ago, when it was not really a game, but one of our most important rites. This rite I am going to describe now, for it is the seventh and last sacred rite of this period given to us, through a vision, by *Wakan-Tanka.*

The game as it is played today represents the course of a man's life, which should be spent in trying to get the ball, for the ball represents *Wakan-Tanka,* or the universe, as I shall explain later. In the game today it is very difficult to get the ball, for the odds— which represent ignorance—are against you, and it is only one or two of the teams who are able to get the ball and score with it. But in the original rite everybody was able to have the ball, and if you think about what the ball represents, you will see that there is much truth in it.

It was a Lakota called *Waskn mani* (Moves Walking), who received this rite in a vision many winters ago. He did not tell anybody about it for a very long time, until one day a Lakota called High Hollow Horn saw in a dream that Moves Walking had received a sacred rite which should belong to all the people. Thus, according to our custom, High Hollow Horn made a sacred tipi on one side of the camping circle; he then filled his pipe in a ritual manner, and with four other holy men, he went and offered the pipe to Moves Walking.

"Hi ho! Hi ho! Hechetu welo, it is good!" Moves Walking said, "What is it that you wish of me?"

"I have been told through a dream," High Hollow Horn said, "that you have received a very sacred rite which will be the seventh rite which the White Buffalo Cow Woman promised us in the beginning. All the people wish you to perform this rite now!"

"It is so," Moves Walking replied. "Announce to all the people that tomorow will be a holy day and that they must all paint their faces and wear their finest clothes. We will have this rite which *Wakan-Tanka* has sent to me through the buffalo!"

Moves Walking then held the pipe to heaven and prayed: "O Grandfather, *Wakan-Tanka,* behold us! You have given to us this pipe, that we may come closer to You. With the pipe we have walked upon the sacred path through this age. We have done Thy will here on earth, and now we will once again offer this pipe to You. Give to us a holy red and blue day! May it be sacred; may all rejoice!"

Moves Walking then told High Hollow Horn and the four other holy men that they should gather together the following things:

a pipe

some *kinnikinnik*

sweet grass

a ball—made of buffalo hair, and covered with buffalo skin

Tapa Wanka Yap: THE THROWING OF THE BALL

a Spotted Eagle feather	a bag of earth
a knife	some red and blue paint
a hatchet	a buffalo skull
some sage	a food rack, painted blue

The five men then left to prepare for the following day, and by now very many people had gathered around the sacred lodge, for they could see that something important was soon to happen. One man said that "this must be the seventh rite, for until now we have had only six, and I believe it will be a game which will represent life. I think they will throw a ball, for I just heard that it is to be a part of the equipment. Tomorrow should be a great day!" All that night the people talked about what was to happen the next day, and everybody was happy, for that which the White Buffalo Cow Woman had promised would now be fulfilled.

Before dawn the next day, all had been prepared, and the floor of the sacred lodge had been strewn with sage. Just before the sun came up, Moves Walking slowly approached the tipi, crying as he walked, for he had been thinking of the six other rites that his people had, and he knew that today the White Buffalo Cow Woman would again be with them. Many people went out to meet Moves Walking, and they also cried as they approached the sacred tipi; Moves Walking entered first, and after sitting at the place where the sun goes down, he cleared a place in front of him with a knife and then asked the helpers to bring a coal from the fire. He took sweet grass, and holding it over the coal, he prayed.

"Grandfather, *Wakan-Tanka,* You have always been and always shall be. You have created everything—there is nothing which does not belong to You. You have brought the red people to this island, and You have given us knowledge that we may know all things. We know that it is Your light which comes with the dawn, and we know that it is the Morning Star who gives us wisdom. You have given us the power to know the four Beings of the universe and to know that these four are really One. We see always the sacred heavens, and we know what they are and what they represent. This day will be a great day, and all that moves upon the earth and in the universe will rejoice. On this day I put Your sweet grass upon the fire which is also Yours, and the smoke which goes forth will spread throughout the universe and will reach even to the depths of the heavens."

Moves Walking brought the sweet grass down on the coal, stopping four times; then he purified the pipe, the ball, the buffalo skull, and all the equipment which was to be used that day.

"O *Wakan-Tanka,* my Grandfather," Moves Walking prayed, "I have used Your sweet grass, and the smoke has spread throughout the universe. Here I will build the sacred place, and the day which is now approaching will see it. They will look at each other face to face. In doing this I am fulfilling Your will. This is Your place, O *Wakan-Tanka.* You will be here with us!

Just as the first rays of the sun began to enter the tipi, Moves Walking picked up a stone axe, offered it to *Wakan-Tanka,* and struck the ground at the center of the sacred place which he had scraped in front of him. Then, offering the axe to the west, he struck that side of the sacred place, and in the same manner he struck the ground at the three other quarters. Then, after holding the axe to the earth, he once again struck the center.

Moves Walking took the knife and slowly scraped the earth from this place which he had marked out and placed the earth at the east; next he took up a handful of the purified earth, and, after offering a small part of it to the Power of the west, he put the earth on the western side of the sacred place. In the same manner earth was placed at the other three directions and at the center. Then, with the earth which he had piled at the east, Moves Walking made a mound at the center and carefully spread it all over the sacred place. Finally, he leveled it off with an eagle feather.

He then picked up a pointed stick and, after offering it to *Wakan-Tanka,* drew a line in the soft earth, from the west to the east; after offering the stick again to the heavens, he drew another line from the north to the south. Finally, the altar was completed by making two lines of tobacco on top of the two paths drawn on the ground, and then this tobacco was painted red. This altar now represented the universe and all that is in it. At its center was

Wakan-Tanka; His presence was really there in the altar, and that is why it was made in such a careful and sacred way.

While Moves Walking was making the sacred altar, he sang the sacred-pipe song (*Cannumpa wakan oloowan*), while another Lakota in the lodge made low and rapid thunder on the drum.

Friend do this! Friend do this! Friend do this!
If you do this your Grandfather will see you.
When you stand within the holy circle,
Think of me when you place the sacred tobacco in the pipe.
If you do this He will give you all that you ask for.

Friend do this! Friend do this! Friend do this!
If you do this your Grandfather will see you.
When you stand within the holy circle,
Send your voice to Wakan-Tanka.
If you do this He will give you all that you desire.

Friend do this! Friend do this! Friend do this!
If you do this your Grandfather will see you.
When you stand within the holy circle,
Crying and with tears send your voice to Wakan-Tanka.
If you do this you will have all that you desire.

Friend do this! Friend do this! Friend do this!
That your Grandfather may see you.
When you stand within the sacred hoop,
Raise your hand to Wakan-Tanka.
Do this and He will bestow upon you all that you desire.

There is much power in this song because it was given to us by the White Buffalo Cow Woman at the time when she brought to us our most holy pipe. This song is used even today, and it makes my heart good whenever I hear or sing it.

As Moves Walking was making the altar and singing the sacred song, a young girl who was to play an important part in the rite was brought into the tipi by her father, and, passing around the lodge sun-wise, she took her place to the left of Moves Walking. Her name was *Wsu sna win* (Rattling Hail Woman), and she was the daughter of High Hollow Horn.

Moves Walking picked up the sacred ball, which had been made from the hair of the buffalo and covered with tanned buffalo hide. He painted this ball red, the color of the world, and, with blue paint representing the heavens, he made dots at the four quarters; then made two blue circles running all around the ball, thus making two paths joining the four quarters. By completely encircling the red ball with the blue lines, Heaven and Earth were united into one in this ball, thus making it very sacred.

He then put sweet grass upon a coal, and over the smoke he purified the pipe and began to pray, holding the pipe stem to the heavens.

"O *Wakan-Tanka,* behold this pipe which we are about to offer. You we know are the first, and You have always been. We shall walk the path of life, carrying in one hand the sacred pipe which You have given us, and in the other hand will be our children. In this way the generations will come and go and will live in a holy manner. This is Your sacred day, for on this day we shall establish a rite which will complete the seven rites of the pipe. O *Wakan-Tanka,* look down upon us as we offer the pipe to You. On this day the four Powers of the universe will be with us. O You, Power, there where the sun goes down, who control the waters, we are about to offer this pipe: help us with your two good days! Help us!"

This tobacco was placed in the pipe for the West, and then pinches of tobacco representing the other Powers or directions, were put into the pipe, with the following prayers for each:

"O You where the Giant lives, who purifies with Your white breath, and You, winged one who guard this straight path, we are placing You in this pipe, and so help us with Your two sacred red and blue days!"

"O You, Power of the place where the sun comes up, and you Morning Star, who divides the darkness from the light, giving wisdom to the two-legged peoples! with You we shall offer this pipe. Help us with Your two good days!"

Tapa Wanka Yap: THE THROWING OF THE BALL

"O You, Power of that place where we always face, from which the generations come and go; O You, the White Swan, who guard the sacred path! there is a place for You in this pipe which we are about to offer to *Wakan-Tanka.* Help us with Your two good days!"

"O You, winged of the blue heavens; You who have strong wings and eyes which see everything—You live in the depths of the heavens and are very close to *Wakan-Tanka.* We are about to offer this pipe; help us with your two sacred red and blue days!"

"O You, Grandmother, from whom all earthly things come, and O You, Mother Earth, who bear and nourish all fruits! behold us and listen! Upon You there is a sacred path which we walk, thinking of the sacredness of all things. Upon You there will be made sacred this young and pure girl, Rattling Hail Woman, for it is she who will stand at the center of the earth, holding the *wakan* ball. Help us, O Grandmother and Mother, with Your two good days, as we offer this pipe to *Wakan-Tanka!*"

With these prayers the pipe was filled and placed against the little blue rack made of forked sticks stuck into the ground. Moves Walking then picked up the painted ball and handed it to the young girl, telling her to stand and to hold it in her left hand and to raise her right hand up to the heavens. Moves Walking then began to pray, holding the pipe in his left hand, and holding his right hand up to the heavens.

"O Grandfather, *Wakan-Tanka,* Father, *Wakan-Tanka,* behold us! Behold Rattling Hail Woman, who stands here holding the universe in her hand. Upon that earth all that moves will rejoice this day. The four Powers of the universe, and also the sacred heavens, are there with the ball—all this Rattling Hail Woman sees. The dawn of the day, and the Light of *Wakan-Tanka* is now upon her. She sees her generations to come and the tree of life at the center. She also sees the sacred path which leads from the place where You always face to there where the giant lives. She sees her Grandmother and Mother Earth and all her relatives in the things that move and grow. She stands there with the universe on her hand, and all her relatives there are really one. O Grandfather, *Wakan-Tanka,* Father, *Wakan-Tanka,* it is by Your will that Your Light is now shining upon this girl. This day we all feel Your presence. We know that You are here with us. For this and for all that You have given us, we give thanks."

Moves Walking then stood before the buffalo skull and spoke to him in this manner: *"Hunka* spirit, today they have given to you a paint which I now put upon you, for you are related to our people, the two-leggeds, and it is through you that they live. After I put this sacred paint upon you, you will go forth with this young girl, and you will give of your grace to all the people."

Moves Walking then painted the buffalo by making a red line around the head, and then a straight line from between the horns to between the eyes. When he had finished this, he went and sat next to Rattling Hail Woman and spoke to her.

"Rattling Hail Woman, you are sitting there in a sacred manner! It is good, for the spirits of the buffalo have come to see you, and, therefore, I shall reveal to you the vision which I have received. In my vision I went towards the place where the Giant lives, and I saw a great people moving as if on a journey. They, too, had their guards, their chiefs, and their holy men of prayer, just as we do. And as I came before these people, they stopped and one of their leaders came forward and spoke to me.

" 'Two-legged, behold these people who are sacred! They are now going to teach an honored young one to walk, and in her life you will see four ages.'

"Then they brought forward a tiny girl, who sat down, and I saw that she was a little buffalo calf. She stood up and began to walk, but then she staggered and lay down. Her people, who I now saw were buffalo people, gathered around the little calf, and one buffalo cow snorted a red breath upon her, and when the calf lay down again I saw that she was now a white yearling buffalo. The mother continued to snort red and to nudge the yearling. When she got up again I saw that she had changed a second time, and was now a larger buffalo. The young buffalo then lay down, but when she got up again she was full grown; and then she ran away over the hill, and all the buffalo snorted, so that they shook the universe. I then saw buffalo at all the four quarters, but they were now people, and I saw the little girl standing at the center with a ball in her hand. The girl tossed the ball to the place where the sun goes down, and all the people scrambled for it and returned it to the center. In the same manner, the girl tossed the ball towards the place where the Giant lives, towards the place where the sun comes up, and then to the place towards which we always face; each time the ball was returned to the girl at the center. The last time the little girl threw the ball straight up, and immediately they all turned back into buffalo, and, of course, none of them were able to catch the ball, for the buffalo people do not have hands as we do. The little girl, who was now a buffalo calf again, took the ball and nudged it towards me, and the leader of the buffalo people then said to me: 'This universe really belongs to the two-leggeds, for we four-legged buffalo people cannot play with a ball; you should therefore take this and return to your people and explain to them that which we have taught you here.' "

Moves Walking then explained this rite to Rattling Hail Woman and to the other people gathered there: "In the buffalo there are four ages, as they have shown me in this vision. Rattling Hail Woman and the buffalo—represented by his skull—shall together go forth from this tipi, and she will throw the ball as I have explained to you in the vision. It is the will of *Wakan-Tanka* that this be done. Do not forget that the ball is the world and, also, our Father, *Wakan-Tanka,* for the world or the universe is His home; thus, whoever catches the ball will receive a great blessing. All of the people must try to catch the ball, and Rattling Hail Woman will be the buffalo calf at the center. She shall now leave, stopping four times as she goes, and each step that she takes will be for the benefit of her people."

All the people had gathered around the tipi in order to hear what was being said; they all were dressed in their best clothes, and everybody was happy. High Hollow Horn walked out of the lodge first, holding the sacred pipe, and after him followed his daughter, Rattling Hail Woman, carrying the ball in her right hand. Moves Walking then followed holding the buffalo skull, and snorting. Four times he pushed Rattling Hail Woman with the skull, and each time red smoke came out its nose. As he did this, Moves Walking sang one of his *wakan* songs.

> *In a sacred manner from all directions,*
> *They are coming to see you.*
> *Rattling Hail Woman has been sitting in a sacred*
>   *manner.*
> *They are all coming to see her!*

Finally, when they stopped the fourth time, High Hollow Horn and Moves Walking stood on either side of the girl, facing towards the place where the sun goes down. The girl then threw the ball towards the west, and one of the people there caught the ball and, after embracing it and offering it to the six directions, handed it back to the girl at the center. In the same manner, the three then faced towards the place where the Giant lives, and the ball was thrown in that direction, all the people scrambling for it, finally returning it to the center. Then the ball was thrown to the place where the sun comes up, and then to the place where we always face, and each person who was fortunate enough to catch the ball was given a horse or some valuable present. The fifth time, the ball was thrown straight up, and there was then a great scramble, until finally one person had the ball and returned it to the girl at the center.

When the throwing of the ball had been finished, High Hollow Horn offered the sacred pipe to Moves Walking, who held the stem towards the heaven and began to send a voice to *Wakan-Tanka*.

"*Hee-ay-hay-ee-ee!* [Four times]. I am sending a voice to You, O *Wakan-Tanka*—to You who have always been, and who are above all things. Father, *Wakan-Tanka*, You are the chief of all things; everything belongs to You, because it is You who have created the universe. Upon this great island You have placed our people, and You have given us the wisdom to know all things. You have made us to know the moon and the sun, the four winds and the four Powers of the universe. We know that the generations come from, and return to, that place towards which we always face, and upon this straight red path leading to where the giant lives we have walked in a sacred manner. And above all, we know that our four closest relatives are always our Grandfather and Father, *Wakan-Tanka,* and our Grandmother and Mother, the Earth. O *Wakan-Tanka,* behold today Rattling Hail Woman who holds in her hand a ball which is the earth. She holds that which will bring strength to the generations to come who will inherit Thy earth; and the steps that they take will be firm, and they will be free from the darkness of ignorance. Rattling Hail Woman stands here holding Your world, and, from this day on, this ball will belong to the generations to come, and they will rejoice as they walk hand-in-hand with their children. Help them to walk the sacred path without ignorance. May the heavens above behold us here and be merciful to us! Grandfather, *Wakan-Tanka!* Father, *Wakan-Tanka!* may we always know and do Thy will. May we never lose this relationship established here! May we cherish it and love it always! O *Wakan-Tanka,* be merciful to me, that my people may live!"

The sacred pipe was then smoked or touched by all who were present, and those who were fortunate enough to have caught the holy ball were given presents of horses or buffalo robes, and all the people had a great feast and everybody was happy, for that which the White Buffalo Cow Woman had promised in the beginning had now been fulfilled.

I, Black Elk, should now explain to you several things that you may not understand about this holy rite. First, it is a little girl, and not an older person, who stands at the center and who throws the ball. This is as it should be, for just as *Wakan-Tanka* is eternally youthful and pure, so is this little one who has just come from *Wakan-Tanka,* pure and without any darkness. Just as the ball is thrown from the center to the four quarters, so *Wakan-Tanka* is at every direction and is everywhere in the world; and as the ball descends upon the people, so does His power, which is only received by a very few people, especially in these last days.

You have seen that the four-legged buffalo people were not able to play this game with the ball, and so they gave it to the two-leggeds. This is very true because, as I have said before, of all the created things or beings of the universe, it is the two-legged men alone who, if they purify and humiliate themselves, may become one with—or may know—*Wakan-Tanka*.

At this sad time today among our people, we are scrambling for the ball, and some are not even trying to catch it, which makes me cry when I think of it. But soon I know it will be caught, for the end is rapidly approaching, and then it will be returned to the center, and our people will be with it. It is my prayer that this be so, and it is in order to aid in this "recovery of the ball," that I have wished to make this book.

for "Preparing a Girl for Womanhood" received, 117; rites for "The Throwing of the Ball" received, 128, 134–35

Wakan, meaning of: 3 n., 4 n.
Wakan-Tanka: explanation of aspects of, 5 n.; goodness of, 35, 36; unicity of, 72; as the center, 89–90, 108; as giver of life, 109; as the center within men, 115; as merciful, 125; always present, 134, 137; *see also* Great Spirit
Wakinyan-Tanka: description of, 39; as guardian of the pipe, 61; *see also* Thunder-Beings
Walker, J. R.: 39, 45 n., 65
Wanagi, explanation of: 8 n.; *see also* soul
Wanbli Galeshka: symbolism of, 6 n., 18, 45, 51; *see also* Spotted Eagle
Wasna, how made: 17, 19
Whistles, eagle-bone: significance of, 71; used in sun dance, 93 ff.
White Buffalo Cow Woman (mythical person): 11, 22, 67, 85, 101, 117–18, 128–29, 131, 137
White Buffalo Cow Woman Appears: 117–26
Wichasha Wakan (Holy man): 44; as distinct from "medicine man," 45 n.
Willow tree, significance of: 31, 32
Wochangi (influence): 59, 62
World Tree, The: 69 n.

▼

▼

Black Elk

Holy Man
of the Oglala

by Michael F. Steltenkamp

Dedicated to the memory of
my grandmother, Lucy Looks Twice,
my mother, Julia Antoinette Steltenkamp,
and all Good Ones of Wakan Tanka.

Contents

▼

▼

Illustrations

Preface

A friend who lived some distance out in the country needed a ride home, so I agreed to take him. He came from a traditional Lakota background.[1] In fact, English was his second language. Driving over dry roads on the Pine Ridge Indian Reservation in ninety-degree weather would make us thirsty, we knew, so before setting out, we bought a can of soda. As we drove along, we emptied the can, and my friend turned toward his window, then stopped: "Mind if I throw this out?"

The question took me by surprise. Here was a young man whose usual behavior reminded me of the prereservation period, when the Plains were free of twentieth-century pollution. A rare moment had presented itself, so I responded by asking: "Did you ever see the television commercial that showed an Indian man in buckskin paddling down a river? When he landed, someone threw trash at his feet, and the Indian man was pictured with a tear on his cheek?" Pensive for a few moments, my friend answered, "Yeah, what's *he* crying about?"

"The commercial seemed to be showing that years ago, before settlers came to America, someone could paddle down a river and not see any trash lying around at all. And if an Indian from a long time ago saw how polluted America had become, he would cry." That was the point of the television commercial as I understood it.

I awaited my friend's reaction. He did not reply immediately; instead, he was taken up in thought. With a look of bewilderment, and with no inflection in his voice, he asked: "You mean I'm not supposed to throw this can out the window?"

I told him I would throw it away when I got home, and he set it on the seat between us.

The matter was closed, but my friend seemed perplexed by the decision. If I wanted to carry an empty soda can back home with me, fine—but doing so was not the choice my friend would have made. He could not identify with his television counterpart. Never again would I view that commercial with my same, previously unchallenged assumptions.

My experience illustrates a larger issue that this work addresses: how the legacy of stereotypes we have inherited obscures the flesh-and-blood individuals who *are* Native people. I pursue this issue by focusing on the life of Black Elk, a "holy man of the Oglala Sioux," who has been characterized in ways that have spawned numerous images of the Indian world that are not entirely accurate (Neihardt 1972). His life story can shed light on the larger, more complex social system within which he lived (Bourguignon 1979:19). Black Elk can tell us much about the Lakota world view, and it is his story, his special role in the panorama of Indian culture, that the rest of these pages address. In the process, far more than just one man's life will be better understood.

When Thomas Mails persuaded "ceremonial chief" Frank Fools Crow to relate his life experiences (1979), readers of that biography met a man who enjoyed unique genealogical, political, and religious prominence among the Lakota.

Besides addressing the United Nations General Assembly during the 1970s on behalf of Indian America, this elder statesman acquired prestige and notoriety among his people as the repository of sacred knowledge. At first unwilling to discuss this information, he relented only when Mails told him that the revered Black Elk, an uncle to Fools Crow, had recounted his own life history years earlier. The fact that Black Elk had chosen this course demanded that Fools Crow reconsider his own position. After all, even for Fools Crow, Black Elk was a beacon. His stature, Fools Crow knew, dwarfed that of all modern religious practitioners, including Fools Crow himself (from whom many others were taking their cue). What Fools Crow did not know was that Black Elk was perhaps the best known of all American Indians.

Black Elk's life and thought were first brought to the public forum in 1932 through the poetic craftsmanship of John Neihardt.[2] After this initial introduction, Joseph Epes Brown transmitted the holy man's knowledge of Lakota religious tradition in a work entitled *The Sacred Pipe* (1953). The numerous reprints of both books (in America and Europe) attest to the appeal of what Black Elk had to say.

Neihardt and Brown portrayed him as a man living in his memories of prereservation life. Born when buffalo was still the staple of Plains tribes, he shared in the victory of Little Big Horn (1876) and witnessed the heartbreak of Wounded Knee (1890). Throughout these summer and winter years, Black Elk grew into manhood. As DeMallie has noted (1984a:124), however, Neihardt and Brown both erred by depicting him solely as a nineteenth-century figure.

Consisting largely of first-person narratives, *Black Elk Speaks* portrayed Sioux life as it existed during the latter half of the 1800s. Like other works of its kind, the biography recounts boyhood memories and early adult experiences, village and family life, religious ritual, and sober reflection. Historical figures such as Crazy Horse, Buffalo Bill Cody, and George Armstrong Custer all come alive in the powerful simplicity of Black Elk's account.

Except for an incident reported in the postscript, *Black Elk Speaks* restricts itself to the downfall of the Sioux as a self-sufficient people. Prereservation days are portrayed as generally carefree times, the Indian victory at Little Big Horn becomes a prelude to reservation confinement, and the 1890 massacre at Wounded Knee is shown as a coup de grace to an entire way of life. His dream, Black Elk said, died with those who fell in this final conflict. In effect, Neihardt casts the holy man in the role of spokesman for all Lakota, if not all Indian people. Dee Brown continued this image when he used Black Elk's grim reflection on the demise of the Sioux as a conclusion for his 1970 best-seller *Bury My Heart at Wounded Knee.*

In *Black Elk Speaks,* the holy man prays to Wakan Tanka (Great Spirit), "Maybe the last time on this earth, I recall the great vision you sent me" (233).[3] He is presented as a very old man, nearly blind, who might well pass away at any moment. That Black Elk experienced so much personal hurt along with his people only adds greater emotional impact to the closing pages of this book. "Noble savage" and "vanishing American" motifs reverberate throughout the final passages.[4]

Sixteen years after Neihardt wrote of Black Elk in this fashion, however, Joseph Epes Brown came upon the very same man and found him still very much alive! Brown asked Black Elk to describe the seven rites of the Oglala Sioux— traditional religious ceremonies belonging to the earlier period but practiced irregularly in recent times. With the publication in 1953 of *The Sacred Pipe,* the holy man's knowledge of ritual was brought to the fore. Once again, readers were understandably touched by what Black Elk had to say.

In sum, the two books portray Black Elk and the social

institutions he so cherished as paralyzed victims of Western subjugation. Doomed to live out his years as a relic of the past and prisoner of irreconcilably foreign ways, the holy man (and his people) becomes an object of pity. Readers are left to conclude that Black Elk lived his first thirty years productively and endured his last sixty tearfully.

Nothing was known of Black Elk's life for the forty years not treated by Neihardt, and except for Brown's eight-month visit in the winter of 1947–48, nothing is known of Black Elk's last twenty years. Essentially, then, sixty years of the man's life are unaccounted for, and readers are left to wonder whether Black Elk participated at all in the twentieth-century reservation world (fifty years of which he knew).

Brown's 1971 preface to *The Sacred Pipe* rightly suggested that what so far has been revealed in the two books on Black Elk only "raises the question as to who, in fact, Black Elk really was" (xiii). Roger Dunsmore (1977) raised the same question, insisting that one of the principal tasks of anthropologists is to understand how people such as Black Elk made sense of the disastrous encounter between Oglala culture and the invading white culture (if indeed they did). Such concerns no doubt have confronted most readers of the moving, though enigmatic, commentaries ascribed to the man in either book. Perhaps readers wonder if people like Black Elk exist any more, or if in fact they ever did exist.

So evocative is Black Elk's characterization that it has been expropriated and utilized on behalf of diverse forms of special pleading. Environmental activists, Indian militants, anthropologists, historians, religionists, students of Americana, and others have gleaned from Black Elk passages that bolster or refute whatever conventional Native theme they choose because, it appears, his representation has become *the* conventional stereotype par excellence.[5] Those aware of this larger frame of reference are thus con-

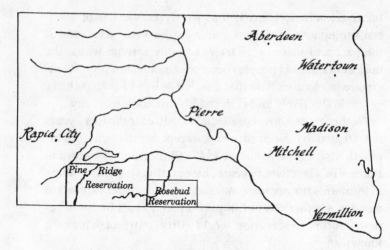

Map 1. South Dakota, showing the Pine Ridge and Rosebud
reservations.

fronted with the task of separating the wheat from the chaff—
discerning whether Black Elk was a kind of "modal man"
of the Sioux, a mystic, or a myth.

A certain irony accompanies the Neihardt-Brown portrayal in that their Black Elk elicits admiration from readers, even though his story represents a kind of personal and
societal death-rattle. Cultural forms after Wounded Knee
are shown to be by-products of a lifeless resignation to non-
Indian ways that the holy man was forced to endure. Many
readers perhaps assumed that Black Elk's life typified the
experience of the Oglala people (and others) on their mark-
erless path from nomadic times to sedentary living. However, only by analyzing the man's *entire* life, within the
constraints of the nineteenth- *and* twentieth-century Lakota
milieu, can we attempt cross-cultural comparisons or interpret Black Elk's socialization and world view.

When I assumed a teaching position on the Pine Ridge
Reservation, I was on the very same terrain that had been

home to the holy man for most of his life (see map 1). Joseph Epes Brown had been one of my college instructors just the year before, so I was eager to seek out (as he had done) living custodians of ancient ways and perhaps learn more about the famous holy man himself.

After only a short time, however, I learned to my great astonishment that Black Elk's prestige in the reservation community was not attributable to the popularity of his two books. Prestige he had, but it was the result of his very active involvement with priests in establishing Catholicism among his people. Older persons remembered him as "Nick" Black Elk, and most knew little (if anything) about the two books based on his life and thought. Those who were familiar with the literature thought it was the work of Nick's son Ben.[6]

Neihardt made passing reference to Black Elk as a preacher in his introduction (*BES,* x) but concentrated his attention on the man's role as a traditional holy man *(wicasa wakan)* of the Lakota. In describing Black Elk only as "a kind of a preacher," Neihardt left the most significant portion of the man's life story unreported.[7] To my amazement, I learned that Black Elk had preached Christian doctrine to his people for the greater part of his life and that he had been formally invested with the office of catechist.

Readers of *The Sacred Pipe* initially are made aware of Black Elk's familiarity with Christianity but are not told its full implications. The simplicity of his testimony is easily glossed over when juxtaposed with the wealth of Lakota religious tradition he proceeds to relate. The holy man is quoted in Brown's 1971 preface as saying: "We have been told by the white man, or at least by those who are Christian, that God sent to men his son, who would restore order and peace upon the earth; and we have been told that Jesus the Christ was crucified, but that he shall come again at the Last Judgment, the end of this world or cycle. *This I understand and know it is true*" (xix, italics added). This creed seems to have been read in terms of Black Elk's being only superficially acquainted with Christian doctrine. As I later learned, much more was involved.

When Ben Black Elk died in February 1973, and as I sang with the Lakota choir at his burial, I felt a great loss. Now that Ben was gone, I thought, a direct family link with the Oglala holy man could no longer be made. The child of so venerable a parent as Nick Black Elk might have shed some light on the questions raised by the old Sioux patriarch. I had barely known Ben, and now he was dead. The book seemed closed on Nick Black Elk's life, and further illumination seemed left pretty much to anyone's speculation.[8]

Such were my feelings when just three months after Ben's funeral, I happened to meet an *unci* (grandmother) who was seated on a bench in front of the Holy Rosary Mission.[9] I asked her if she perhaps had attended school at the mission years earlier, when only one building served as the entire educational complex. The question prompted her to take a long look at the grounds and seemed to take her back many years to another time and another style of life. Her wrinkled face bespoke a glimmer of nostalgia as she replied: "When I was just a little girl, I came to school here, and so did my brother Ben. Since he passed away, this school dedicated its yearbook to his memory." This is how I met Lucy, Black Elk's only surviving child.

We spoke awhile, and I asked if I might visit her someday. I explained that I was a teacher at the Red Cloud Indian High School and was attempting to relate her father's story to the students. I felt that she might be able to help me understand more deeply just who her father was.

Lucy said she would be happy to explain as much as she could about her father and that I could visit her whenever I wished. We shook hands and parted until two weeks later, when the spring rains had ceased and country roads permitted passage.

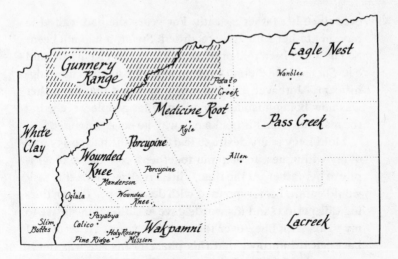

Map. 2. Pine Ridge Reservation, with districts and villages.

Lucy's home was an old log house roughly four miles north of Manderson, South Dakota, a small town on the Pine Ridge Reservation (see map 2). When I arrived for our first meeting, Lucy suggested we sit under a shelter of pine boughs that her husband, Leo, had constructed. There we could speak uninterrupted by the smaller grandchildren who were playing around the house.[10]

As I interviewed her, I based my questions on material drawn from *Black Elk Speaks* and *The Sacred Pipe*. Lucy brought me up short by saying she had never read either book and that she knew very little about her father's life as a young man. The more I referred to the books, the more I realized Lucy had other things on her mind. I was beginning to think she did not really wish to have me visit or to ask questions about anything. Finally, sensing our encounter would soon be over, I asked if there was anything she felt should be known about her father that was not already known to people.

It was then I learned of a dream Lucy had carried with her

ever since her father's death. For years she had waited to have her father's life fully recorded. So far, it had not been. So far, it had been told only partially by John Neihardt, and *The Sacred Pipe* did not capture what she felt was most significant. Moreover, Lucy was disappointed that her father was now being misunderstood and that people were using the material from his books in a way he never intended.

I told Lucy of my desire to learn what she had to say and of my willingness to help put together a conclusive biography of her father. At the time, I little realized what this task would entail. I corresponded with Joseph Epes Brown during this period, and his words gave additional incentive to my visits with Lucy over the next few years. He wrote: "I have felt it improper that this phase of his life was never presented either by Neihardt or indeed by myself. I suppose somehow it was thought this Christian participation compromised his 'Indianness,' but I do not see it this way and think it time that the record was set straight."

Brown suggested that the record be set straight, and it was clearly Lucy's intention throughout the course of my relationship with her to do just that. She had long desired to undertake such a project and, from that time on, looked forward to my visits. In her declining years, Lucy knew that not much time remained for her to fulfill the vision of relating her father's life story.

After several years of interviews, visits, and correspondence, I read to Lucy my translating, transcribing, compiling, editing, interpreting, and polishing—a methodological luxury her father (and other Native consultants, I am sure) did not enjoy. She was quite satisfied with our collaborative effort, and I was pleased to have mediated the preparation of a written text that had included many disparate, and sometimes disconnected, means of inquiry (i.e., taping sessions, planned and unplanned visits, solicited and unsolicited letters, family gatherings, and chance meetings).

Other consultants upon whom this work depends knew

Black Elk personally. Most of his intimates were either long dead, however, or seriously infirm, so necessity required my attending to a senior generation that was fast slipping away. It was within their camp that the substance of Black Elk's life and thought was best preserved.

Her brother Ben was now gone, and Lucy's health was not good. The Neihardt-Brown portrait of her father was, these long years after his death, being invoked by people (both extended-family members and outsiders) who did not really know him. In turn, these people were espousing social actions, religious sentiments, and practices she knew her father would not so readily affirm.[11] Hence, I was eager to learn more about Black Elk's life and thought, and Lucy was long ready to pass on what previously had been left unreported.[12] In addition to being a biography of Black Elk from the viewpoint of his daughter and friends, this inquiry will illuminate corners of the Lakota world that have heretofore been shadowy or indeed misrepresented.

Stated more directly, the tendency has been to compartmentalize Black Elk's life and thought into an era untainted by non-Indian social or religious currents. Such a tack is, quite simply, easier to pursue, since it avoids having to analyze disparate influences that reside beyond the Lakota world. The fact remains, however, that the holy man lived well beyond the Wounded Knee tragedy, and he did so with much vitality. Black Elk's life goes beyond the neat construct of total nativism on the one hand, or complete absorption of Western ways on the other. His biography is not a profile in syncretism but is, rather, an example of reflexive adjustment to new cultural landscapes that previously had not been explored.

The conventional assumption regarding Lakota history is that chameleonlike, a pastel world changed to moribund gray in the years after Wounded Knee. A "people's dream" had died, and their once-vital lifeblood clotted with each passing year. Poverty and depression hung heavily upon the now-hunched shoulders of a proud "warrior society," and the already-fading pulse of a people in despair lessened more and more. A grim and spectral reality was this Indian culture, and it very much clashed with an America whose global supremacy was beginning to emerge.

Before and after the massacre of Wounded Knee in 1890, many Lakota indeed suffered a malaise of spirit over several decades that certainly took its toll on their morale. And yet, the holy man lived—animatedly, serenely, lovingly, spiritually—through all of it. The contention of this work is not to disprove the anomic realities that have characterized so much of the reservation period but rather to explain how persons like Black Elk were able to face such odds and come to terms with them. The following pages seek to understand how a stereotypical Plains medicine man of the nineteenth century could experience so many perturbations of life-style, meaningfully integrate new patterns of activity, and live out his days more or less happily.

Here is the story of a now-famous medicine man whose life was altered in a dramatic encounter at the deathbed of a dying child. A ritual specialist from one religious tradition confronted an "intrusive other," and life was never again quite the same. Depending upon one's point of view, such was Black Elk's fated destiny, fortuitous chance, bad luck, or providential call. Whatever perspective one adopts on this chapter of the man's life, it needs to be understood that what seems a radically abrupt break with tradition is, at its core, an unfolding of reality that the holy man was predisposed to cope with, comprehend, assimilate, and address with considerable satisfaction. Plains culture itself was the source of this preadaptation.

Rapid settlement of the West eliminated many of the identifiable features of prereservation life. These features truly had a substance of their own, and their loss can only be imagined by we who are removed from those times and places. Nonetheless, by examining Black Elk's life, we can appreciate Lakota experience from perspectives that heretofore have been overlooked. And so, this biography does not just offer some telling facts about one man's life. It provides new glimpses of how, in fact, an entire group carried on against challenges that are today still menacing.

Many years have elapsed since the writing of this biography was first undertaken. Apart from the Pine Ridge residents quoted in this book, there are numerous others who in some way helped see it through to completion. I acknowledge their special, unsung contribution, and my heart shakes hands with theirs. Moreover, I am especially grateful to Raymond J. DeMallie of Indiana University, whose scholarship set standards to emulate and whose assistance produced better revisions. Similarly, Charles Cleland, Robert McKinley, John McKinney, and Charles Morrison of Michigan State University and Daniel J. Gelo of the University of Texas at San Antonio provided helpful suggestions and clarifications. Gilbert Cymbalist and Randy Lukasiewicz contributed important supplementary material, as did Mark G. Thiel of Marquette University's Archives, and the late F. W. Thomsen of Dana College. Jesuit Fathers Raymond Bucko, Bernard Fagan, Michael Flecky, Paul Manhart, Paul Prucha, Ronald Seminara, John Staudenmaier, Paul Steinmetz, Glen Welshons, and Theodore Zuern offered helpful perspectives on the history of the Lakota. Finally, gratitude is extended to John Drayton from the University of Oklahoma Press, whose role as editor was eclipsed only by his role as friend.

MICHAEL F. STELTENKAMP

Bay Mills Reservation, Michigan

▼

chapter one

▼

Lakota Culture

In order to understand Black Elk's later life, it is necessary to understand the cultural system within which he was born and the social organization with which he was familiar. Before achieving notoriety as an individual, the holy man was an anonymous participant in Native American Plains life, as that life was conventionally defined by his particular group. These initial pages flesh out the identity of a people whose very name has elicited controversy and confusion. By addressing this issue of name, and then the people's social configuration and history, this chapter serves as a kind of ethnographic primer for readers who are unfamiliar with Black Elk's cultural context.

Residents of the Pine Ridge Reservation variously refer to themselves as Sioux, Siouxs, Indian, and Lakota. Other, maybe somewhat faddish phrases such as "natural peoples," "Native American," "original people," and so forth are usually employed by nonresidents. Different persons simply use different terms. However, "Lakota," "Sioux," and "Indian" are the names most commonly used.

Books on the subject have noted that "Sioux" was actually the shortened form of an Ottawa word "Nadowessiwag" (spelled different ways within the literature), which meant "little serpents" (Baraga 1973:264). The Iroquois apparently loomed as a larger threat to Ottawa existence and so were called "Nadowe," or "big serpents." This people's regard for the Iroquois did not linger, linguistically at least, as did the well-known, surviving expletive "Sioux"— the name that adhered, over time, to Black Elk's people.[1]

Whatever its origin, "Sioux" eventually became the colloquial English word used when Lakota referred to themselves. Only in recent times have the "Sioux" begun to eschew associations with this foreign name bequeathed by their Woodland neighbors and reinforced by popular usage. Researchers have followed their lead and now employ the term "Lakota" when referring to these people.

In ages past, they referred to themselves as *oyate ikce ankantu* (literally "people native superior"), and diverse groups that composed the nation "considered one another kin" *(taku kiciyapi),* while regarding others as "inferior" *(ihukuya)* (Walker 1982:3). At first glance, such designations seem to imply a heightened degree of ethnocentrism. Monographs that take this linguistic approach, however, have neglected to show that something more is operative within the terminology.

The fuller meaning of *oyate ikce ankantu* relates also to one of the origin stories, according to which the people emerged from a lower world, with their appearance on earth implying an ascendance on top of, or above, the "inferior" realms below (*ankantu* also means "above"). This mythical underpinning of Lakota identity has been probably overlooked because of the recurrent displays of ego, or bravado, that so often characterized their behavior (Hassrick 1964:32). The earliest visitors to Lakota territory, and those who followed, never failed to mention the Sioux as being exceedingly proud (Catlin 1844; Chittendon and Richardson 1905;

DeVoto 1953; Parkman 1950). More important, perceiving themselves as "above" people was a reminder to all (variously internalized) of their cosmic identity—of whence they came and what destiny was assured, at the behest of the Sacred. It is this mind-set, or worldview, that will be seen as pivotal in the life of Black Elk. It allowed him and others to maintain a transcendent perspective on life.

Regarded as snakes or enemies by their opponents, as Sioux or Sous by Europeans, and as kin by themselves, this geographically widespread group defined its membership, generically, as being allies or friends. Herein lies another aspect of nomenclature that needs attention. Namely, three principal divisions existed among this people that, taken together, constituted the group as a whole. They did, however, maintain their own unique identities, while a loosely felt alliance existed between the divisions.

Although anthropologists have for years lumped the people under the label "Dakota," this word technically applies only to the most eastern group. Hence, those closer to their Woodland origin were Dakota, while slightly further west were the Nakota. Finally, the largest and more well-known division was the High Plains Lakota, Black Elk's people. The group to which one belonged could be detected (among other ways) by listening for the respective *l, n,* or *d* sounds in speech (e.g., *kola, kona, koda* = "friend").[2] Furthermore, the divisions *(otonwepi)* comprised subgroups (indicated below), which came to be known as the seven council fires *(oceti sakowin)*, although the historical reality of this latter designation is subject to debate (Little Thunder n.d.).[3]

The Seven "Council Fires"

Dakota	*Nakota*	*Lakota*
Wahpekute	Ihanktonwan	Teton
Mdewakantonwan	Ihanktonwanna	
Wahpetonwan		
Sistonwan		

Just as the nation was thus divided into seven groups, so were the Lakota-Tetons. Like the nation, these Teton groups (called *ospaye*) were each assigned a specific place within the camp circle *(ho-coka)*.

In terms of felt identity, a given individual experienced belonging at the most immediate level. This identity did not negate, however, a more expansive self-definition. A person such as Black Elk, for example, might order his sense of belonging in at least five successively larger circles (Walker 1917:97–98):

1. *ti-ognaka*   household
2. *wico-tipi*   camp
3. *ti-ospaye*   band
4. *ospaye*   division
5. *otonwe*   blood-related tribal division

Today, these Plains folk are understood to be a geographically widespread, linguistically differentiated, nomadic and semisedentary people whose organizing principle was the camp circle. The group as a whole was conceived thus, as were the Teton of the west. Moreover, within this division was Black Elk's subgroup, the Oglala, who also comprised seven segments. The eastern divisions, with whom the Lakota had sporadic contact, were similarly arranged. Hence, daily life was carried on within a local camp, and the social configuration of this grouping eventually expanded outward to include all of the *oyate ikce ankantu*.

As central as the notion of camp circle was to Lakota life, its composition has been difficult for observers to pin down. "The encampments are not always defined in descriptions of Dakota [sic] social organization because they were not permanent the year round and were constantly shifting in band membership. . . . The encampments are also confused in historical literature with the smaller bands and sometimes with the larger subtribes" (MacGregor 1946:

52–53). Since this observation was made, however, the social universe of Black Elk has been studied in greater detail (due in large part to the interest generated by Black Elk himself).

Semisedentary villages were not uncommon to the eastern Dakota (earthlodges were maintained in some instances), but their presence among the Teton was unknown (Eggan 1966:45–77). Lakota camps did not remain in one spot year-round and did not always keep a fixed membership. Fluidity of composition was due to both internecine struggles and climate. In warmer weather, groups tended to come together; in winter, the large groups disbanded into smaller parties. This pattern of aggregation and dispersal reflected, appropriately enough, the exact seasonal behavior of the buffalo, the people's primary subsistence resource.

The buffalo was indeed significant, as the following extended listing of the uses of its various parts in Lakota culture clearly demonstrates.[4]

Beard: ornamentation.

Bladder: pouches, medicine bags

Blood: soup, pudding, paint

Bones: fleshing tools, pipes, knives, arrow points, shovels, splints, sleds, war clubs, scrapers, quirts, awls, paintbrushes, game dice, tableware, toys, jewelry

Brain: food, hide preparation

Buckskin: cradles, moccasins, winter robes, bedding, shirts, belts, vessels, leggins, dresses, bags, quivers, tepee covers, tepee liners, bridles, backrests, sweatlodge covers, dolls, mittens, tapestries

Chips: fuel, diaper powder

Fat: tallow, soap, hair grease, cosmetic aids

Gall: yellow paints

Hair: ropes, hairpieces, halters, bracelets, medicine balls, moccasin lining, doll stuffing, pillows, pad fillers, headdresses

Hind leg skin: preshaped moccasins

Hoofs, feet, dewclaws: glue, rattles, spoons

Horns: arrow points, fire carriers, spoons, headdresses, cups and ladles, toys, powder horns, signals, medications

Liver: tanning agents

Meat: immediate use, sausages, caches, jerky (dehydrated), pemmican (processed)

Muscles: glue preparation, bows, thread, arrow ties, cinches

Paunch liner: meat wrappings, buckets, collapsible cups, basins, canteens

Rawhide: containers, shields, buckets, moccasin soles, drums, splints, mortars, ropes, sheaths, saddles, blankets, stirrups, bull boats, masks, lariats, straps, caps, snowshoes

Scrotum: rattles and containers

Skull: Sun Dance, medicine prayers

Stomach liner and contents: medicines, paints, water containers, cooking

Tail, teeth, tongue: whips, switches, brushes, ornaments, combs, choice meat

Tendons: sewing thread, bowstrings

Because of the nature of Teton camps, which alternated between fission and fusion, early observers found it difficult to understand their structure fully. Diligent research, though, has provided a fairly good understanding of how camps functioned, knowledge of which has benefited both the academic community and heritage-minded Lakota. Black Elk's generation derived their identity from, and themselves defined, the lifeblood of camp tradition, which eventually led to the contemporary reservation settlement pattern.[5]

In terms of leadership, the popular notion that Indian leaders were "chiefs" and their followers "braves" represents colloquial convenience at the expense of a more sophisticated grasp of Lakota terminology. It is true that, in recent times, the English word "chief" has often been used by Tetons themselves when referring to leadership roles, but this contemporary usage is not entirely consonant with the tradition. Black Elk himself was accorded this title, posthumously, by "some people in Rapid City," who provided his grave with a special headstone that read "Chief Black Elk."[6] Yet, the prereservation period was not so gratuitous in the bestowal of such honors. The public forum required more formal structuring.

Lakota lifeways were perhaps attributable, in large measure, to earlier events within prehistory that link the people with the equally famous Iroquois. This "league" of tribes seemed intent upon subduing their neighbors (Morgan 1962), the belligerence fanned by a felt, religious imperative, namely, that of bringing all people into one fold (the league's) as prescribed by the prophet Deganawidah (Hunt 1967; Wallace 1969). However, Iroquois militancy might have been motivated more by mercantilism than it was by a mercenary, spiritual fervor. That is, the league found itself caught within the French and English confrontation in North America, which forced woodland groups to cast their lot with whoever offered the most profitable incentives. At stake for France and England were fertile lands and a lucrative fur trade. At stake for the Iroquois was survival.

This struggle affected Black Elk's ancestors, a people whose shrouded origins seem to have been in the woodlands east of the Missouri River (Lehmer 1977:25–43).[7] Whether Iroquois aggression was due to religion, revelry, disposition, dispossession, economics, self-preservation, or a combination of all these, their sorties against the Chippewa and other groups of the Great Lakes region prompted population movements westward. What eventually became known as High Plains tribes were the descendants of folk who were probably socialized in an entirely different terrain.

Since all of this history entailed many actors in a production that took over two centuries to unfold, and since none of this drama bore the scrutiny of eyewitnesses who could in turn recount every deed found wanting or proven worthy, reasonable conjecture must ultimately be relied upon when proposing how people and events came to be the way they are (Oliver 1962). Hence, the Lakota are seen as one of many groups who converged within the Plains ecosystem, having been pushed from ancestral lands encroached upon by well-armed whites and adversarial Indians (Newcomb 1950). The aftershock of this displacement was somewhat mitigated by finding a bountiful region that provided new opportunities, but the beacons that guided adaptation were more the vagaries of experience than the wisdom of tradition. The historic period brought constantly shifting circumstances, which forced each generation "to create their own patterns of behavior" (Barrett 1984:96). Black Elk was not spared this experience. It was to serve him especially well in later, more harrowing years.

Demographic convulsions of the frontier era created for Plains groups a kind of utilitarian behavioral mode whereby expedience vied equally with convention. As a result, people like the Lakota cannot be regarded as persons inextricably bound to age-old lifeways that, if displaced, guaranteed cultural collapse. Challenges were indeed massive, but the people were accustomed to a longstanding struggle to survive.

Aided in their migration by the growing ubiquity of horses and guns, these people fanned onto the Plains like the buffalo upon which they subsisted. In fact, their adaptation was so complete that Clark Wissler concluded Plains culture to be "timeless"—extending back into the primordial past. In the case of the Oglalas, however, horses were acquired around 1750, and the Missouri crossed in about 1775. The Kiowa and Crow were extirpated from the Black Hills, which thenceforward became the sacred possession of the Lakota (Powers 1975:28).

The heart of social life that beat within the more out-wardly observable cultural traits was everyone's sense of relatedness to others and, ultimately, to the universe as a whole. Ethnographies have often addressed this organic facet of social intercourse when using such terms as "de-scent," "marriage," "kinship terminology," and "geneal-ogies," but much can still be learned, as DeMallie has in-dicated: "A study of Lakota kin terms that strictly used the genealogical method . . . [or] that strictly used Mor-gan's method of interviewing . . . would simply miss the complexity of Lakota life" (1979:235). DeMallie further implies that this complexity is at the heart of the Lakota worldview itself. As a result, even though "adequate expla-nations of kinship, marriage, and descent" are lacking, it is necessary to search for how the Lakota reckoned, con-trolled, and constructed their relatedness to one another and their environment as a whole (Powers 1975:36). Only after making this effort can the social sentiments inter-nalized by people such as Black Elk be fully appreciated.

Concerning marriage, one was advised to "go to the top of a hill and look for a wife on the other side." This wisdom was bolstered by the aphorism, "Do not choose a wife from the corner of your household" (Powers 1975:35). Members of the camp *(wico-tipi)* and band *(tiyospaye)* regarded one another as kin *(otakuye)*. Hence, dutiful youth sought eli-gible mates outside their own band so as to avoid incest *(wogluze)*. Moreover, emerging youth would be told stories that reinforced the social pattern by illustrating how mar-riage regulated by hormones led to one's demise. As Lévi-Strauss noted, oral narratives confirmed "the pre-eminence of the social over the natural, the collective over the indi-vidual, [and] organization over the arbitrary" (1969:45).

Elopements occurred from time to time, and individual preferences in choosing a mate were acknowledged. How-ever, a young man ordinarily courted both the girl and her family. Ultimately, then, Lakota marriage was an exogamous union that cemented an alliance between two *tiyo-spayes*.[8]

When Black Elk was growing up, the conventional court-ship consisted of males vying for the privilege of standing under a blanket with the desired, closely chaperoned maiden. (Virtuous women were prized, and so attracted more suit-ors.) Charms would be worn, flutes played, and gifts ex-changed in a scenario that allowed the girl and her family to decide who the best choice would be. Eventually, the maiden's brothers negotiated a price for their sister that, once agreed upon, was ratified by a feast. The price in-volved goods such as horses and robes, and perhaps in-cluded taking up initial residence with the bride's family. The feast was called *winyan he cinakakupi,* or "he wanted that girl, so they gave her to him"—an understatement if there ever was one, given the social and economic dimen-sions of this very ritualized courting process (Hassrick 1964:114–18).

Marriages produced genealogies, but the fictive compo-nent of Lakota social relations was just as important, per-haps even more so. When DeMallie observed that "Lakota kinship cannot be understood [solely] . . . in terms of the traditional categories of descent and marriage," he was, in fact, calling attention to the variegated ways this people "familialized" their universe (1979:222). One could be "made a relative" through a ceremony known as *hunkapi,* a rite that conferred family status upon the initiate, who was subsequently treated as being a father, brother, sister, and so on. (Brown 1953:101–15; Walker 1982:5–6). Sim-ilarly, relationship terminology was applied to offices within social groups and to those for whom one had "feeling" or those whose behavior merited it. Terms were also be-stowed on nature (earth, sun, moon, etc.), and the Great Spirit (Wakan Tanka) was itself addressed as Grandfather (Tunkashila).

Like other peoples, the Lakota considered it dreadful to

be without relatives, even though the possibility of such a nightmare was quite remote. In some form or another, familial connectedness was an operative feature wherever one looked. Whether as a visionary ideal, perceived reality, or calming assurance, the phrase *mitak oyassin* (usually translated "all my relations" or "all are relatives") was employed throughout life in the course of ritual gatherings. Year-round and lifelong religious ceremonies were a kind of perpetual goading of everyone to actualize relatedness (Sandoz 1961).[9]

Dovetailing with the above were associations one made en route to gaining status and prestige within local and larger communities. This was accomplished by gaining membership in what the literature refers to as sodalities, warrior societies, or simply societies. The Lakota word for these groups was *okolakiciyapi,* and a good number of them remained vital throughout the historic period (Wissler 1912). A variety of shaman organizations also existed (i.e., different rituals with practitioners for each), along with women's guilds or groups, (whose focus was generally religious or handicraft specialization).

These sodalities were not strictly age-graded, and a person could belong to several of them at the same time. At about the age of seven, one was invited to join a group, with full membership coming later. Officers were elected and served for specific periods of time. Meanwhile, camaraderie was the trademark of these organizations, and sentiments were fostered that blossomed into terminological designations like "brother," "cousin," "uncle," and so forth.[10] Such persons were role models who, as war and pestilence whittled away the population, became few in number as time passed. It will later be shown that the early missionaries capitalized on this social construct and established comparable organizations that today are still in place (see chapter 4).

Despite Wissler's argument that Plains culture was timeless, other observers noted contrarily that adaptation might well have been the key characteristic of peoples who forged a new life out of earlier, prairie patterns (Mooney 1907:361; Kardiner 1945:47). As mentioned before, part of this overall strategy was an egalitarianism that, among the Lakota, certainly prevailed. Authority roles could in fact be more titular than real. Parkman observed long ago that, should the chief "fail in gaining their favor, they will desert him at any moment; for the usages of his people have provided no sanctions by which he may enforce his authority" (1950: 115–16). Whether in noncoercive leadership, rugged individualism, or social groupings that nurtured a militant esprit de corps, Plains living for the Lakota fostered social mechanisms and elicited behavior that seemed best suited for survival in an ever-difficult environment.

Leadership had to be innovative under these conditions, and standards from the past were not always suitable. In all probability, they were found wanting at times. Militancy, if only for purposes of protection, was a sine qua non of every group who competed for survival in this new locale, and this context needs to be underscored, since the popular opinion exists that these peoples were inherently bellicose. Their *new* relationship to a *new* environment required *new* ways to make relatives out of aliens. Hence, there was an expansive quality within Lakota kinship that was itself a mode of adaptation that historic documentation has fixed but that was in fact still forming or evolving for this non-static Plains culture.

Much of the preceding has focused on the more apparent traits of Lakota social organization. Although such an overview is necessary for fully understanding how daily life was orchestrated for the culture's participants, it is equally necessary to keep in mind the religious sentiments that were ritualized and nourished on a daily basis within the Lakota universe. For the sake of brevity, it need only be mentioned that throughout the historical period virtually every observer of, or participant in, Lakota life cited the people's reflexive reliance on what Western scholarship would classify as "religious observance."[11]

Whether their adversaries were human or animal, their opponents alive or inanimate, the Lakota struggle for a safe niche was sustained by a resilience that made them spirited foes. This resilience enabled groups to negotiate the successful exodus west, permitted individuals to sacrifice themselves for the common good, and was an intangible armament within their arsenal of subsistence. It had unbounded limits and was rooted in the belief that all Lakota had access to, and could acquire, supernatural power and purpose. Before, during, and after the vision quest, seeking this power and purpose remained of paramount importance in one's life. For many, if not most, it seemed the only constant within the changing internal and external environments that accompanied people into the reservation period.

The Lakota thought their continued survival was as contingent upon a relationship with the Sacred as it was upon the forces they faced in everyday profane life. This essential feature of the Lakota worldview becomes transparent only after a careful scrutiny of persons such as Black Elk, whose generation strove to pass on this legacy. The unqualified assumption exists that religion was one of the major cultural "traits" among a myriad that were extracted from the Lakota world in the contact situation. The contention here is that, on the contrary, religion was part and parcel of adaptation for many. Black Elk's life will spell out how such a religious identity was the underlying attribute that remained fixed for an otherwise nomadic people of the Plains.

▼
chapter two
▼

Genealogy

The nineteenth-century Lakota world sketched by Neihardt was foreign to Lucy's experience of family life, and thus she alluded to it only fragmentarily. This pattern surfaces throughout her account, and its first appearance is in the text that follows. In it, we are lifted into the last century and are matter-of-factly introduced to Black Elk's family as it existed when Plains culture was at its zenith. Ironically, those were years of warfare, which, in varying degrees, was a leitmotif of Plains existence from the beginning.

As her father had done with Neihardt, so does Lucy refer to Black Elk's father. Dying in 1889, he was placed on a scaffold, which was a customary burial procedure. Included within her family's genealogy was Crazy Horse (Tasunke Witko). Among many Indian people today, he is regarded as a heroic figure, whose name represents resistance to white oppression (although his representation on a U.S. thirteen-cent stamp issued on January 15, 1982, was for the less provocative purpose of acknowledging Native leadership). Killed at Fort Robinson, Nebraska, in 1877, his body was secretly disposed of by family members, and many persons have searched for his remains since that time, hopeful of recovering some tangible keepsake of the free spirit that so defied captivity (Sandoz 1942).

In Lucy's narrative, other members of the Black Elk family are likewise given attention. Neihardt may have judged them extraneous to the movement of his story, but such persons would not be so excluded by Lakota narrators. One's personal identity, for good or for bad, was largely fashioned by the individuals who composed the familial community *(tiyospaye)*. Its distinct members fostered one another's values, attitudes, and existential perspective. Such is why Lucy acknowledged the different people who were part of life's daily routine within her father's world, and the world of her own home life (Medicine 1969).[1] Here Lucy recounts her family background:

My father had five sisters and one brother, but I knew just two of my aunts. My grandfather was wounded in the leg at the battle of the one hundred slain soldiers and was crippled, so my father was the man of the house.[2] He was the one who had to get out and hunt.

My father's brother died a long time ago, and I never knew him. When I was old enough to understand, I'd see my father praying and crying on a hill. He used to do that. My grandma told me, "He's crying for his brother." His name was Wicegna Inyanka or Runs in the Center. Somebody named him that when he went on the warpath.

My one aunt, Jenny Shot Close, died when I was maybe three or four years old. She was sickly and had tuberculosis, but she was really nice. She used to comb my hair. My other aunt was Grace Pretty Bird, and she is buried beside my grandma. She was a nice, quiet woman who had two children—a boy and a girl. I remember playing with my cousin, and she used to treat me mean. She'd hold me by the arm and swing me till I got dizzy. Then my grandma would really get mad. My cousins both died of tuberculosis while they were young.

I don't know where my grandfather is buried because they always used to travel a lot in the old days, and he died back then. So they made a scaffold for him somewhere.

My father always said that Crazy Horse was his second cousin, and he's dead too. My father's mother was named Mary Leggins Down, and she died in 1915. I don't know why Neihardt called her White Cow Sees. I never heard that name before. It wasn't my grandma.

During his life, my father married two times. The first marriage was a common-law marriage to a woman named Katie War Bonnet, who died in 1901. She had three boys: William, who died in infancy around the year 1895; John, who died of tuberculosis at the age of 12 in 1909; and Ben, who passed away in February of 1973.

My father's second marriage was to my mother, whose name at birth was Between Lodge but was later changed to Anna Brings White. She was a widow who was left with two children from her first marriage (to a man named Waterman). These children were Agatha and Mary, and my father adopted Mary when he married my mother in 1905. Agatha was too old to be adopted. But my sisters both died of tuberculosis in 1910.

From the marriage of my father and mother, three children were born. I was the oldest, and only girl—born in Manderson, South Dakota, June 6, 1907. My brother Henry died in 1910 while still an infant. But my brother Nicholas grew up and married, but he had the accident—that tragic accident. He burned to death in 1959 while sleeping in a small shack over in Nebraska.

I guess that since my brother Ben is now gone, it's up to me to relate a little history because I'm the only one now surviving of Black Elk's children—the same Black Elk people have read about in the books Black Elk Speaks and The Sacred Pipe.

Both in *Black Elk Speaks* and *The Sixth Grandfather*, "White Cow Sees" is given as Black Elk's mother's name, without explanation. DeMallie, however, has showed that there existed alternative renderings for people's names.[3] Lucy's reference to Leggins Down was said as offhandedly as one might say "Jones" or "Smith." Baptismal records note that Mary Leggins Down was born in 1844.

Given the nonverbatim mode in which Black Elk's words were recorded (DeMallie 1984b:32), it is possible that Neihardt chose a name that simply sounded exotic or mysterious (at least more exotic and mysterious than "Leggins Down"). Or perhaps Ben Black Elk, who replaced Emil Afraid of Hawk as translator, substituted this name instead of his grandmother's real one. Maybe it was simply an older name that Lucy had never heard spoken. Whatever the case, Lucy was not pleased that her brother had served in the capacity of translator, as she felt he took liberties with what her father intended to say.

Why *Black Elk Speaks* took the form it did is an interesting study in itself. According to DeMallie,

*Black Elk told Neihardt very little about his later life . . . as a missionary. . . . Neihardt was curious about why Black Elk had put aside his old religion. According to Hilda, Black Elk merely replied, "My children had to live in this world."
. . . For Neihardt, the beauty of Black Elk's vision made the formalism of Christian religion seem all the more stultifying, and he seems to have accepted Black Elk's pragmatic explanation at face value. (1984b:47)*

Contrary to the above is Brown's opinion that revealing Black Elk's Christian participation was somehow seen as compromising the holy man's Indianness. That is, Neihardt avoided the issue and simply focused on the premodern era, highlighting "the end of the trail" and "vanishing American" themes. Similarly, "Black Elk's pragmatic explanation," taken at face value, may well have prompted Neihardt not to probe any further. However, hindsight now shows that Black Elk's full life story would ultimately be more intriguing. In taking the pulse of the holy man's true sentiments, the pages to come will show that "the formalism of Christian religion" was not an issue.

After all, Lakota religion (like others) also had much formalism, and varying preferences in the matter of religion (as in leisure, sports, etc.) may account for why some people embrace one form and some another. That is, what is life-giving for one may simply be stultifying for another.[4] Later it will be shown that "the beauty of Black Elk's vision" (subjective as such a description might be) lies beyond the stenographic notes of Neihardt's daughter, or the poet's depiction of it in the chapter of a now-famous book. These and related issues that bore upon Black Elk's life will become more transparent through the recollections of those who knew him best.

In the comments that follow, Lucy refers to an "addition" her father gave Neihardt. Since no such document exists within the poet's papers, her reference has remained elusive. Whatever the addition was, it appears to conflict with the pragmatic resignation implied by his statement that "my children had to live in this world."[5] She said:

My father related to John Neihardt an addition to his book, but they never put it out. Afterward, he realized this and wanted the last part of his life also told—his life as a Christian man praying. My father wanted it known that after he quit his medicine practice, he became a catechist. But this man [Lucy pointed to a picture of John Neihardt] really believed in the Indian religion. . . .

I shall try with all my ability to relate this untold history of my father, and I have felt guilty at times not doing this as a memorial for him. When my brother Ben was alive, we always wondered if we should do something like this. We got this idea after my father's death, and I have waited for an opportunity to relate the entire story of his life as a holy man.

My name is Lucy Looks Twice now, but I was Lucy Black Elk before I was married. And I am the only living child of Nick Black Elk. Many people have already read about my father's life as a medicine man in Black Elk Speaks *and* The Sacred Pipe. *So, I'd like to tell about the rest of his life— the many years not talked about in either book. The greater part of his life was spent as a Catholic catechist whom I knew as a meek and loving father. This is the story I know about and want to relate. This needs to be done while I am alive. My father would have wanted me to do this.*

DeMallie's efforts in *The Sixth Grandfather* certainly illumined much of Black Elk's life that previously had not been told. Besides providing a verbatim account of the Neihardt documents, the work also addressed issues that came to bear on Black Elk during his catechist years and as a result of his involvement with the poet laureate. Consequently, what follows is a kind of necessary reprise from the holy man's family and friends, who witnessed, and participated in, the events and concerns that composed this special person's life. The chapters here thus constitute an important companion volume that completes, as it were, a trilogy of portraits.

This is the final reckoning of a man who, because of his literary legacy, will remain forever the clearest voice from an Indian America that predated the modern era. Perhaps because his boyhood memories recaptured a time that seems less complex than succeeding periods, perhaps because the world he described was ecologically more pristine than what was to follow, and perhaps because his words encouraged us "to emphasize the best that dwells within us," Black Elk retains a privileged place within the constellation of luminaries whose light has been transcultural (Deloria 1979:xiv).

His decades-long appeal, however, has been based on relatively scant biographical detail. As a result, his image may be so firmly entrenched that this portrait might at first seem disappointing to those who imagined him to be someone other than he was. Nonetheless, Lucy and friends of Black Elk desired very much that this fuller story be told and that his sacred vision be fleshed out in its totality. Far from intending to be iconoclastic, these intimates of the holy man sought to provide a better understanding of Black Elk himself and of the times within which he lived. In their opinion, his image would become even more appreciated than it already was.

Encounters with Lucy and other contributors often included words or references that, for non-Lakota, need definition or clarification. Whereas chapter 1 addressed some of the terms defining Lakota culture as a whole, these pages consider certain terms that figure prominently in discussions about Lakota religion. Contemporary medicine's emphasis on holistic health might well have taken its cue from this Plains people (Vogel 1970).

Just as the word "doctor" is collectively applied to such divergent roles as dentist and heart surgeon, so too is the term "medicine man" (from the French le médecin, "doctor") when colloquially referring to specialists found within Lakota society. Today, however, "practitioner" or "medicine person" now appears in the literature, since there also were—and are—women healers. In reality, a particular person's gifted power would be sought for addressing specific ailments or needs.

Among the Oglala today, the "medicine man" (pejuta wicasa) is also commonly regarded as a "holy man" (wicasa wakan), although the two roles traditionally have been separate (Brown 1953:45n; Walker 1917:152; Walker 1980:91–92). That is, the former referred to healers who used herbs or applied certain skills for curing. The latter term implied one's acquisition of mystical power, which was either put to work on behalf of a patient or was the reason why such a person could preside at certain ceremonial occasions. Time and practice have obscured precise usage of the terms by Lakota speakers and others. Yet, in spite of this change, Lucy's narrative rightly characterizes her father as a *pejuta wicasa* before his work as a catechist. (The same phrase applied to osteopathic and allopathic physicians of the non-Lakota world.)[6] Current parlance would accord her father the title of *wicasa wakan* once he became a catechist, a phrase likewise designating the priests with whom he worked.

Having dreamed of lightning, the Lakota were obliged to undertake the *heyoka* (clown) practice, lest they be struck down by lightning. The term itself refers to the "Dakota god . . . represented as a little old man with a cocked hat on his head, a bow and arrows in his hands and a quiver on his back. In winter he goes naked, and in the summer he wraps his buffalo robe around himself" (Buechel 1970:174). As the definition suggests, behavior of the *heyoka* was profoundly nonconformist, and humor depended upon one's ability to act contrary to all norms (Thomas Lewis 1970:7–17; 1981:100–104; Starkloff 1974:74).

At first glance, *heyoka* participation within the Lakota religious system might seem to be a peculiar mixture of secular and sacred conceptions. Such a commingling, however, has been (and still is) present within the larger, so-called world religions. Its obvious manifestation is the ubiquitous Trickster figure (Radin 1956). According to Hyers (1969:7), the rationale for so curious a phenomenon is that:

The comic spirit is fundamentally a certain attitude toward and perspective upon life. The essential element in relation to the sacred is the periodic suspension of seriousness and sacrality . . . and the realization of the playful, gamelike quality inherent in all human enterprises, however holy.

Comedy in fact plays with both the categories of reason

and irrationality, of order and chaos, of meaning and mean-
inglessness at the heart of reality itself.

In specifically addressing the *heyoka* cult within Lakota
religious tradition, Black Elk lends support to the Hyers
contention. "You have noticed that the truth comes into this
world with two faces. One is sad with suffering, and the
other laughs; but it is the same face, laughing and weeping.
When people are already in despair, maybe the laughing
face is better for them; and when they feel too good and are
too sure of being safe, maybe the weeping face is better for
them to see" (*BES*, 159–60). The *heyoka* provides the har-
monizing element to a human existence charged with emotional and psychological extremes and so keeps in check
one's tendency to distort reality. A kind of native therapist,
the *heyoka* helped people keep things in perspective (Brown
1979:58).

Whether coincidental or the result of instruction, Black
Elk's reflections on laughing and weeping curiously parallel those of Ignatius Loyola, founder of the Jesuit order (to
which Black Elk's priest-friends belonged). Referred to as
states of "consolation" or "desolation," periods of calm
and chaos were addressed at length by the sixteenth-cen-
tury mystic (Puhl 1963:141–50). Jesuits since the time of
Ignatius have been schooled in this spirituality, and they in
turn frequently teach it to others. Hence, the traditional
Jesuit understanding of this duality either fashioned Black
Elk's thinking on the subject or simply dovetailed compati-
bly with an older, Lakota approach (or perhaps both).

The following commentaries include references to the
heyoka practice and to that of *yuwipi*, the traditional ceremony associated with Black Elk in his precatechist days.
Yuwipi refers literally to "transparent stones" used in ceremonies conducted by modern-day Lakota shamans, although the word has also been rendered "to wrap around"
(Buechel 1970:656; Powers 1982:6). Its precise etymology

is unclear today. Whatever its origin, the ceremony itself, which is performed in total darkness, consists of a specialist, bound firmly within a "star quilt," who calls upon diverse spirits, which often appear as glimmering flashes. Throughout the meeting area, animal sounds and human voices are heard, having been summoned by the practitioner. Future happenings might be foretold, missing persons located, or diagnosis and cure of a given person's illness might be offered. On rare occasion, however, nonbenevolent purposes, or *hmunga* (to cause sickness), might also be the thrust of particular *yuwipi* gatherings. At the conclusion of the ceremony, the adept is seen freed of fetters, with the release being attributed to the action of spirit helpers.

Many Oglalas today regard the *yuwipi* man as representative of the old-time religion, vestiges of which are present in the ceremony. Oral history and research, however, point to non-Lakota origins of this "shamanic cult institution" (Bogoras 1904:164; Densmore 1970:44; Powers 1982; Wallace 1966). Nonetheless, "Yuwipi and Yuwipi-like rituals continue a tradition whose roots lie in the nebulous past" (Powers 1982:8). Practitioners today might be called by the umbrella term "medicine man," or by the more precise "Yuwipi."

Lucy's understanding of her father's early involvement with these older traditions is as follows:

Before being converted into the church, and before he became a catechist, my father was a medicine man. I wasn't born at that time, and he didn't talk about it very much. I remember he told us that he and his partner, Kills Enemy, were heyokas, or clowns. This clowning was actually done by him and his friend as a trial stage for them. To live the life of a heyoka for one year was a promise they had to fulfill. If they succeed in one year, then I believe they could become medicine men.

John Neihardt called Kills Enemy "One Side" in that book, but he really wasn't called that until he was an old man. He got that name because he used to wear a hat all the time, and it always sat crooked on his head. Before that, he was always Kills Enemy to us.[7]

He didn't talk about his medicine practice very much. However, he did say "I was kind of good at it." I almost believed him sometimes. Once I asked him, "Father, do you believe in this yuwipi?" And he said "No! That's all nonsense—just like the magicians you have in the white people. It's just like that. Praying with the pipe is more of a main thing. If a man prays with the pipe, why, people would kind of pray along with him. But this other one, yuwipi, it's just like a magician trying to fool. I know because I've done it myself."

One of my father's medicines could be found by standing out on a hill in the darkest night. He used it for curing tuberculosis. When there's no moon, you can see it. That medicine just glows. The yuwipi man uses this same medicine in his ceremony.

Once he was fooling around with his friend I mentioned earlier, Kills Enemy, and they were going to shoot an owl that was above their camp. That owl was just bothering them during the night, so they got a fire going and started loading up. They filled cartridges themselves at that time.

Just then, they were so close that a man said, "You guys! Don't get close to that fire. It's going to explode for sure!" Just then, when he said that, one of the sparks hit the powder, and everything shot up in his face. So that's where he almost lost his sight, and he's been partially blind ever since.

I got that information from Joe Kills Enemy. He was old enough to hear when his father and my father visited and talked about what they did in their early lives. He's way older than I.

I always thought he got his blindness while he was a heyoka with Kills Enemy. What I thought was that my father suggested they put a loaded shell in the ground, smash it, and see how far it goes down in the ground. Instead, it exploded up in his face.[8] He did a lot of things like that.

In his early years, my father had been a warrior. He was in the Custer fight, and he was in this massacre [Lucy pointed down the road toward Wounded Knee]. My father said that when all those soldiers got killed at Little Big Horn, he and a bunch of boys his age would go around and pick pockets of the dead. He said some of them found money, but they didn't know what it was.

About Wounded Knee he always said, "I was there to witness after it was over. I saw all those women and children and old people. The soldiers shot at them with their guns, and they all just laid there in the big draw. Something awful! They had no weapons—and those children massacred like that." My father carried wounded persons—women and children—over the hill to safety. They claim he said, "Today is a good day to die!" But he never actually said that. It was Crazy Horse who hollered those words. My father was young then, so he wasn't the one.

Black Elk's comment on the *yuwipi* practice is not shared by all Lakota people. As in any profession, motivation for one's involvement differed among individuals.[9] Contemporary practitioners have a sincere following, however, and their regard for the tradition is high. Persons such as Lucy might locate the *yuwipi* practitioner's special medicine and use it for other purposes, but it is still regarded as the substance out of which "spirits" take their form.

Black Elk's actual blinding is another biographical point that might never be fully ascertained. Aside from the two accounts mentioned above, another exists that tells of Black Elk's divining for water. Having placed gunpowder beneath a hole filled with water, Black Elk announced he would make water issue forth from the ground. Touching a spark to the fuse, he remained too close to the eruption, and his face was peppered with water, dirt, and gunpowder. This version was volunteered by a Manderson resident who questioned the reliability of the other accounts.

Regarding the war cry "today is a good day to die," most presume the now-popular statement refers to patriotic sentiment. That is, warriors should always be willing to die while proudly defending their families and home territory. Indeed, such was probably at the heart of the phrase when skirmishing the cavalry. An unsolicited interpretation offered by an Ottawa woman, however, carried a different meaning. "We Indians have an expression 'today is a good day to die.' It means that we should be ready to die on any given day. We should always be prepared to die, and have no regrets. That's why it's important to begin each day fresh, and not let past problems or present distractions cloud how God wants us to live." (Note that the speaker restricted this expression to "we Indians.")

Her comment is illuminating in that it shows how Black Elk material has been used by other native groups to the extent that even a war cry would be a source of reflection.[10] Whereas militants utter the phrase almost threateningly, the Ottawa woman gave a more religious interpretation. Who knows how the cult-film hero "Billy Jack" intended the phrase to be understood? At one point, the lead character solemnly announced that "today is as good as any to die!"—the Black Elk material once again authoritatively quoted, albeit erroneously, to sanction what Hollywood purveyed as authentic Indian ideology.

With the preceding traditions emerging from the material on her father's life, Lucy suggested that a visit be arranged with an old friend of Black Elk's who was still living. Mr. John Lone Goose could recall those earlier times and could provide additional commentary that was reliable.

▼

chapter three

▼

Conversion

The journey from Pine Ridge to Rushville is a little over twenty miles, and the drive is a scenic one through rolling Nebraska hills that undulate with dark, green, conifer splashes. Along the winding highway, mule deer frequently fall prey to startled automobiles. Billboards, restaurants, and residential areas suddenly appear, and within the new vista lies Parkview Nursing Home—a small facility appended to the town hospital.

John Lone Goose had been paralyzed from the waist down (the result of a car accident seven years earlier) and, because of his great size, needed the attention that only an institution such as a nursing home could provide. Apart from the paralysis, his health was excellent. He accepted his condition with serenity and said that prayer enabled him to carry on without being bitter.[1]

John's immediate family was all deceased, and more distant relatives seldom visited. Residents of the home were predominantly non-Indian, and his beloved reservation was far away. A wise elder who spoke softly and with openness,

John commanded a reverence or admiration that was easy to bestow. It was apparent that he was quite prepared to pass on.

During the course of an obligatory cigarette (a modern ritual of friendship probably rooted in the older tradition of sharing a pipe), John recounted the following indignity he suffered when placed first in a Hay Springs, Nebraska, nursing home: "I had braids that long [pointing to his waist]. They cut them. I don't know why they do it. Want me to cut my hair—that's why they do it. But I never asked what they did with my hair. The long braids! Those long braids. It wasn't quite like mine now. They were all black—coal black. But I don't know what they did with it." John's former appearance did not come as a surprise because Lucy had already spoken of him, and because one of the Jesuits referred to him in an unpublished manuscript from the 1930s as "the Giant Indian with long hair!" (Sialm n.d.:86).

Whereas braid-wearing today is common and generally reflects the trend in cultural resurgence, John was from a time when braids were still part of the living tradition. He was literally the last of a kind who could speak from the summit of many years. His was an authoritative perspective because of a long-standing familiarity with persons, places, and events.

After a short while, he came around to talking about times past, and his opening remarks include reference to the Rosebud Reservation—a large territory allocated to the Brule division of Lakota (Hyde 1961; Grobsmith 1981). Smaller in size than Pine Ridge (its western neighbor), Rosebud was the site of activity that closely paralleled Oglala history (Hyde 1937). In fact, relatives of any given family might be spread throughout the two reservations. Jesuits, government personnel, and Lakota regularly commuted between the two regions (and still do).

Spotted Tail, a famous Brule leader, requested Jesuit presence on the Rosebud, and in 1886 the order established

the St. Francis Mission. Since that time, it has served as a
school and religious center much like Pine Ridge's Holy
Rosary Mission, which was founded in 1888 at the request
of Red Cloud (Olson 1965).[2] One of the Rosebud's early,
well-known personalities was Father Digmann, who baptized John. Born in 1846 in Eichsfeld, Germany, Digmann
came to the United States as a priest in 1880. At the in-
sightful request of his superiors, Father Digmann organized diary notes into a readable commentary on his life as
a missionary among the Lakota from 1886 until 1930 (he
died in 1931). Available to researchers through Marquette
University's Archives of Catholic Indian Missions, this unpublished document contains sketches of early reservation
life that are incredibly graphic.[3] Future research on Lakota
experience of the decades around the turn of the century
should hereafter take into account this priest's unique contribution, now that it is accessible.

John provided a page never entered in Digmann's diary.
Perhaps it was not worth including from the Jesuit's perspective, as it was just part of an ordinary routine. For John,
however, the event meant everything. His parents told him
about it, but John spoke of the incident as if he were a
credible witness of the proceedings.

*On April 17, 1888, my father and mother went to Sunday
Mass in the morning at St. Francis Mission. I was in my
mother's womb at the time. While the Father was saying
Mass, and while they were sitting there waiting to get their
Holy Communion, my mother fell sick and said: "I'm going
to go out for a little while. I'm going to be right back." So
she went outside the church, spread her shawl, and sat
down. Right there—outside the Catholic chapel at St. Francis—I was born.*

*Since my mother didn't come back into the church, my
father came out to see where she was. He found me and my
mother laying there, so he went to tell the Mother Superior*

about it. Pretty soon, all the Sisters came out and took me up in the Sister's room, washed me, cut my cord, and dressed me up. They washed my mother too. At about eleven o'clock I was baptized by Father Digmann. I was the youngest one in the family—and there were fourteen of us. Now, I'm the last one still living. All my aunts and uncles, all my brothers and sisters, they all died. I'm the only Lone Goose left. There are no more by that name.

Here was Lone Goose, the one-time infant, christened "John" by Father Digmann.[4] Here was the long-haired helper of Black Elk whose great size occasioned laughter-provoking memories, such as when he and Black Elk were burying a fellow Catholic. Ever so involved with the cemetery ritual, big John Lone Goose, moving backward, lost his footing and preceded the casket into its grave. His body wedged tightly in the ground, John required the assistance of many mourners to gain release. Tears were turned temporarily to laughter through the slapsticklike misfortune of their kind-hearted brother.

Here now was the aged John Lone Goose, a gentle man who did not share the fame of his celebrated colleague and who did not have much earthly existence remaining. He provided the following recollection:

I first met Nick around 1900—when I was a young boy and he was not a Catholic. I don't know what they call him in English, but in Indian they call him yuwipi man. Sam Kills Brave, he's a Catholic, lived close to him. And before Nick converted, Kills Brave would say, "Why don't you give up your yuwipi and join the Catholic church? You may think it's best, but the way I look at it, it isn't right for you to do the yuwipi." Kills Brave kept talking to him that way, and I guess Nick got those words in his mind. He said that after Kills Brave spoke to him, he wanted to change.

Corroborating John's testimony, Lucy fleshed out the incident that changed her father's life. A key figure in this episode (and for some years after) was the Jesuit priest Joseph Lindebner. Born in 1845 at Mainz, Germany, he came to Pine Ridge in 1887 and worked there until his death on October 4, 1922.[5] The priest's small stature inspired Black Elk and others to call him affectionately Ate Ptecela, or "short father," (a phrase Lucy used interchangeably with the more formal Father Lindebner). Sina Sapa, or "Black-robe," was the traditional Lakota reference to Catholic priests, who most of the time wore black soutanes, or cas-socks. Episcopalian clergy were called white gowns, and Presbyterians were known as short coats.

When Lucy narrated the following pivotal experience of her father's life, family members listened intently:

Sam Kills Brave, Louis Shields, and my father organized this Manderson community. Like we say, there is the White Horse community, White Bear community, Crazy Horse community, and others.[6] These men organized so they could help each other farm and carry on other business. Kills Brave was the main one, the leader or chief. That's the way it was in olden times. Kills Brave was already a Catholic, and he used to tell my father to make up his mind about his religious practice.

That's when in 1904 my father was called to doctor a little boy in Payabya—seven miles north of Holy Rosary Mission. The boy's family wanted my father to doctor their son because they heard he was pretty good at it. So, my father walked over there carrying his medicine and every-thing he needed for the ceremony. At that time, they walked those long trails if they didn't have a horse.

When he got there, he found the sick boy lying in a tent. So right away, he prepared to doctor him. My father took his shirt off, put tobacco offerings in the sacred place, and started pounding on his drum. He called on the spirits to heal the boy in a very strong action. Dogs were there, and they were barking. My father was really singing away, beating his drum, and using his rattle when along came one of the Blackrobes—Father Lindebner, Ate Ptecela. At that time, the priests usually traveled by team and buggy throughout the reservation. That's what Ate Ptecela was driving.

So he went into the tent and saw what my father was doing. Father Lindebner had already baptized the boy and had come to give him the last rites. Anyway, he took whatever my father had prepared on the ground and threw it all into the stove. He took the drum and rattle and threw them outside the tent. Then he took my father by the neck and said, "Satan, get out!" My father had been in the hundred-and-one show and knew a little English, so he walked out.[7] Ate Ptecela then administered the boy communion and the last rites. He also cleaned up the tent and prayed with the boy.

After he was through, he came out and saw my father sitting there looking downhearted and lonely—as though he lost all his powers. Next thing Father Lindebner said was, "Come on and get in the buggy with me." My father was willing to go along, so he got in and the two of them went back to Holy Rosary Mission.

Ate Ptecela told the Jesuit brothers to clean him up, give him some clothes—underwear, shirt, suit, tie, shoes—and a hat to wear. After that had been done, they fed him and gave him a bed to sleep in. My father never talked about that incident, but he felt it was Our Lord that appointed or selected him to do the work of the Blackrobes. He wasn't bitter at all.

He stayed at Holy Rosary two weeks preparing for baptism, and at the end of those two weeks he wanted to be baptized.[8] He gladly accepted the faith on December 6, 1904, which was the feast day of Saint Nicholas. So they called him Nicholas Black Elk. After he became a convert and started working for the missionaries, he put all his medicine practice away. He never took it up again.[9]

My father said that what he was doing before he met Ate Ptecela was the work of the Great Spirit, but that he suffered alot doing it. As a matter of fact, he had ulcers and had to be treated for them shortly after he started his missionary work. The Jesuits sent him to a hospital in Omaha, and he was on a diet for two or three months until the ulcers cleared up. When he converted, knowing about Christ was very important to him, and receiving communion was what he really held sacred.

People who used to be treated by him when he was a medicine man started coming to him. They asked him about the new religion he belonged to, and he explained to them what it meant. Many followed his example, and he instructed them in the new faith.

The scene sketched by Lucy was discomforting, as it seemed consistent with the oftentimes trite depiction of ill-mannered missionary versus innocent native. Taken at its face value, Black Elk's story ratified books, movies, and popular opinion that so often portray missionaries as close-minded zealots bent on destroying Native culture (Terrel 1979), and as having little of what today would be called compassion, cultural sensitivity, or ecumenism. Far from being something positive, Black Elk's experience seemed more of a deathblow to his true spirit.[10]

Lucy insisted, however, that her father did not resist Lindebner's intrusion upon the ceremony and was not angry or enraged. He did not harbor resentment and did not give in to despair. She regarded his conversion story as rather amusing and understood the event to be a great occurrence in her father's life. Moreover, she had difficulty understanding why her *takoja* did not join with the others present, who laughed and smiled in hearing of the incident. Here was an amazing story and humorous tale being told (she thought), but he had remained expressionless while listening!

Apparently, the factors most important to Black Elk on

this occasion were these: (1) a holy man was present, (2) the holy man's powers were known to be very strong, (3) resistance to such power was unthinkable, (4) Black Elk regarded his power as negligible by comparison, and (5) he was predisposed to changing his religious practice. That the priest was of another culture, that he was a white man, and that he was seemingly so indiscreet, pushy, or insensitive were not important. What mattered was Wakan Tanka, whose action was apparent and could not be challenged. Such was, at least, the tentative interpretation for a story that captivated two distinct listening audiences for two widely differing reasons.

According to Lucy, her father had "suffered a lot" while practicing as a medicine man and had experienced quite a bit of inner turmoil. This experience, along with Kills Brave's entreaty and a persistent stomach disorder, reinforced Black Elk's desire to seek some kind of relief. He knew that something was not right in his life, and the symptoms were, minimally, social, physical, and psychological. After his visit to the hospital, during which time he received the Catholic sacrament of the sick, Black Elk undertook the work of a catechist, and his ulcers were never again bothersome. Lucy said that her father felt "the son of God had called him to lead a new life." The Christian Lord known as Wanikiye had "selected him" to do this work.

In the opinion of several Manderson residents who heard Lucy's account of the story, liberties were taken in telling what probably transpired. Although no one claimed to speak with certitude, it was commonly assumed that medicine men such as Black Elk would not allow themselves to be pushed around in that fashion. Similarly, the priest had a reputation for being very kind and gentle and could hardly have been the ruffian portrayed.[11] All agreed, however, that something out of the ordinary occurred in Black Elk's life, although the exact details were quite difficult to pin down.[12]

Digmann and Lindebner knew one another well, and their work on both reservations was similar in scope. Allowing for idiosyncratic differences, Digmann's experiences and reflections may have paralleled those of Ate Ptecela. He wrote the following about his first encounter with a Lakota medicine man:

A pagan Indian . . . called for a priest to baptize his dying child. I went with him on horseback to his camp, about three miles from the Mission. One of our school girls, already baptized, had dressed the one-year-old boy nicely and put a small crucifix on his breast. He was asleep. After we had said the Our Father, the Apostle's Creed, I baptized the child "Inigo." For a couple of days he had taken no nourishment, as the mother had no milk.

A boy went with me to the Mission to get milk and medicine. Mother Kostka, who was a good nurse and had knowledge of medicines, wished first to see and examine the sick child. We went on foot under the parching heat of the sun to the Indian camp, the white veil of the Sister was soaked with perspiration. A short distance before the log cottage, Grace Anayela met us saying: "The medicine man is conjuring the sick child, I do not want to be present." Arriving at the door, we heard their singing, beating the drum. . . . What a spectacle! In a corner of the room, the father was sitting with the naked child in his arms. Along the wall four conjurors were crouching, with their faces painted red and yellow. One of them had returned from an Eastern school, understood English fairly well and spoke it tolerably. Him I addressed first: "George, you here?" He had asked me already before to baptize him. Then I continued in Sioux the best I could at the time, "Give up your devil's work. The child is baptized and belongs to the Great Spirit." George said: "Do you want that one of us shall die?" "You will not die, get out of here." They, however, continued their pow-wow, singing and ringing pumpkin shells. On my repeated begging they finally kept quiet. Mother Kostka examined the little patient and wanted to make hot poultices.

The conjurors had spread out on the dirt floor of the loghouse their medicine bags. There were also bowls with water, and a pan with burning coals. To gain room, I removed . . . the deerskin bags, gave the water to the Sister, and put the coals in the stove to start a fire. Horrified they looked at me, thinking perhaps that the Evil One would hurt me. George flung the satchel of the Sister out of the open door. The scared mother took the sick baby outside, the Sister followed. George, angry, grasped my arm to put me out, but I stood the ground. In the presence of them I told the father of the child, not to allow them to continue their conjuration, and not to let their leader take the child to his house. They promised. The firmness seemed to make an impression. George became cool. He said he did not believe himself in this pow-wow but there was money in it. They make the parents pay in ponies, blankets, or other valuables, while at the Mission and at the Agency they would get medicine gratis. (MACIM:8–9)

A similar situation is reported for April 6, 1909, wherein Father Lindebner himself is mentioned. Digmann wrote:

Osmund Iron Tail called me out of Catechism class saying: "Jim Low Cedar would die today." He was going to the agency to get a coffin. James was a boy of ten years, had been at the Mission over two years, but owing to a slow fever was allowed to go home. We told his mother, who had been baptized not long ago: "Call the physician and give his medicines. If you know of any good Indian medicine, you may also give it, but do not allow any conjuration, sacred songs, etc. of the medicine man." Iron Tail told me that she had first done so, but seeing that the Whiteman's medicine did not improve him, she had called for an Indian Medicine Man. Now, Father Lindebner had visited the sick boy and

*administered to him Extreme Unction but could not give
him yet the Holy Viaticum. When then the medicine man
came making arrangements for his pow-wow, Little Jim
peremptorily refused it saying: "The Little Father [Lin-
debner] has anointed me; I don't want to be conjured, I
want to go to heaven." When Iron Tail reported this, I said
within myself: "Jim, you deserve also Holy Communion."
Arriving there, I found him fully conscious and glad to receive the Blessed Sacrament. After a short preparation and
prayers, he received his Lord for the first and last time with
visible devotion. Three hours later he took his flight, to see
Him in heaven.*

It is not surprising that Lindebner encountered Black
Elk under the circumstances he did. According to Digmann,
"The sickbed is the field, where the physician (medicine
man) and priest (missionary) often meet. We had a special
eye on the sick, not to let them go without baptism. Several
of these died soon after baptism, and the opinion was spread
by the medicine men that pouring on of water had killed
them"(8).

Such scenarios were commonplace, it seems, as the Lindebner obituary illustrates.

*On one occasion, he broke through the ice while crossing
Little White River, and one of his horses was drowned. Father Lindebner himself was almost frozen to death, yet the
same night he borrowed another horse and made his way to
a dying Indian. Only three or four years ago, when over
seventy years of age, he made a sick-call trip of four hundred and twenty miles in the face of a keen blizzard that
brought the thermometer well below zero . . . three years
ago, the writer was returning from a trip with the holy old
priest, when on nearing the mission we were informed of a
dying man some miles back on the road. We returned forth-
with to the Indian's cabin and found the patient lying on*

blankets and pillows on the ground outside his house. After Father Lindebner had done what he could for the poor fellow, the latter begged us to sing some Indian hymns for his consolation and encouragement . . . for an hour we sang all the hymns we knew and some, I fear, we didn't know. The result was more noisy than harmonious. But it seemed to please the sick man. (IS1923:84–86)[13]

Lucy was not familiar with the Digmann material. Rather, she simply reported the tale told by her father. Perhaps Lindebner was indeed too gentle a soul to match the conversion story's persona, and perhaps Black Elk would not have tolerated anyone's intrusion upon his religious ceremony. Perhaps the type of experience Digmann reported in his diary was well known, and maybe Black Elk's otherwise undramatic conversion story drew more listeners when garnished with details from somewhere else. Maybe the type of interaction Lucy reported frequently occurred, however, and simply did not elicit controversy at all (as it does for those removed from the times and places).

Black Elk's story might belong to a special genre, namely, an oral narrative telling a biographical truth via incidents that never actually happened quite as reported. Lucy, for example, could relate the story and, with her family, appreciate its import. Unfamiliar with this form of communication, a non-Lakota could listen to the story with disbelief or chagrin and consequently miss the point intended.

Lucy told of her father's conversion on several occasions, and she never failed to mention that "dogs were there, and they were barking." Her words appear to be straightforward in their description of events, but more seems to be at work than Black Elk (or Lucy after him) simply recounting a play-by-play account of what occurred. The inclusion of barking dogs is a significant embellishment that would lend additional force to the story among Lakota listeners. As William and Marla Powers have written:

*Dogs are considered useful for protecting the house from
the incursions of strangers, as well as for announcing the
presence of friends. Anyone living on the reservation soon
becomes accustomed to dogs barking all night long, and
the reason for their nocturnal howling is frequently discussed the next morning, because dogs herald not only the
presence of humans but that of ghosts as well. In Lakota
. . . the expression sungwapa, "dog barking," is a metaphor for any general commotion. (1986:7)*

By saying that dogs were barking, Black Elk (or Lucy) perhaps used a type of literary formula that established a frame
of reference for the conversion event. Spirits were present,
and they signaled that something important, extraordinary,
or mysterious was unfolding. The dramatic effect of this
narrative element would be lost on a non-Lakota audience.
It thus is probable that the tale falls within a traditional
genre, one that authenticates the experience itself.

Religion particularly might lend itself to this narrative
form, as Christianity has an analogous story within its Scripture. Judaism's Saul was en route to Damascus to perse-
cute Christians when all of a sudden he was knocked to the
ground and blinded (through, it is assumed, divine inter-
vention), leading him to change his name (to Paul) and religious practice (to Christianity). Christian fundamentalists
might interpret Paul's experience literally and assume that
he had in fact been knocked down and then blinded, physical events that ultimately led to his conversion. Other Christians, however, might look beyond the extraordinary details of the account and simply conclude that Paul was
somehow profoundly changed or converted on this occasion. Lucy even mentioned that her father's experience was
like Paul's.

Black Elk's own presentation of the drama of Payabya,
whether whole or partial in its statement of concrete fact,
unambiguously signaled for him the decisive call from

Wakan Tanka through a Wanikiye Blackrobe. Such was
the basic import of the holy man's experience, and his life
after this event constitutes the most solid testimony to such
an understanding. Such an understanding can embellish
or delete whatever it was that actually represented the life-
changing occurrence near a dying child in 1904.

Paul Steinmetz said of Black Elk's conversion story that
the experience resulted in an "integration of the two religious traditions on a deep emotional and even unconscious
level" (1980:158–59). DeMallie asserted otherwise. He noted
that Black Elk's conversion was "unquestionably genuine"
but that the acceptance of Catholicism placed him "beyond
the onerous obligations of his vision" (1984b:59,14). As
this study progresses, a more curious and complex series of
experiences will be shown to unfold within the holy man's
life that beg a more expansive interpretation than those
proposed thus far.

An initial building block of reinterpretation can be exca-
vated from the classic ethnography of religious experience
by psychologist William James (1961). His work was one of
the first to address conversion as a phenomenon to study
instead of an experience simply to take for granted or dis-
miss as psychological instability. His observations are
apropos of Black Elk's life: "To be converted, to be regen-
erated, to receive grace, to experience religion, to gain assurance, are so many phrases which denote the process,
gradual or sudden, by which a self hitherto divided, and
consciously wrong, inferior and unhappy becomes unified
and consciously right, superior and happy, in consequence
of its firmer hold upon religious realities" (James 1961:160).
As was the case with Black Elk, "religious aims form the
habitual centre" of one's energy after such an experience
(165). As a result, it is not surprising that questions surface
in regard to the facts of Black Elk's conversion story. According to James, "Neither an outside observer nor the
Subject who undergoes the process can explain fully how

particular experiences are able to change one's centre of energy so decisively" (165).

A more contemporary evaluation of this process can also help explain what was at work in Black Elk's life. Proudfoot has said that it is not the subject matter of religious experience that is as important as the explanation of it given by the individual (1985:231). Being ineffable, such experiences beg articulation through symbol or metaphor, through poem or story, or through whatever mode that one can utilize as a vehicle for expression. Black Elk's conversion narrative seems to have been a product of this very personal, and very profound, experience.

▼

chapter four

▼

Catechist

The overview of Lakota culture in chapter 1 indicated that men and women highly valued their participation and membership in warrior, curing, dancing, hunting, handicraft, and other special-interest groups. In the postreservation period, however, these sodalities began to disappear (Lowie 1948:294). As they did, Lakota Catholics were organized into two religious organizations known as the St. Joseph and the St. Mary societies, and these groups were received quite favorably. They assumed a prominence formerly reserved by the traditional associations.

Louis J. Goll, S.J., onetime director of the Jesuit community at Holy Rosary Mission, related this history of the *okolakiciyapi* (societies) of St. Mary and St. Joseph:

The Benedictine Fathers working among the Sioux . . . organized two societies, one for men, under the patronage of St. Joseph, the other for women, under the protection of the Mother of God, and called them the St. Joseph and St. Mary Societies.

The Jesuit Fathers introduced these societies in their mis-sions. Accordingly, the Catholic Brules and Oglalas would meet every Sunday, whether or not a priest had come to them for services. One man, elected and approved for that purpose, led in a kind of lay-service: hymns were sung, and specified prayers were recited. This finished, the presi-dent ("grandfather") gave a well-thought-out address on an article of the Creed, on the sacraments, or on the Com-mandments of God. This done, he would appoint two or four men as speakers on the same subject. Such was the meeting of the St. Joseph Society.

The St. Mary Society also had its program. The presi-dent ("grandmother") would address all present. She, too, would appoint two or four speakers, there being excellent speakers among these Indian women, able enough to drive home a lesson for men and women alike. Then the grand-mother would give a resumé and hand back the presidency to the grandfather. (1940: 36)

Throughout the year, meetings were held and were well attended. Besides gathering for prayer and song, members would discuss religious issues and plan parish activities. After the first fifty years, membership in the societies de-clined, and the core participants became the now-elderly children who had been born in the early reservation period. The ebb and flow of religious involvement in recent times, however, has made the fluctuation unpredictable. Other institutional expressions have also arisen—most nota-bly, in Catholic circles, the Tekakwitha Conference, a na-tional organization named after the Mohawk maiden whose piety was reported in *Jesuit Relations* (Kenton 1954:293–95).

The major annual event planned by the societies was the Catholic Sioux Congress. This three-day gathering of Cath-olic Sioux from all the reservations first started in 1891 at the Standing Rock Reservation, on the border of North and

South Dakota, and has occurred every year since then at
different locations selected by the membership.

Usually held around the Fourth of July, this religious
convention was instituted by the missionaries for several
reasons. In earlier times, many Lakota would gather yearly
and celebrate their unity against the backdrop of the Sun
Dance. Building on this older religious tradition, which
was outlawed in 1881, missionaries organized the summer
congress as an opportunity for new church members to see
and support one another in their faith (Goll 1940:39–43).
Moreover, it was felt that an event so specifically tailored to
Native interests would be a more suitable celebration for a
people to whom Independence Day had little or no meaning. Generally, the agent would distribute thirty head of
cattle to the tribe for purposes of celebrating the national
holiday. When congresses first started, the Catholic population requested that these cattle be given to the societies!

Before automobiles were in much use, caravans of wagons could be seen taking society members and their families to the assigned rendezvous, with each family carrying
its own camping equipment. Shortly after arriving, as many
tents as wagons dotted the hills of the congress site—Oglalas
from Pine Ridge in one section, Brules from Rosebud in
another, and so on.

Three days of praying, singing, receiving sacraments,
exhorting, and friendly visiting would ensue. Well over
three thousand Lakota participated in this event fifty years
ago, although attendance has steadily decreased. As recently as thirty years ago, nearly a thousand representatives were present, but this number dropped to a couple
hundred just a decade later. Even so, those who still attend
the event have an eager anticipation long months before it
occurs.[1]

Society members have lamented the dwindling number
of congress participants, and their concern has been evident since the 1940s. In that Lucy's generation represents

the mainstay of the societies, younger members stress the need to update the event's proceedings and focus more religious activities around Lakota youths. However, such reforms as the speaking of English rather than the traditional Lakota, or initiating a youth congress, have repeatedly been voted down.

Black Elk's involvement with this unique institution was considerable. Being a catechist, his duties included organizational details, preaching, and instructing new converts. This ever-active participation in society work and congresses molded Lucy's religious formation. Tenets cultivated by her father were absorbed during early childhood, as the following recollections show:

We'd go along with him to the congress and the Catholic general meetings, and all the catechists would show up. On all kinds of Catholic holidays—Easter, Decoration Day, Christmas, New Year's—the catechists would get together at their parish chapels and have services. And on these occasions I often heard my father instruct the people about Scripture.

He related Scripture passages to things around him, and he used examples from nature—making comparison of things in the Bible with flowers, animals, and even trees. And when he talked to us about things in creation, he brought up stories in the Bible. That's why he was a pretty strong Catholic—by reading the Bible.

On one occasion, my father and the old faithful catechist Fills the Pipe were attending a meeting and were camped side by side. Fills the Pipe had a crippled wife, who could hardly do anything. So one night, my father was coming back to his camp when he heard someone hollering.

A lady was hollering, so my father went down to see what happened. Anyway, this Fills the Pipe had been hauling water from the creek, and he fell just as he came up with the buckets full of water. Again, he slipped and fell.

The third time, his lady just couldn't take it, so she sat

*down and started hollering. That's when my father went
down to help this poor old man carry his water. That's the
way these catechists ran into hardships with their families.*

Building upon what the culture already had in place, the
societies established leadership roles and communal activities for the Catholic population. Their success also was
enhanced by a Catholic clergy who "held a somewhat more
tolerant attitude toward Indian ritual and custom" and
who, "being celibate, were more mobile" than their Protestant counterparts (Marty 1970:9–10). Furthermore, religious
nomenclature (i.e., Father, Sister, Brother) employed by the
Catholics also sounded a positive note for Native listeners,
whose social universe was glued together by kinship.[2]

Where Native deacons and priests today serve as clergy
among the people, catechists were the lifeblood for the
societies (and the Catholic population as a whole) in times
past. According to Duratschek (1947:206–7), these men
were:

*selected for their intelligence, good character, and zeal,
[and] were the agents who carried out whatever the missionaries proposed. They met periodically with the priest
who instructed them in what they were to teach those
natives whom the missionary would not reach the next
week or two. On the Sundays when Mass was not offered in
their districts, the catechists led the prayers and hymns of
the gathering, be it in a tepee, log house, or chapel. After
reading the Epistle and Gospel for the day, they instructed
the people. When necessity arose, it was the catechists who
baptized and who buried the dead. They visited the sick
and informed the priest when anyone was in danger of
death.*

More was involved with this type of religious commitment, as Lucy's memories of her father show a man who

took this responsibility so seriously that for many years it was a way of life the family as a whole accepted as their own. But Black Elk was not an exception, or was not alone, in pursuing this course within the new order of twentieth-century Plains life, as the recollections that follow indicate. Lucy recalled:

I don't know why they did this, but even the Episco-pals chose the medicine men—like my father's uncle over here. You'll probably hear about him later on. Black Fox they call him.³ He was a medicine man—a great one. And here he got converted to the Episcopal church, became a preacher, and even became a deacon before he died.

A good number of the early catechists were medicine men—like Paul and Joe Thin Elk. But they quit and turned back to the old ways. One of them told my father: "Brother, I am turning back to the old medicine." And my father answered: "That's up to you." As I said earlier, after my father was baptized, he promised to do away with his early practices. Since he was a catechist, he lived up to it. He never gave up his prayer or what he was taught.⁴

At the time, we had a three-room log house with one room for my grandma, who died in 1915. My father raised horses and pigs, while my mother had chickens and a milk cow.⁵ They plowed up the ground and grew potatoes, corn, beans, and other vegetables. My mother helped him with this, and we seemed to have enough food, because my father built a cellar in which they kept most of it. Although he drew only ten dollars a month for his missionary work, it seems we never went hungry.

Right after his conversion, he went back and was sup-posed to take care of the Manderson district. He gathered all his friends, called a meeting, and then asked his friends and relatives to help him build a place—a little house in which to have Mass when the father comes. Somebody do-nated a horse to them, a work horse, which they traded for

logs. They then built the first St. Agnes Church and meet-
inghouse. It wasn't too big, but at least they had something
ready for the priest. And so that's where my father started—
right from that little log house. He was the first catechist of
St. Agnes Chapel. They appointed leaders and had a big
Christmas party—giving presents to all the older people, the
real old ladies and real old men. They called them by
names and gave them presents individually.

After the Jesuits baptized several in each district, they
pretty soon began to get men like my father to be catechists.
In every station they appointed two or three catechists to
work with them. These laymen were trained to conduct ser-
vices, read Scripture on Sundays, baptize if necessary,
visit the sick, and bury the dead. But most of all, they were
trained to teach the Catholic faith.

There were catechists in all those little communities like
Grass Creek, Rocky Ford, White River, and Pine Creek. I
know Alec Two Two was the catechist in Wounded Knee,
which at that time was called Brennan, South Dakota.
William Cedar Face and Kills Enemy were the catechists in
Grass Creek, while Frank Gallego was down in Rocky
Ford. Silas Fills the Pipe took charge of the community out
there at Red Shirt Table, while Joe Horn Cloud took over at
Potato Creek. John Fool Head was at Slim Buttes. Many
others were also catechists at the time of my father, like Red
Willow, Jim Grass, Louis Mousseaux, Daniel Broken Leg,
Willie Red Hair—and Ivan Star Comes Out was at Our Lady
of Good Counsel on the other side of Oglala on the White
River. Men were catechists from all the different districts.
And when it came along that my father was called away to
other reservations for missionary work, Paul Catches took
his place.

Since my father was one of the first catechists, the Black-
robes might come for him at any time to go on a trip. So
right away he had to work—and he worked. They used to
come for him very often, and he was really willing to accept

any kind of trip they were supposed to make—even in the coldest weather. He would go with Father Lindebner or Westropp or Father Henry Alder, and people would come to them, attend Mass, and even have their young ones baptized. There would be converts, and he would teach them.

The Catholic church in Manderson today is still named St. Agnes. Unlike its cabin predecessor, it now is a larger, white, wooden structure looking like a typical country church. The meeting hall behind was dedicated to Black Elk's memory. However, the sign that commemorated this, which reported his tenure there as a catechist, was torn off the building not long after the 1973 occupation of Wounded Knee—according to popular suspicion, by members of the American Indian Movement (AIM).

Black Elk's friend Paul Catches was the father of Pete, who also became a catechist. Now a practicing medicine man (Zimmerly 1969:46), Pete is no longer formally involved with church work, even though his ties with Jesuits are still strong. The ceremony he conducts is not *yuwipi* (as some local people charge) but rather that of *wanbli* (eagle), performed largely for healing purposes.

Pete's ceremonies (or sings, *lowanpi*, as such occasions are also called) are easy to confuse with those of *yuwipi* (Feraca 1962). In the darkness of a small cabin, with participants sitting cross-legged on the floor, he orchestrates an entrancing, prayerful, sensory experience that includes singing sounds and faces touched with light brushes of eagle feathers and water droplets. He does not, however, get tied up (as reported for the *yuwipi* ceremony earlier). Persons present utter prayers of thanksgiving (or need) in a room so pitch-black that the atmosphere is one of disembodied voices. Pete has often been the guest of priests and other interested parties at meetings that address differences and similarities of Lakota and Christian religious tradition (Stolzman 1974, 1986).

Catechists at the Catholic Sioux Indian Congress, 1911, at Holy Rosary Mission. Black Elk is sixth from left, wearing moccasins.

Another highly respected reservation elder was Ben Marrowbone, a man whose ties with the past were far more intimate than those of most residents. He was from the generation of Lakota patriarchs whose parents were the last to experience nomadic Plains life. During his active years, Ben worked as a catechist, undertaking this labor when Black Elk was still an active missionary himself.

Lucy thought Ben perhaps could add to her own narrative, since he was known to be very devout in his religious practice and was considered a "true traditional" within the reservation community. He was one of the leaders pressing Lakota claims that the Black Hills be returned to the people. Mixing Lakota with English, he used hand gestures to lend power to what his words communicated. He was just as willing to discuss those days long past as he was of speaking to government officials about the Black Hills (maybe hoping both would be, somehow, returned before his death). According to Ben Marrowbone:

I drove the team, and we used to start from here [Holy Rosary Mission is across the road from Ben's cabin]. We'd go

Catechists attending the Catholic Sioux Indian Congress of
July 1920. Black Elk is in bottom row, far left.

to *Slim Buttes, Wanblee, Sand Hills, Eagle Nest, and every
district. It took three or four weeks sometimes. I was tired
when we came home.*

*There'd be no meetinghouse or no church, so we'd bring
bedrolls. Brother used to bake a big loaf of bread for us,
and we'd take a box of chicken, some potatoes, and sauerkraut too.*[6] *We went to every house in a district, and
we stopped before sundown. We would talk to each other.
"You want to stay there overnight?" "Sure!" You see, different people would want us to come in. Some people had a
bedstead, but sometimes the father and I would sleep on the
floor. We'd spread our bedrolls and sleep together.*

*One time we went to bed about eight o'clock. It was a
cool night, and we had a bedstead to sleep in. Father Lindebner nudged me as we fell asleep and said: "We aren't
alone. Little animals are sleeping with us." That bed was
filled with little bugs.*

*In the morning, strong coffee would already be cooked—
and we'd have to drink it. And grease bread, we'd eat it
too. Father then offered Mass at that house and people*

nearby would come. They'd explain their confession, their sins before God. Remember, everybody makes mistakes, so we tell Almighty, and he forgives them. The people understood this, and they truly believed it.

John Lone Goose adds:

That book, Black Elk Speaks, *just talks about the olden way. But I remember every detail of what he did because I was with him—not every day—but every time the father would come over, or when he would teach somebody who wanted to be a Catholic. I was there to help him.*

The priests gave him instructions in the faith, and Nick said he wanted to teach God's word to the people. So he kept on learning, learning, learning. Pretty soon, he learned what the Bible meant, and that it was good. He said: "I want to be a catechist the rest of my life. I want it that way from here on!"

So he went around as far as Norris, Kyle, Potato Creek, Porcupine, and all those districts. He'd go around preaching with Father Buechel, Father Lindebner, Father Perrig, Father Louis, Father Henry, and all those old priests. Lots of people turned to the Catholic church through Nick's work.

He never talked about the old ways. All he talked about was the Bible and Christ. I was with him most of the time, and I remember what he taught. He taught the name of Christ to Indians who didn't know it. The old people, the young people, the mixed blood, even the white man—everybody that comes to him, he teaches—from the Bible, from the catechist book, from his heart.

He was a pretty good speaker, and I think Our Lord gave him wisdom when he became a Christian. For even though he was kind of blind, his mind was not blind. And when he retired and was sick, he still taught God's word to the people. He turned Christian and took up catechist work. And he was still on it until he died.

Left to right: John Lone Goose, Father Sialm, and Ed White Crow at Manderson, 1928. (Courtesy of the Buechel Memorial Lakota Museum.)

Lucy contributed these memories:

Sometimes he'd be in bed and somebody would come saying there was a person dying who wanted to receive the sacraments. And so, even at night he'd go and pray for them. If they were already baptized and had been receiving the sacraments, he would call for the priest in the morning. Lots of times he would have to ride to Holy Rosary Mission [thirteen miles distant] on horseback in order to get a priest to come and administer the last rites to a sick person.

During the times he was home, he'd go on sick calls or have prayer services for other families. When someone needed to be baptized, he would call the priest. Or if there was a Mass, he would serve it. On Sundays, when the priest couldn't make it for Mass at a particular chapel, the catechists were trained to read Scriptures, put on a prayer service, and make a sermon. My father did these things and learned all the prayers by heart. And in lots of cases, when the priest was not there, he administered baptism.

The people really liked to sing with my father, and Mr. John Lone Goose would play the organ—by ear. Whenever they had Mass there, he was playing for them. They right away caught on to the singing, and they really liked to do Indian hymns.

Of course, my father never had any experience in this kind of work before he was baptized, but still—right away he understood what it meant. He had poor eyesight, but he learned to read Scripture and prayer books written in the Indian language.[7]

Pretty soon, I was so interested.

As a small girl, I was trained in praying those Lakota [i.e., Catholic] prayers and Lakota Indian hymns by my mother. She taught me how to read in Indian too. She really taught me a lot in praying and singing. I wanted to receive Holy Communion, so I really tried my best. Well, my father and mother thought I was old enough at the age of seven years.

Ever since I was six years old he trained me in prayers—Indian prayers—and Indian Catholic hymns. There's one song—the first song he ever taught me was this song here. I'll sing it right now.

Wakantanka lila waste
Slolyeic iya cin ce;
Oyas tanyan iyuskin po,
Niucantepi nicila.
Lakota oniyatepi,
Koyan ekta up ye;
Jesus niyuhapi kta ce
Heon oyas nicopi.

O God most good
Who wants to make himself known,
All rejoice rightly,

He asks of you your hearts.
You Lakota are a nation,
Quickly may they come together;
Jesus would have it so,
Because he has called you all.

My father liked it. I guess that's why I like it.

They told me that I was baptized the same day I was born. I was born a Catholic the same day I was born a Christian. And my father raised me a Christian-Catholic. That's the only thing I was taught by him.

I made my confirmation in Rapid City at the Immaculate Conception Cathedral. Of all my father's children, there was Ben, my younger brother Nick Jr., and myself—he had us really trained in the Catholic church. We had to do what he asked, and we had to attend Mass every Sunday.

Today I have a great devotion to the Sacred Heart, I myself. One time my younger brother Nick had a hemorrhage. He was bleeding from the nose. He was dying. I didn't know what to do, so I knelt down. My father and mother were broken up—saddened—so I knelt down with them. We prayed the rosary and the Sacred Heart prayer.

While he was laying there, my brother said: "I want some prayers said to St. Theresa." I don't know why he said that, so I said a prayer to the Little Flower of Jesus. Afterward, when he got well, he told me he saw that Little Flower—that Theresa. He said: "I know it was her."[8]

Not all of Lucy's recollections were as dramatic as the above. In fact, Black Elk had some humorous experiences that Lucy found quite memorable. When she related the episodes that follow, the family members present took great delight in hearing them. By contrast, the day-to-day routine of her father's life at Oglala (a community to which he was assigned as catechist) is more soberly stated in Father Buechel's diary. The entry for December 23, 1928, reads:

"Mass, sermon & 12 Holy Communions at Oglala. Drove home. On the way, Black Elk & I prayed for Mrs. Charles Eagle Louse who is sick" (MACIM). Other dates, containing scant information, show Black Elk sponsoring for baptisms and present at various religious gatherings.

Lucy continues her stories:

My father was appointed catechist at Oglala, so we moved there. My father would often have services and come home by himself real late at night. My mother would leave a lamp burning near the window so my father could find our house— as it was out in the country. Anyway, one night my father came walking home, but all he saw were tall trees and bushes. My mother had forgot to light the lamp, and my father was lost.

He started shouting "hey, hey," but my mother was sound asleep and didn't hear him. I woke up right away and poked my mother saying, "Mother, there's my father shouting outside." So she got up, opened the door, and saw my father about ten feet away from the house looking the other way. You see, his sight wasn't too good at the time, and he didn't know he was so close to home. That's why he was shouting for help.[9]

On another dark night my father came home riding our big white horse Baloney. Baloney was so well broken that you could just let the reins drop and he wouldn't move— he'd just stand there. When my father came home, he got off the horse and went to open the corral we had nearby. After he opened the gate, he turned around and was really scared. A white ghost with big black eyes was right behind him—looking at him. My father real quickly punched that ghost in the nose, and was he surprised to see Baloney run off! You see, he didn't realize that Baloney had followed him to the gate and had turned to face him. That horse didn't come back until the next day.

Father Henry Grotegeers used to ride a motorcycle when he went around to say Mass. My father was at Holy Rosary Mission one day, and Father Henry asked if he would help assist at the services in Oglala. So my father got on the back of the motorcycle, and the two of them started off. When they got to the church, Father Henry couldn't stop the motorcycle, so he headed for the racetrack that used to be there. They went around and around that track until Father Henry decided to head back to the mission. My father held on all the time wondering why they couldn't stop.

On the way back to the mission, Father Henry changed his mind and figured he would stop that motorcycle by driving it into a bank. So he crashed into a bank on the side of the road, and he and my father were thrown off. My father shouted at Father Henry, "You nearly killed me!" But when he told us the story afterward, we all laughed and laughed.

Another time, one of the missionaries came along to get my father for a trip. So my father said: "I'm going to get my clean clothes on." He was in such a hurry that he rushed to the suitcase and started dressing. They [Lucy's mother and father] must have both used the same one, for when he put on his underwear, he was wearing those things [Lucy points to the chest area]. It was my mother's underwear he put on!

He was mad. He went to my mother and said, "Woman, put your things in a separate place from here on!"

And another time, during Christmas, he was resting. For any big feast or holiday that came along we used to stay overnight in the addition to the meetinghouse. So everybody was getting ready for the Christmas party—putting up the tree and preparing for services. When they were ready for prayer to begin, they called my father.

Right away he went and got his coat and threw it over his shoulders. All the coats were hanging on nails. So there he was leading prayer in front of all the people on that cold night—wearing my mother's coat, which had real high shoulders.

When he finally sat down, one of the men near him said, "Cousin, you've got a nice coat on. Where'd you get it?" My father then went over to my mother and said, "You hang your coat someplace else!"

My father went with Father Westropp way over to the Cheyenne agency, and they had to cross the Cheyenne River. When they got there, it was flooded, so my father said, "Father, I don't think we'll be able to cross it." But Father Westropp said, "No, Nick, God is going to help us. He'll take care of us." So they went into the water.

Well, it was so high that the horses were swimming, and they were just barely hanging on to the buggy. All their belongings just floated away—their Bibles, prayer books, bedding, and even their food. On the other side were some people who came to rescue them.

These people took Father Westropp and my father to their camp, and everybody's clothes were just all soaking wet. They clothed them, fed them, and gave them a place to sleep. They even gave them hats—cowboy hats. So that's the kind of life they had in those days.

When he was older and retired from his church work, my father did that inipi, that sweatlodge, with some other men. Georgie was outside and in charge of opening the flap when they needed air. Well, we had a windmill nearby, and Georgie went and climbed it just when they wanted that flap opened. I heard them shouting for Georgie, but he couldn't get down. Since that sweatlodge was for men only, I didn't want to open the door, and I told them Georgie couldn't get down. I wasn't going to open that door. After I said that, my father shouted right away, "Daughter! Open that flap now or we'll burn up in here!" By that time, Georgie had climbed down and could open the door—so they *were really glad to finally get some relief. It was really hot inside.*

One time, he went and took his buggy and team to the store. As you know, he was a pretty talkative man—so while he was there, he forgot about his buggy and team. After he came out to go home with his groceries, his team and buggy were gone! They had left him and went home. After he got a ride, he found them back at our place.

Another time, he rode to the store and left his horse in the front. He then came home, but forgot that his horse was tied up on the rail.

Although Lucy regarded the above incidents as simply humorous happenings from many years ago, those related to wife and horses suggest another level of meaning at play. Several of the episodes show, in one form or another, an indirect reproof (*heyoka*-like) administered by Black Elk to two types of creature with whom he had to contend. Layers of interpretation aside, however, everyone who knew Black Elk recalled him as a man with a good sense of humor.

Even in the account of his participation at the massacre of Wounded Knee, Black Elk made a statement that reflects his *heyoka* upbringing. Finding soup in a deserted *tipi* north of Pine Ridge, he and his friend stopped and helped themselves to it. Soldiers were in hot pursuit of the two men, and bullets whistled in and about the *tipi*. After one bullet struck too close, Black Elk casually stated, "If that bullet had only killed me, then I could have died with *papa* [dried meat] in my mouth" (*BES*, 224–25). Neihardt (or Ben) may not have detected his statement as being intentionally humorous—an example of comic relief during a narrative of woe. Similarly, readers of the early Black Elk material might so solemnize his utterances as to miss this comic facet of his personality. It was preeminent, however, in the memory of those who knew him.

▼

chapter five

▼

Missionary

Black Elk was a catechist whose efforts were not restricted to the Pine Ridge Reservation. As the following recollections show, he was employed as, and enjoyed being, "a kind of a preacher" among groups other than his own. Lucy recalls:

The Jesuits also took my father to other different tribes—even though he couldn't understand their languages. He instructed Arapahos, Winnebagoes, Omahas, and others—teaching them the Catholic faith with the help of an interpreter. At that time, these tribes were going for peyote and had been influenced by their neighboring tribes. But he converted a lot of these people.[1]

Sometimes I would have to sing in front of the Catholic gatherings. I had always been with him—I and my mother, and also my younger brother—and he would say to me, "Never be ashamed to pray or sing, because if it's for God—praising him and praying to him—you'll be rewarded by his blessings in the future."

So I learned a lot through him—and understanding. If it wasn't for him, I don't know what I would have done. Through his teaching and training me, I stood strong in my faith. There's something about this Christian life never failing. If anything went wrong with my children, if he prayed, I knew everything would be alright. He had a way, since he said he loved little children.

Even though he ended up with a lot of sufferings and trials, he still went strong—even when two of his children died and he had two caskets in the church.[2] He stood by, still preaching because he was loved by everybody.

One thing he always hoped and prayed for in those days was that a Sioux boy would become a priest and a Sioux girl would become a nun. And I think he was rewarded because I've known a girl from our district who became a Sister. And from the reservation, there are several of them.

He sure was interested in that kind of life. Everything in the Scriptures he understood. He knew. Members of the St. Mary's Society always came to him for advice and asked him what church work they should do in the future.

One of the Jesuits with whom Black Elk had considerable interaction was Eugene Buechel. Born in Germany in 1874, Buechel first arrived among the Lakota in 1902 at St. Francis Mission. From that time until his death in 1954, he worked with the people of Rosebud and Pine Ridge as a missionary-priest-linguist and was held in very high esteem. In 1923 he published *Bible History,* and in 1939 *Grammar of Lakota.* Having taken extensive field notes during his many years on both reservations, Buechel's collection of Lakota words and definitions remains unmatched. Jesuit priests compiled his notes into a dictionary in 1970, which remains today the authoritative reference on the Lakota language.

His name is legend among older Lakota speakers, one of whom said: "We can't teach the young people how to

talk Indian. The only man who ever spoke it perfect was
Father Buechel, and he's dead." Another aged consultant
recalled speaking to Father Buechel and not knowing the
old words used by the priest. Buechel kept a diary during
his many years, which contains, aside from pastoral concerns for the area, a daily statement about the weather
(MACIM).[3]

On November 14, 1906, Father Buechel made the following entry in his diary: "Nick Black Elk had come to collect
money at an issue in Rosebud. As it came off later, he made
three days retreat. I gave [it] to him. He asked 'How is it
about eating during the retreat? The Indians do not eat during their recesses.'" The incident here reveals Black Elk's
attempt to understand his newer religious practice against
the backdrop of his older one. Fasting was common to both
traditions.

Lucy could not assign a date to an experience that her
father spoke about in later years, but it occurred at St. Francis Mission and might have taken place at the time of the
retreat mentioned above, or during other visits there, which
continued for years.

*My father was at St. Francis when they were going to have
a burial of a little baby in a casket. They brought the one
that died into church, so he went in and sat down to pray.
That casket was there in the church overnight, and they
were going to have it buried the next day.[4]*

*My father was in the church that night when a certain
Sister kept coming to the casket. Three times she came. Finally, she asked my father to tell the rest of the mourners
that she wanted the casket open so she could see the little
baby that was in there. I guess they let her.*

*They opened the casket, and they found the baby was
alive! And this Sister, my father told us, must have had a
special sense for that child. Anyway it was a girl in that
casket, and she grew up to be an older woman.*

Before his departure in 1916 as a missionary to India, Fr. Henry Westropp, S.J., authored a pamphlet entitled *In the Land of the Wigwam: Missionary Notes from the Pine Ridge Mission* (MACIM). In this very brief, fifteen-page account of his experiences among the Lakota, he refers to Black Elk's work as a catechist in much the same fashion as did Lucy. He wrote:

Many of the younger men who are capable are given duties as catechists, and many of them are and have been faithful companions for years, gladly abandoning wife and family for weeks at a time to help the missionary in his work. One of the most fervent of these is a quondam ghost dancer and chief of the medicine men. His name is Black Elk. Ever since his conversion he has been a fervent apostle, and he has gone around like a second St. Paul, trying to convert his tribesmen to Catholicity. He has made many converts. At any time of day or night he has proved himself ready to get up and go with the missionary. On any occasion he can arise and deliver a flood of oratory. Though half blind, he has by some hook or crook learned how to read, and he knows his religion thoroughly. On one occasion a preacher asked him if he thought it right to honor the Blessed Virgin. The following dialogue took place. Black Elk asked him:
    "Are the angels good people?"
    "Yes."
    "And St. Elizabeth, is she good?"
    "Yes."
    "And the Holy Ghost?"
    "Yes."
    "Well, then, if all these honored her, why should not I?"[5]

When she was a small child, Lucy accompanied her father to other reservations where he was assigned. One was the Wind River Agency of Wyoming, home of the Shoshone and Arapaho. Here he worked out of the St. Stephens Mission, which, like the other Jesuit institutions, served as an educational facility and religious center. Another sojourn was at the Marty Mission (Duratschek 1947:273–311), a similar operation directed by Benedictine priests some two hundred miles east of Pine Ridge. Not particularly apparent in this part of the account, but poignant in its telling, was Lucy's profound admiration for her father and his work.

Staying at Marty was less challenging than at other places, and the Yankton people with whom they lived were particularly receptive to Black Elk's visitation. Both Lucy and her father enjoyed their time among the Yankton and returned often to encourage the developing faith-community. Lucy continues:

When I was three years old, my sister Mary died. She and Agatha used to go to Holy Rosary, so when we went to St. Stephens in Wyoming, I used to go around and cry trying to find her. I thought she was among those Arapaho girls.

Finally, they thought I was going to be sick, so my father spoke to the superior and said he was going to bring his family back home. Just before that, my younger brother Henry died.

Later on, my father and James Grass went back to the Arapahos, but that tribe had been quarantined against what they called "sores"—which was the German measles. They stayed around until the quarantine was lifted and wanted to get in contact with the main leaders. But most of them were on peyote, especially the Shoshones, so my father and Grass gave up on them and got ready to leave.

Then a chief of the Arapahos came into where my father was staying, grabbed him by the chest, and made the sound of a bear. Then it looked as if he wrapped something up and threw it out. The chief then said, "You're not strong or brave enough to go through with us. We were thinking about your Christianity. We were having a meeting thinking about you." That man said he would bring his people for instruction.

So my father went to get a permit from the agent. During the quarantine, they couldn't have any gatherings, and the agent still didn't want to give them permission for dances. My father got the permit for the church gathering, but he had also told the people to bring their Indian costumes to Mass so that afterward they could have a feast and dance. He knew they liked the dancing. So some of them even wore their Indian costumes to church. That was the only way they could have their dances for a while. A lot of them joined the church and got baptized—even peyote people.

That's when they first started Christmas night dancing. Everyone would go to midnight Mass, then have a feast, and then dance. They'd break up real late. After my father retired, he and Jim Grass visited them. They found out that they continued that dance—only now it was for an entire week up until New Year's. I don't know if they still do that.

When I was small, maybe five or six years old, the missionaries appointed my father and three others to go east. The places I know he went were New York, Boston, Washington, D.C., Chicago, Lincoln, and Omaha. They were trying to lecture for the Oglala Sioux who were becoming Catholics and who were in need of chapels and other things. Somebody served as interpreter for them.

After this trip, he told us about his experiences. He said, "In some towns, we'd go down the street or to some special occasion and some white people would throw rotten eggs or tomatoes at us. That happened in some places, but in others a lot of people were real good to us." I think he meant the kids were bad to them. He even visited prisons, like Sing Sing in New York. He tried to talk to them and convert them.

At one place he said he was up there talking and saying to the audience: "You white people, you came to our country. You came to this country, which was ours in the first place. We were the only inhabitants. After we listened to you, we got settled down. But you're not doing what you're supposed to do—what our religion and our Bible tells us. I know this. Christ himself preached that we love our neighbors as ourself. Do unto others as you would have others do unto you." At that early time, he said those words. He told us that when he was finished speaking, everybody clapped.

He told me about the white people he had met when he was in the East. He said they were coming like a big river through the land and that I must try and learn at least how to speak English so I could get along with them and compete with them. He didn't hold anything against them, but he always cautioned us to keep our land and work on it—like we're doing now. We have a garden and have had one every year.

When I was six years old, we went to Marty, South Dakota—where the Marty school is now located. There was a house for the catechist to stay in, and my father was the first one to use it. He went around with Father Westropp instructing and baptizing the people. On Sundays they have Mass, and my father would serve for it. He knew how to serve.

We stayed there over a year, and I used to play with the Yankton Sioux children. When I came back home, my friends all laughed at me because I talked like a Yankton. Also during this time, the little Yankton children and myself, we all learned the Latin responses for Mass. After he retired, my father used to put my kids to sleep by singing one of the Latin high Masses. It would work too. You just had to say something to him once, and he caught on.

Black Elk himself recounted his missionary experiences in a publication that circulated around this time. Apart from simply reporting what he did, the catechist would also pass on to readers his religious philosophy, as the following selection shows:

I have seen a number of different people—the ordinary people living on this earth—the Arapaho, the Shoshone, the

Omaha, the tribe living in California and Florida, the Rose-
bud, the Cheyenne River Sioux tribe, the Standing Rock,
and our own, the Oglalas. The white men living in all these
places—I have said prayers for their tribe. I'm really moved
that I was able to travel to these places and meet people that
are very friendly. . . . In all these, good things come from
God because of your faith. The United States—all the peo-
ple—should have faith in God. We all suffer on this land.
But let me tell you, God has a special place for us when our
time has come. (Sinasapa Wocekiye Taeyanpaha, July 15,
1909)

Because of his time in Europe and travel throughout the
States, Black Elk developed a worldview that included more
than the Lakota Reservation experience. This background
provided him with new perspectives, religious and intel-
lectual, that later proved advantageous in his work as a
catechist. His travels gave experiential substance to what
he said.

How Black Elk's missionary journeys sometimes got
started is revealed in the following correspondence
(MACIM). In it, another style of self-expression is attributed to the holy man, quite unlike that fashioned by
Neihardt some twenty-odd years later, and by someone else
just a year later. Similarly, his work among the Shoshone is
cautiously acknowledged by a missionary who mentions
Black Elk was good, but not as effective as one of the men
who accompanied him (i.e., Grass).[6]

Writing in English through an interpreter (of questionable grammatical skills) to the director of the Catholic Indian Missions, who was stationed in Washington, D.C.,
Black Elk sent the following letter in 1908:

Dear sir. Wm H. Thatchman
if you wants have a church in your country why I wish
you let me know.

We was in saint Stephen Wyoiming. and we make have a church. so.

if you wants same is that. why you let me know.
and shonshone indians they wants to me to do it same
you remember me in prayers your friend
   Nick Black Elk, Manderson S.D.

A year later (September 7, 1909) a better interpreter seems to have been found, as Black Elk again expressed an eagerness to be on the road doing church work.

Rev. Father Wm H. Ketcham
Washington D.C.
My Friend
It is long since I have not written to you. About two things I want to speak to you. The Assiniboins in Canada want the prayer. They want to see me very much.

The other thing is this: I want to take care that many children in North and South Dakota join the Society for the Preservation of the Faith.

Therefore I want to go round for 2 or 3 months. I want to hear what you think about that. My sister died.
With a good heart I shake hands with you
Nic. Black Elk
Address: Manderson P.O.   S. Dak.

In a 1915 letter to the Bureau of Catholic Indian Missions now in MACIM, Father Westropp described Black Elk as a catechist who was "doing great work," and in an exchange of letters (one by Black Elk), the matter of catechist's salary is raised. *The Sixth Grandfather* reported that their pay was five dollars a month (1984b:16), whereas Lucy said her father received ten. The Bureau of Catholic Missions "thought it was $15.00," while Westropp and Black Elk understood it to be twenty-five dollars! Perhaps Lucy's recollection was, after all, one related to the disparity between negotiating parties (i.e., a difference of ten dollars). Or perhaps the wage simply changed over time. Whatever the amount, Lucy made it clear that her family was not in need.

Marquette University's Catholic Mission Archives contains other letters exchanged between Fathers Ketcham, Westropp, and Buechel related to Black Elk's missionary trips and compensation for them. As director of the Bureau, Ketcham was besieged with correspondence from missionaries and catechists nationwide, which included a flood of reports and requisitions. In Black Elk's case, the catechist would write of journeys to different reservations and his efforts to promote the faith. Generally, he would ask for Ketcham's continued support of the trips and mention the need for some kind of travel expense.

Ketcham would then try to corroborate Black Elk's comments with the priests out in the field. Both Westropp and Buechel affirmed the catechist's labors but cautioned the director against subsidizing him beyond what they had already provided. Westropp's 1909 letter, referring to Black Elk as Uncle Nick, assured Ketcham of the catechist's prosperity and, as in Buechel's letter of 1912, noted the frequent tendency of such men to beg. An evaluation of these exchanges given by DeMallie is that "holding to Christian doctrine, he practiced the virtue of charity to the fullest. On the other hand, he was able . . . to fulfill the traditional role of a Lakota leader, poor himself but ever generous to his people" (1984b:23). This understanding, and not a more critical one, seems apropos as Black Elk's reports from Manderson, published in *Sinasapa Wocekiye Taeyanpaha,* reveal him zealously committed to the work of catechist. That is, his toils were not self-aggrandizing. The content of these articles reflects what Lucy described as the gist of her father's preaching (more excerpts of which appear later on).

Lucy often relayed information that presumed knowledge of persons and events connected to Pine Ridge history. She did not realize the need to explain a cultural vocabulary unique to her Lakota upbringing and probably wondered why her father's biography could not be drawn together after one session. Some of her references needed clarification, as in the case of the Ghost Dance.

At times called the Messiah Craze, the Ghost Dance of the 1880s was a Native religious movement whose most vocal adherents were from among the many Lakota bands. Rooted in the teachings of a Nevada Paiute named Wovoka (also known as Jack Wilson), the Ghost Dance was received as the answer to a prayer. Suffering from confinement to a drought-stricken reservation, and dying from disease and starvation because of inadequate food allotments and failed crops, a good number of Lakota fervently embraced a doctrine they heard would end such misery (Mooney 1896).

Word was received that a second coming of the Christ was close at hand. Whites had killed him years earlier, so this time he would deliver the Indian people, restore their buffalo, raise the dead, and vanquish their foes. Wovoka is reported to have preached a doctrine of nonviolence and resignation, but among the Lakota his teachings took on a militant cast that eventually produced tragic consequences (Utley 1963).

Besides gathering to dance for a return of the dead, people like Short Bull and Kicking Bear advised that a speedier end to their troubles would occur if "Ghost shirts" were worn and resistance asserted against whites.[7] The shirts were thought to have the power of deflecting bullets, and any form of submission to reservation law would only delay liberation. Consequently, a hostile atmosphere prevailed throughout Lakota country in 1890 as growing numbers looked with longing to the spring of 1891 (when deliverance was expected). Meanwhile, government injunctions against these ideas and practices seemed only to underscore their validity. The oppressors knew they were doomed, or so went the thinking, and the exhaustive, trance-producing dance became the order of the day. Father Perrig's diary reported for December 15, 1890, that "Fr. Craft has seen last night the ghost dance performed in the Rosebud Indian camp. He found it to be alright, quite Catholic, and even edifying" (MACIM). Unfortunately, this perspective was not shared by government personnel.

Sent to intercept Big Foot's band of Minneconju dancers, cavalry troops mismanaged surrender negotiations and precipitated the now-infamous massacre of Wounded Knee on December 29, 1890. After a mass burial of over two hundred men, women, and children, and with the spring of 1891 giving birth only to the summer, protective shirts and a second coming became dreams-turned-nightmare. The Ghost Dance hope was dead, even though the conditions that produced it were not. The following account can be understood better with this history in mind, since Black Elk interacted with persons who were very involved with Ghost Dance activities and knowledgeable of the Christian themes it included. In Lucy's words:

At one time, Father Lindebner said to my father: "Nick, go over there, and I'll have Mr. Fills the Pipe go along with you to instruct a very old lady so she can be baptized pretty soon. I'll come along later."

My mother said I wanted to go, so my father hooked up the team and we went down the creek below Manderson toward Rocky Ford. When we arrived there, this old lady was in a little log house shack all by herself—next to a bigger house where the people who took care of her lived.

We went in and she greeted us, and my father instructed her. Afterward, Father Lindebner came.

My father asked the old lady, "Unci" (that means Grandma), "do you want to be baptized and join the church?" Right away she said, "Yes, everybody is getting baptized, so don't leave me out." She said she was willing to answer every question they asked.

So my father said, "Do you believe in the Catholic church?" She said, "Yes." And then he said, "Do you believe in Jesus Christ, who came down from heaven?" And she said, "Yes, I know that long time ago." Right away she looked at Father Lindebner and said, "But I heard the wasicus [white men] were bad, so they killed him." We'd take that as a joke today, but they didn't. They just went on instructing her, and pretty soon she was baptized and willing to receive communion.

After that, although she was pretty old, she walked to St. Peter's Church.[8] I guess she really believed in the faith, because she used to walk slowly, but she always did get there to receive her Communion. Then she'd walk back to her shack again.

She was really rewarded with a happy death. The priest was there, and she received her last rites and communion. And that's one I witnessed myself.

Another time Father Lindebner came over to baptize my grandma and her cousins. They were all living together and were ready to be baptized because they had already been instructed. And again there was my father and his friend (he says it's his cousin) old man Fills the Pipe, who was trying to make them say the Acts of Faith, Hope, Charity, and the Act of Contrition.

He was trying his best to make them say the prayers along with him, but they were kind of blundering. Fills the Pipe would tell them: "Say after me." And one old lady would repeat, "Say after me" each time he'd begin a new sentence.

They were going so slow that I took my fancy little cup. I had it ever since I was a small girl. I took my cup, filled it with water, and went around baptizing my three grandmas. That Father Lindebner—I really like him. He just stood there looking at me pouring water on each one and said, "Hurry up with the prayers, Lucy has already baptized all the old ladies!"

I guess I really took to everything, and I'll always thank my father for training me and giving me a good Catholic life. But that's the way they were. He and my mother were really interested in church work.

In those days it was fun to get a lot of the older people baptized. Sometimes they'd understand, and sometimes they wouldn't. They might ask a woman what name she had chosen, and she might say "Jacob," or some other man's name. Or one man said, "I want to be called Julia." So, things like that happened in the old days.

Since my father and mother trained me as a helper, I had to teach the younger people. I had to go along with my father to teach them prayers in Lakota—like the Our Father and Hail Mary. And I had to tell them stories in the Bible, like when the Lord was born in Bethlehem.

Anyway that's the way I followed them around. And my father told me to do my duty as a Catholic—go to Mass, receive the sacraments, and never forget to thank Wakan Tanka for the blessings and benefits he has bestowed upon me. He always said, "To live close to God is more enjoyable than to live easy—with all the pleasures and riches—because such things never will reach to heaven. One thing is never lie, too, because you will lose all your honesty toward God and your neighbors."

When I took communion, I knew that Christ came into my heart. He was present on the altar, and he came to my parents and my heart. I used to play with my dolls and make believe they received communion. I'd dress them in white and put that little veil on them and make believe they made their first communion.

I also used to go out in the garden when I was a little girl and shake hands with the corn stalks. "Good morning," I would say to these creatures. And I would pray with them.

Another time there was going to be a Christmas Midnight Mass, so my father told me to go to bed early. He said that "tonight Jesus comes into the church"—and we all believed exactly that (since Christianity had just been taught to the Indians). Anyway, I got up, dressed, and went into church.

After I went out of the house, my mother must have put a doll above my bed as a present. I also had a stocking hanging there, so they filled it up with candy and nuts, and on top of it they put a big apple. When I returned from Mass, I didn't notice anything. I just went to bed. I didn't look around.

Next morning, my father sang an old song with the words: "Get up and see what you've got above you." He was singing that, and I knew he meant me. So I looked up, and here that doll was hanging there. And my stocking was filled with candy and things I really enjoyed. That was the first time I ever had a doll. Later I went to school at Holy Rosary, and Father Buechel gave me a doll too—a nice little doll that I had for a long time.

When Lucy started school, she lived at Holy Rosary Mission the better part of a year. Apart from holiday sessions, she would see her parents when they came to visit. Upon completion of her eight years of formal education, Lucy remained at home until her marriage. Efforts to secure a more detailed pattern of her father's life always met with a calm restatement of information already recorded. Namely, when not actively engaged in teaching, preaching, or other time-consuming church activities, Black Elk maintained his home and attended to responsibilities he had as the head of a family. Lucy continues her recollections.

Well, it came to pass that my father said I must attend school at the Holy Rosary Mission and that I couldn't go along with them on the missionary trips. He said, "Now since you're a girl and not a boy, I want you to take music lessons and learn all you can. So after you get out of school, you're going to be playing for the Mass and for all Catholic gatherings. That way you can serve God. If you were a boy, I would have you trained as a catechist."

So I did. That way I thought I would please my father. Yet, I learned afterward that the Sisters who taught me music actually worked for the service of God, and it was actually a heaven-sent talent that I learned from the Holy Rosary Mission.

I was an organist for the last thirty-four years, and sometimes I still play when I'm in a good mood—but sometimes I have a little rheumatism, so I hardly ever play anymore.

When we went to the Holy Rosary Mission, my father and mother didn't even notice that I wore my beaded moccasins. I also wore a velvet dress that had ruffles on it, and my hair was long. So my father brought me to school, and my mother stayed home because she hated to see me go.

Father Buechel went and got a box with a big red apple on it and said, "I got something that you'll really like." So I looked in the box and there was a doll—the kind that slept. My dad was there to see if I was going to cry—because my mom told him to take me back home if I did. But I passed him and went to the school clothing room with Sister Genevieve. She took away my moccasins and gave me some real thick shoes, black stockings, and a big heavy dress with ruffles.

I was at Holy Rosary when my grandma died, and I didn't know anything about it until my father, mother, and baby brother came to visit me. My mother had her hair all down, like in the morning when you get up, and it wasn't braided. She wore black, and when she saw me she hugged me and was crying as she said, "Your grandma died."

When Lucy related the above incident, her words were slowly and solemnly uttered. The loss of her grandmother some sixty years previously seemed painfully immediate.

Black Elk, in front, with his wife, Anna, and Lucy, with her hands on boy's shoulders, after a "home mass" near Oglala in 1937. (Courtesy of Heritage Center, Red Cloud Indian School.)

▼

chapter six

▼

Life Story

Lucy could recall very little about Neihardt's visit with her father, but Father Sialm's diary reflects a viewpoint held by some within the Catholic population at the time *Black Elk Speaks* was first published in 1932. Some objected to the book not so much on what was related but rather on what was left out. Neihardt's supposed life story covered only twenty-four years of the man's life, which they felt was an injustice to Black Elk. Nothing had been mentioned about his long years of labor as a Christian missionary among his people. Excerpts from Sialm's diary illustrate this rather strongly felt position.

Concerning Black Elk's relationship with Father Sialm and other Jesuits, Lucy said: "Oh, he liked all of them, even though they said Father Sialm really got after him sometimes.[1] But he didn't mind that. Father Sialm was my confessor, but I didn't know much about him." Lucy's sentiments regarding the publication of *Black Elk Speaks* paralleled those expressed by Father Sialm, but she and the priest's successors have come to value Neihardt's work as an important contribution to Lakota heritage, however incomplete its rendering of Black Elk himself.

Placidus Sialm, born in 1872 in Disentis, Switzerland, first came to Pine Ridge in 1901. He died there in 1940. His use of the word "pagan" should be understood here and elsewhere to mean a person who has not been baptized into the Christian faith. He wrote in his diary as follows about Black Elk:

He was very zealous . . . and went much around with Fr. Westropp. He became catechist and traveled to other reservations under direction of Fr. Westropp. He was well educated in the faith.

Nic Black Elk could have finished the book with a fine chapter of his conversion. But Neihardt did not want that. . . . Nic as Catholic did more for his people than as medicine man before. Nic was in his best years when he was converted and he knew that the Gospel was clearer than his dream. Nic had many fine speeches about the Catholic faith in big assemblies, at congresses in several places. But all that did not suit Mr. Neihardt.

For quite a few years Nic Black Elk made the Catholic retreat under Fr. Sialm and what he learned then was more than all the dreams of the Indian medicine men. After one of these retreats Nic Black Elk came to Fr. Sialm with the solemn declaration: "We Indian catechists have resolved never to commit a mortal sin." It was Nic in the name of all who made up the resolution. In our great procession of Corpus Christi, Nic Black Elk was prominent in leading the real Indians in their costumes in the procession. It was perhaps the greatest exultation of his heart when he saw so many Indians following up to Corpus Christi Hill in Oglala and in Manderson in perfect order and knowing & firmly believing that the living Christ was among and with them all to bless them & their country. He saw then more horses lined up than in his dream. [See chapter seven for a discus-

sion of Black Elk's "vision," here referred to as a "dream."]
With 9 years Nic Black Elk could for a truth not count the
horses which he pretended to have seen in the dream. But
perhaps it was rather Mr. Neihardt who by all force put
things together to suit his own purpose. Black Elk cannot
read the book as it stands and cannot object against the
forceful contortion of the poet.

The greatest injustice, however, is that Black Elk is left
under the impression that now as an old man he is in despair
about fulfilling his destiny for his people. He has done won-
derful good work for the truth & the way & the light which is
Christ, and His one holy catholic apostolic Church. We, as
missionaries whom Black Elk calls Fathers, are obliged to
protest against the injustices done to Black Elk—one of the
worst exploitations ever done to an honest Indian. This book:
Black Elk Speaks has no "placet" and no "imprimatur"
from Black Elk. It could fairly be put into the class of not
only exploitation, but what is worse, of stealing—plagia-
rism—material for a book, cleverly done, a kind of kidnap-
ping the very words of a man . . . and translating them into
a new language to disguise the fraud.

We missionaries have learned the language of the Indi-
ans. We lived with them not only a few months. We know
their good and bad qualities. But we feel that the Indians
have sacred rights to be respected. If a book cuts out the
very best from a man's life under his very roof: this is not to
be left unchallenged. We know that Black Elk would not
conclude his narrative as did Mr. Neihardt. His son Ben
Black Elk said that the last chapter was not in the intention
of his father. [2]

Black Elk did not divest himself from Christianity to fit a
poet in such a manner as to stand before the world as a real
old time pagan. It badly befits an old man to dissimulate.
In the old Book we read of a man in his old days who would
not dissimulate but would rather die to keep his good repu-
tation and to be an encouragement to young people than a

stumbling block [2 Macc. 6:18–31]. Black Elk knows that story. He is man enough and Christian in addition as not to fall back from the holy command which was delivered to him by his missionaries. He knows better than Neihardt the words of Peter II, 2:22. Black Elk knows all those truths and stands for them. If it were in his power he would solemnly protest against this book, especially against the last chapter added without one consultation by the writer.

Let him speak as a pagan up to 1900—but after baptism Black Elk solemnly protests to stamp him again a pagan. In the last 30 years since we knew Black Elk this Indian stands up as a Christian, knowing & professing Christ the true Messiah and his only church with Peter, the Rock, as guide & light. It is wonderful to have a solemn Declaration of Black Elk with regard to his firm & solid Catholic faith signed by himself & declared before the whole world. This Declaration should stand in every new edition of Black Elk Speaks. The members of his parish St. Agnes Manderson & all the Catholic Indians on Pine Ridge Reservation will gladly testify that Black Elk is one of their true & sincere members & should not stand before the world now in his old age as an old time pagan and medicine man. Black Elk is a true Christian.

Such a declaration was finally made but never reached the presses as a postscript. In short, feelings were hurt, as the following document reveals.[3]

Holy Rosary Mission
Pine Ridge, S. Dak.
January 26, 1934
Black Elk Speaks Again—A Last Word
I shake hands with my white friends. Listen, I speak some true words. A white man made a book and told what I had spoken of olden times, but the new times he left out. So I speak again, a last word.

I am now an old man. I called my priest to pray for me and to give me holy oil and the Holy Food, the "Yutapi Wakan." Now I will tell you the truth. Listen my friends.

In the last thirty years I am different from what the white man wrote about me. I am a Christian. I was baptized thirty years ago by the Black-gown priest called Little Father (Ate-ptecela). After that time all call me Nick Black Elk. Most of the Sioux Indians know me. I am now converted to the true Faith in God the Father, the Son and the Holy Ghost. I say in my own Sioux Lakota language: Ateunyanpi—Our Father who art in heaven, Hallowed be thy name—as Christ taught us to say. I say the Apostle's Creed and I believe every word of it.

I believe in seven Holy Sacraments of the Catholic Church. I myself received now six of them: Baptism, Confirmation, Penance, Holy Communion, Holy Marriage, and Extreme Unction.

I was for many years a regular companion of several missionaries going out campaigning for Christ among my people. I was nearly twenty years the helper of the priests and acted as Catechist in several camps. So I knew my Catholic Religion better than many white people.

For eight years I made the regular Retreat given by the priest for Catechists and I learned much of the faith in those days. I can give reasons for my faith. I know Whom I have believed and my faith is not vain.

My family is all baptized. All my children and grandchildren belong to the Black-gown church and I am glad of that and I wish that all should stay in that holy way.

I know what St. Peter said about those who fall away from the Holy Commandments. You white friends should read 2 Peter 2:20, 22. I tell my people to stay in the right way which Christ and His church have taught us. I will never fall back from the true faith in Christ.

Thirty years ago I was a real Indian and knew a little about the Great Spirit—the Wakantanka. I was a good dancer and I danced before Queen Victoria in England. I made medicine for sick people. I was proud, perhaps I was brave, perhaps I was a good Indian; but now I am better.

St. Paul also turned better when he was converted. I now know that the prayer of the Catholic Church is better than the prayer of the Ghost-dance. Old Indians danced that kind for their own glory. They cut themselves so that the blood flowed. But Christ was nailed to the Cross for sin and he took away our sins. The old Indian prayers did not make people better. The medicine men looked for their own glory and for presents. Christ taught us to be humble and to stop sin. Indian medicine men did not stop sin. I want to be straight as the black-gown church teaches us to be straight to save my soul for heaven. This I want to do. I cheerfully shake hands with you all.

    signed: Nick Black Elk
         Lucy C. Looks Twice
         Joseph A. Zimmerman, S.J.

Concerning the above declaration, DeMallie thought its translation tended to "slant the document slightly more in Christian idioms" and so retranslated it for *The Sixth Grandfather* (1984b:61). A second document, written eight months later (appearing below), shows that a certain dissatisfaction, difficult to assess, continued to linger after the book's publication.

Joseph A. Zimmerman, a signatory to the first letter, was a Jesuit priest who figured prominently in the life of Black Elk and other Lakota over many years. He was born in 1884 in Westphalia, Wisconsin, and spent thirteen years at the St. Francis Mission before coming to Holy Rosary in 1930. Hoping that Black Elk would not be misrepresented again, he did not look favorably on an upcoming visit with Joseph Epes Brown. But where Brown would remember Zimmerman as somewhat of an impediment to fieldwork, medicine man Pete Catches considered the priest "a saint who I pray to."[4]

As to the purpose for writing not just one, but two, decla-
rations, DeMallie suggested that some of the missionaries
were disturbed by the Neihardt portrayal and did not let
the matter rest. He goes on to speculate that Lucy was perhaps "the actual author of the letter" (1984b:62n). Written
from Oglala on September 20, 1934, it reads:

Dear Friends:
Three years ago in 1932 a white man named John G.
Neihardt came up to my place whom I have never met be-
fore and asked me to make a story book with him. I don't
know whether he took out a permit from the agent or not.
He promised me that if he completed and publish [sic] this
book he was to pay half of the price of each book. I trusted
him and finished the story of my life for him. After he pub-
lished the book I wrote to him and ask [sic] him about the
price which he promised me on the books he sold. He an-
swered my letter and told me that there was another white
man who has asked him to make this book so he himself
hasn't seen a cent from the book which we made. By this I
know he was deceiving me about the whole business. I also
asked to put at the end of this story that I was not a pagan but
have been converted into the Catholic Church in which I work
as a catechist for more than 25 years. I've quit all these pa-
gan works. But he didn't mention this. Cash talks. So if they
can't put this religion life in the last part of that book, also if
he can't pay what he promised, I ask you my dear friends
that this book of my life will be null and void because I value
my soul more than my body. I'm awful sorry for the mistake I
made. I also have this witnesses [sic] to stand by me.
I'm yours truly
Nick Black Elk
my name is not Amerdian [sic] but he is lying about my name

Basing his evaluation of the above documents on correspondence between Ben Black Elk and Neihardt, DeMallie

further noted the family's expressed respect for the author. (Ben even named a son after the poet.) Within this correspondence, mention is made of other catechists' being "opposed to—or perhaps jealous of—the book" (1984b:62), particularly one Emil Afraid of Hawk. Ben wrote that Emil "has been loading the old man about lots of things. The old man felt uneasy for a while. But he is perfectly satisfied, very glad to hear you are coming again." Given this information, DeMallie's conclusion regarding Lucy's involvement is a logical one. Other factors came into play, however, which Lucy painfully reported.

As mentioned earlier, there was some disagreement at the time of Neihardt's visit as to who his interpreter should be. According to Lucy, and corroborated by others, Emil's role as interpreter was short-lived, as Ben wished to have involvement with the project. Lucy's brother Ben thus became a moving force behind Neihardt's accumulation of data, but Lucy found herself at odds with her brother as to how the whole matter was being handled. Emil and Lucy dissociated themselves from the enterprise on grounds similar to those of the missionaries—that is, the highlighting of Black Elk's earlier years at the expense of his later ones.

Knowing of Ben's eagerness for further visits, and knowing about the above correspondence of Ben to Neihardt, Lucy would certainly advocate yet another declaration from her father (she made no reference to writing it herself). DeMallie recognized that the document was "difficult . . . to assess" and that "the motive for writing it is not clear." But given the date of the first declaration (January) and the date of Ben's invitation to Neihardt (June), and taking into consideration Lucy's resistance to her brother's involvement, it is not at all surprising that September finds Black Elk once again trying to clear the air. Unfortunate as this father-daughter-son interplay might be, it was nonetheless a reality Black Elk had to contend with during the book's writing and after its production.[5] In essence, the second letter is again Black Elk's, written in the midst of his children's disagreement. Appeasing both sides, the holy man seems to have ultimately steered a course that was as accommodating to as many parties as possible. A visit by Neihardt would be welcome, and Black Elk's identity as catechist would remain intact.

Who said what appears to have been a matter not easily laid to rest, since it also bore upon *Black Elk Speaks* itself. Joseph Epes Brown said in personal communication that while working on *The Sacred Pipe,* he had reason to correspond with John Neihardt, and that the poet insisted his depiction of Black Elk was greatly embellished and was only "based" on the holy man's recollections. (Supplementary material was apparently gleaned from other sources.) Similarly, instead of keeping the original title of his work, Neihardt requested in 1972 that it be changed to *Black Elk Speaks,* "as told *through*" the author. The 1932 edition had "as told *to*"—an important change that can be easily overlooked by readers. Nonetheless, in Brown's opinion, the book seemed greatly indebted to Black Elk. (Some Lakota, however, attribute much of the information to Ben.)

This publishing history, and the different perspectives that have accompanied it, is at times difficult to evaluate. However, one thing is clear. Lucy's father was not a stoic warrior preoccupied with a mythical past, nor was he an otherworldly mystic unconcerned with the pressing issues of everyday life. Instead, Lucy's account, combined with recollections of those who knew Black Elk, reveals the compelling personality captured in the Neihardt work and does so, simply, in a fashion that reads a little more down to earth.

The "forceful contortions" spoken of by Father Sialm were actually the prerogative of Neihardt in his choice of emphases. Whatever the poet may have embellished, whatever data he fictionalized into misleading or ambiguous conclusions regarding Black Elk's worldview, he still managed to discover and reveal much of the substance that made the holy man who he was. Before meeting Neihardt, Black Elk's destiny as an internationally known mystic could only be the imaginative dream of an old grandfather. After learning about Black Elk's entire life from this more intimate perspective, however, one wonders if the disclosure of his story from start to finish just might be a phenomenon not guided solely by human design. It is indeed intriguing that a man's vision still unfolds these long years after his death, revealed to countless persons far removed from his place and time.

Consonant with Father Sialm's earlier remarks, Father Zimmerman sent out a missionary appeal letter that emphasized Black Elk's role as catechist.

The Jesuit Fathers . . . trained him for his many years as a catechist to his race—twenty-seven years on the Pine Ridge Reservation—two years at Yankton Agency—one year at Sisseton Agency—and one year at St. Stephens, Wyoming, among the Arapahos. His rare gift of making clear the Catholic teachings won many inquirers. One of the old missionaries believes him responsible for at least four hundred conversions. Old age, blindness and the seven miles between him and the nearest Catholic Church prevent him from often hearing mass, so at times I promise to say mass at his home. Then he sends out word and gathers in the entire neighborhood, and as in his old time catechist days leads them in hymns and prayers.

Reminiscent of the meeting between Neihardt and Black Elk, Zimmerman recalled the holy man's greeting upon the priest's return to Manderson after a three-year absence: "Every day I saw you in my prayers. I knew you would come back. When I looked and saw you, I could not believe my eyes, and tears rolled down."[6]

In this same vein, Neihardt reported the following concerning his introduction to Black Elk: "'That was kind of funny, the way the old man seemed to know you were coming.' My son remarked that he had the same impression; and when I had known the great old man for some years I was quite prepared to believe that he did know, for he certainly had supernormal powers" (BES, x).

Lucy commented on Black Elk's ministry:

Once, after he retired, my father told me about the years when he first became a catechist. He said the people would scourge him with vicious words and make fun of him, since he had been a yuwipi medicine man. The people made a lot of vicious talk concerning him, but he held on and did not go back to his old ways.

There's a couple or three times, he said, that people would chase them out of the house—not wanting to have them in there. They belonged to this peyote clan (at that time they were really going strong). So they chased him out and even threw their books out. That's the kind of life he led, and those were some of the hardships he faced during his first years as a catechist.

My father told me: "At first, they called me names. They called me yuwipi man and said that I was the devil. But I was a catechist, so I never paid any attention to them. Pretty soon, they quieted down and started coming to me, working with me, and associating with me. I found out that the ones who did say those bad things about me were the ones most easily converted into the church. They'd come and talk to me and tell me this problem and that problem, and by just looking at their faces I could understand what kind of people they are in their hearts."

He said that "at first the little ones listened to me more than the older people. I was always willing to talk to them about God and about our Lord, who was born and died for all of us men. The little ones, the children, were really glad every time I had a service. They enjoyed it. It was the little children who were interested, who came, and listened to me. One of the greatest things God rewarded me with was the little ones. I was always loved by little ones. It seemed like God said, 'Let the children come to me' [see Luke 18:15–17], for that's the way it was. I still think that since I have become a grandfather, why I still am loved by little ones."

So that was always his main teaching. When he taught, he said, "Unless we become as children, become like those little children"—he would point to some—"we cannot enter the Kingdom" [Matt. 18:3]. That was his main topic.

Whenever they'd have a meeting—they always liked to have meetings at that time in the early life of the Sioux Catholics—they liked to hear about God and about Christianity. So they liked to have meetings. At that time, the regulations were very strict, so they didn't associate with the other denominations or have anything to do with divorced persons. They didn't allow them in the meetings.

At all Catholic gatherings—celebrations or meetings—they were bound to have my father lecture on something about the church. One of his favorite subjects was on the words "What does it profit a man if he gain the whole world and suffer the loss of his soul?" [Matt. 16:26]. That's one of the things I'll always remember about him teaching during those years.

My father would really stand out there preaching with all his might. He'd tell me, "It's pretty hard to be teaching the people. But still, I feel good when I get through. It seems I feel so good that I can just feel at ease when I finish instructing them—even though at first it's like doing heavy labor. Maybe Our Lord helps me to put on inspiring preaching."

I remember a relative of mine used to come over and used to gossip about her aunts and uncles. She used to talk about them and complain about them. So before she left one day, my father said to her, "Daughter-in-law, the strong person doesn't speak sharp words about their neighbor, or other persons. People hear such words and they like to hear them—

Black Elk speaking at Joe No Water's home, 1928. (Courtesy of the Buechel Memorial Lakota Museum.)

then they somehow feel satisfied. Seems like all they want to do is hear bad things."

My father gave her an example. He said: "It's like a dog who gets so hungry at times it goes out and gets all sorts of bones. Even if they're dry and rotted, he carries them back to the house and just piles them up stinking. The dog thinks there's real meat on the bones, he picks them up to eat— they're messy and not good for him at all. That's the way it is with people. They like to hear and speak harsh words all the time in all places."[7]

"You yourself, if you believe in God, should just forgive others. Don't mention anything about them. The people you complain about might just be ignorant. They themselves want to do good for you because they see you talk nice about them. They see you don't even care what they said to you. That way they'll be back in the religion and do things you respect. And when they're dead, you can say nice words about them."

That's what he told that lady. That's the way he talked— in a nice way so she wasn't offended. After my father said this to her, she was really getting along good with her relatives right up until they died.

When Lucy narrated her memories, the spirituality Black Elk imparted to her became more manifest, and a different perspective on the holy man gradually unfolded. The grandmother being interviewed was at one time a little girl—the dearly loved and only-born daughter of Black Elk's two marriages. Whatever religious practices or impulses Lucy possessed, and whatever spiritual sentiments she expressed, all were received through the counsel of her father. Black Elk's little girl, now a woman with grandchildren of her own, had clearly been the special recipient of her father's spiritual legacy—entrusted to her from birth and daily manifested within the context of household and reservation life.

▼

chapter seven

▼

Sacred Visions

In Lakota tradition, "visions of real significance could come to a child of ten and twelve years and might affect the course of his life" (Hassrick 1964:281). Never taken lightly by their recipients, such visions still retained a forceful hold on people quite advanced in age. A vision often prescribed particular obligations and brought special power to the person receiving it (Lowie 1963:170–75).

At the age of nine, Black Elk received a great vision, and Neihardt vividly narrates its details in an early chapter (*BES*, 17–39). Referred to as the living heart of the book and Black Elk's life, one commentary notes that an "attempt to describe it would do it injustice" (Waters 1984:187). *Seeing with a Native Eye,* a popular anthology of essays dealing with Indian religion, was even dedicated to the vision (Capps 1976).[1] This childhood experience is shown as haunting Black Elk's conscious life, and the holy man repeatedly asks of Wakan Tanka if he properly sought the vision's fulfillment. The book's concluding chapter movingly suggests that Wakan Tanka answered Black Elk's question affirmatively (231–34).

Cast in imagery typical of other Plains Indian visionary accounts, Black Elk's is difficult to comprehend. He himself spent a lifetime trying to actualize its promise. When DeMallie compared the stenographic record of Neihardt's vision interviews with what was presented in *Black Elk Speaks*, he found that a certain amount of condensation was effected, a few creative liberties taken, and clarity of interpretation elusive for both texts (1984b:94–99). Yet, a key to interpretation of the vision, perhaps unknown to Neihardt and other commentators, surfaced in Black Elk's life at the time of his conversion.

In an attempt to communicate Catholic theology nonabstractly, early missionaries made use of a picture catechism. On a strip of paper about one foot wide and several feet long were contained illustrations depicting what Christians have traditionally called salvation history. Goll described this mandalalike device as follows: "Beginning with the Blessed Trinity and Creation at the bottom of the strip, the student follows the connected pictures of God in heaven at the top. The Apostles Creed, the life and death of Christ, the Church, the sacraments, the theological virtues, the capital sins—all are there between two roads, a golden road leading to heaven and a black one ending in hell" (1940:30).[2] Native catechists were instructed as to the chart's meanings by means of individual and group lessons conducted by priests, and by written explanations in both English and Lakota.

Although differently drawn catechetical charts were employed by both Protestant and Catholic groups, the Two Roads Map (as it was popularly called) in use among the Lakota was a colorful, engaging depiction of human beings and preternatural creatures. The pantheon of Judeo-Christian figures is arresting, as winged angels and bat like demons are pictured fluttering about the course of world history. Crowds of people are variously portrayed—at the mercy of natural disaster, in the clutches of a leviathan monster, under the embrace of a grandfather-creator, and all in seemingly constant motion. In short, the Two Roads Map imaginatively captured in picture form the basic world-view of traditional Christian theology.[3]

Black Elk used the Two Roads Map during his life as a catechist, and many references within his vision correspond directly to the old picture catechism. Some of the surprising parallels include thunder beings, a daybreak star, flying men, tree imagery, circled villages, a black road, a red road, friendly wings, an evil blue man living in flames, a place where people moaned and mourned, emphasis on the people's history, and gaudily portrayed, self-indulgent individuals. Other, more detailed segments of Black Elk's vision are either explicitly or implicitly present on the Two Roads Map.

Psychologist Carl Jung (1970) highly regarded *Black Elk Speaks* and was particularly intrigued by the vision that Neihardt described. Had he known of the map's existence, Jung would have attributed the correspondence to humanity's "collective unconscious," that is, humanity's sharing of "a common, inborn, unconscious life inherited from the distant past, expressed in archetypal (universal) images and symbols" (Stauffer 1981:56).

Black Elk's closing utterances on Harney Peak allude to the picture catechism as he prays about his vision. He says to Wakan Tanka: "The good road and the road of difficulties you have made to cross; and where they cross, the place is holy" (*BES*, 232). These road references are made not just here but also in the earlier vision and later with Brown (1953:7n). However, all one can conclude from these isolated passages is that traditional Lakota could symbolize the virtuous life as being on a kind of "good red road," and evil behavior, or difficulties, as being on a black one.[4] Walker's turn-of-the-century interviews (1980:187, 189–90,

215, 232, 235) verify the color associations, but in Black Elk's case much more obtains.

That the good-evil dualism is found on the Two Roads Map is not particularly noteworthy. More important is the color symbolism and the notion of good and evil roads. Running the length of the map is a "way of good" and a "way of evil," both of which intermittently touch the map's center. The roadlike center section is directional, with the black rungs on the lower half representing the centuries before Christ, and the red ones on the upper half the centuries after him. In light of these depictions, Black Elk's references seem to take on additional meaning.

According to both the vision and the map, the forces of evil have always contended with those of good. The vision's repetitive references to red, and red's association with the good, make the map's Christ-event critical. That is, the map's red section is identified with the Christian era. It seems to be the path Black Elk prays his people might find and follow.

In Neihardt's unedited transcript, Black Elk is reported as describing his vocation in terms that are clearly compatible with both the map and his long years of labor as a catechist. He says: "I had been appointed by my vision to be an intercessor of my people. . . . I'd bring my people out of the black road into the red road. From my experience and from what I know, and in recalling the past from where I was at that time I could see that it was next to impossible, but there was nothing like trying. Of course probably the Spirit world will help me" (DeMallie 1984b:293). Given the imagery at work here, (i.e., from the black-colored, pre-Christian era into the red-colored Christian era), Black Elk's self-understanding was clearly that of a leader of his people into Christian times.

Black Elk's conversion, along with his work as a catechist, was embraced as a more sober life-trajectory than the feverish activity that accompanied his Ghost Dance involvement. The Messiah Craze might then be seen as a kind of theological transition period. It served as a prelude to Black Elk's later acceptance of a belief system that bore concepts with which he was already familiar. Moreover, presented pictorially, the earlier vision was coherently ratified by being placed in a more global context. Whatever its definitional shortcoming, Neihardt's emphasis on such universal concepts as right conduct, human harmony, peace, and friendship was in fact an accurate reflection of themes within Black Elk's vision. The vision was, however, enhanced by the substance of a salvation history that was succinctly delineated on the Two Roads Map.[5]

A patent difference between the vision and the map is that the north-south red road and the west-east black road of Black Elk's vision do not bisect one another on the catechetical chart. The map's two roads appear as distinct routes separated by illustrations of Christ's life. (Interestingly, though, the vision imagery depicts these roads in the form of a cross.) So too, the map's black section is not strictly designated as one of troubles, any more than the red road is designated as good (even though "good," or "better," would be implied as the Christian era eclipses its prehistory). Finally, the catechism's specifically marked paths of good and evil never intersect with the red and black sections.

Nonetheless, reflecting on his vision in later life, Black Elk's comments to Neihardt sound as if he might just as well have been talking about the Two Roads Map and the instructions he received concerning it. In Black Elk's words, "It was the pictures I remembered and the words that went with them. . . . It was as I grew older that the meanings came clearer and clearer out of the pictures and the words; and even now I know that more was shown to me than I can tell" (BES, 41).[6] Why Neihardt asked Black Elk's friend Standing Bear to sketch pictures of the vision is difficult to understand, as they are not Black Elk's and are in fact distracting. Instead, if the Two Roads Map had been in-cluded, this present discussion would have been started years ago.

A comparison of the map and the vision could become a lengthy study in itself. In fact, the temptation exists to find a complete one-to-one correspondence between the two. Yet, although the vision of the picture catechism and Black Elk's private vision are similar, enough different nuances exist to cause some hesitation in seeing things that actually might not be present (especially since he might have taught from maps that, though closely resembling one another, had varying details). Ultimately, though, the propositions here are supported by recollections of Lucy and acquain-tances of Black Elk.

Maybe Neihardt unknowingly transcribed Black Elk's description of the map as the latter blended into it an ear-lier vision or clothed it in Lakota imagery. Perhaps Black Elk condensed a number of visions and used as an inspira-tional force the Two Roads Map, from which he taught for three decades. Or did time simply obscure the vision he once had, so that the holy man wove into his account some elements from the catechism? Comparison of the two re-quires the reconstruction of such possibilities.

When Brown visited Black Elk, he found that the holy man was still haunted by his vision, whatever its source (1953:xv). Neihardt did not fabricate its impact. As was common in Lakota society, Black Elk had received a vision, and it provided him an abiding sense of mission.

Black Elk's poignant religious experience during boy-hood set him in quest of its fulfillment. Years later, after much heartbreak and disappointment, he found himself doctoring a dying child near Payabya. The encounter with Father Lindebner and subsequent exposure to the strangely familiar picture catechism confirmed in what direction the rest of his life would lead. Black Elk's vision seems to have been a foreshadowing of what was later amplified *via* Ghost Dance themes and the Two Roads Map. Whether this ultimately is a case of mysticism, clairvoyance, creative imagination, fiction, or coincidence remains an engaging speculation that will never be confirmed.

Although charting the cognitive patterns at work in Black Elk's life is somewhat speculative, the suggestions here seem likely. If the vision was reported accurately, its similarity to the picture catechism underscored its prophetic place within Black Elk's life. Whether the Neihardt account is Black Elk's superimposition of the map on his vision (or vice versa) will probably never be known for sure; if some blending occurred, however, it was done so because Black Elk regarded the two as part of a continuum. The accounts that follow reveal Black Elk's vision as he came to interpret it, one whose entire meaning could be understood only in light of the Two Roads Map.

Lucy described the map as follows:

I remember Ate Ptecela used to bring a kind of map—with a red road and a yellow road on it. And my father taught me what it was—the good road and the bad road. He would pray, "Canku wan luta akan napata—on the red road we want to walk—I, my relatives, my children, and grandchildren." He learned the idea of the black road when he was a catechist.

One time Father Lindebner came and said "Lucy, let me see what you learned about this map." Right away I rolled it out and said, "Father, sit down. I'm going to teach you something." My father had taught me about it, and I was really good at telling about it.

In the words of Ben Marrowbone:

Black Elk used the Two Roads Map to teach the old people. He would show that in the beginning, God created every-

Two Roads Map, like the one used by Black Elk. Such maps were used at Pine Ridge as early as 1911. Printed by Catholic Press, Ranchi, India. 8" x 36". (From the collection of Michael F. Steltenkamp. Photo by Tudor Studio.)

Black Elk using the Two Roads Map to instruct children, ca. 1935. (Courtesy of the Buechel Memorial Lakota Museum.)

thing. And then all these pictures would help them understand easier. He would teach the old people about the seven sacraments, and that cross. Crucified, hanged between heaven and earth, was the Son of God.

So on every church you see a cross—great worship. This is why Christ came: to build his church on a rock of strength, to stand in place of him. Nick Black Elk explained this church to the people—this great church. He explained and they understood.

John Lone Goose also reflected on the map.

He'd teach them that map many times. He carried one. So everytime we go teach, he'd go down the Two Roads. He taught them how to go to heaven and how to be a Christian man. On another road, they would go to hell.

Father gave him a Two Roads Map, and he taught from it the rest of his life. One road was black and is the devil. The other is yellow—the very good road to heaven. He'd show the people that some go this way, and some go the black road. Some people believed it and turned around and became a catechist. He turned lots of souls to our Lord away from hell.

If he took it in his grave, I don't know. I didn't see that road map any more after he died.

Lucy tried to explain some of the parallels between Christianity and traditional Lakota religion that she and her father recognized.

He and Father Buechel would talk. They talked about my father's visions . . . and the Sun Dance, and all the Indian ceremonies that my father said were connected to Christianity. My father said we were like the Israelites, the Jews, waiting for Christ. And some Jews didn't want to accept Jesus as God.

He said all these ceremonies connected. They knew, somehow, that in the future our Lord Jesus Christ would come one day to his people. Well, actually they didn't see him, but he did come. And the missionaries brought the teachings of Our Lord. They knew, somehow, in the future they would learn this. And they somehow already practiced it in the Sun Dance. That's the way he took it.

Like they say, "Pagan way, adoring the sun"—but it's not that. He told me. They pray and say to the Great Spirit, "Without any sinful thoughts or actions, we're going to do this for you." That's the way they feel when they do these Sun Dance ceremonies. They purify themselves—that's why they wear the sage crown, which resembles the crown our Lord wore—and they start dancing. So the Indian, early before sunrise, had to stand there and had to go with the sun— watching it until it went down. That's the suffering, you see. And some of them even shed their blood. Christ did that too, before he died on the cross. That was the way he suffered.[7]

No woman was allowed to go near because Eve was the first one to come with sin. That's why women were behind the men and weren't allowed to take part in the Sun Dance.

But I don't know if my father totally understood it that way. Only one place could a woman be a part of it, and she had to be a virgin.

This Sun Dance made them suffer from sunup till sundown. They prayed to the Great Spirit and suffered from fasting for three days and not drinking water. Our Lord fasted forty days. They want the Great Spirit to accept their sacrifice because what they want to do is for the sake of their people, for their sick ones, for a richer life, enough to eat, and enough health. That's the way they pray, so the Great Spirit will watch and take care of them.

So Christianity, they already did practice it—in a way that wasn't really too much against the rules of the church. Of course, there were a lot of ceremonies along with it—like the fathers have Masses and all these special days and celebrations. But still, my father was pretty much the new religion.

Central to the spirituality of the Lakota, in particular, was a sacred pipe *(cannunpa wakan).* Use of this ritual instrument was a crucial feature of every religious ceremony, which Brown well reported in his work with Black Elk. Calling so special an object simply a peace pipe, as is often done, is a misnomer.

A legend well known to the Lakota says that Buffalo Cow Woman (a heavenly, mysterious, and beautiful lady) came many generations ago, bearing what appeared to be a child. In the course of events, however, the bundle she brought was unwrapped and found to hold the Sacred Calf Pipe. As time passed, the holy lady revealed how the pipe was to be used and the seven rites that were to be observed by the people. Furthermore, all subsequent pipe usage was to recall this special revelation. Regarded as a particularly sacred and unique gift, a ritual pipe became synonymous with Lakota religious practice. (Small pipes were used for leisurely occasions.) It ensured the people of communication with Wakan Tanka.[8]

Among the early missionaries, attitudes concerning the pipe varied, paralleling the thought of modern Lakota people themselves. Some regarded the pipe as a sacred symbol within the religious heritage, while others saw it as dysfunctional in the twentieth-century world. Arguments regularly arise today in Native contexts pitting Christian tradition (or even peyote tradition) against the pipe tradition; one group or another typically has members who cannot reconcile the blend (Steltenkamp 1982:21–49).[9] The accounts that follow can contribute to further discussion in such circles.

According to Ben Marrowbone:

A heavenly woman once came and gave us a pipe. Every family had to keep a pipe of its own—use it every day, at night too. That woman gave it to us and told us to talk to the Almighty—pray for whatever we need—for rain or good crops. You didn't have to see any great vision. The Almighty hears you. Take this pipe. Pray that he hears you. That's what the holy woman said. That kind of order was given our grandfathers. So they followed.

Before he converted, Nick Black Elk talked to Almighty God with that pipe. He learned that the same God talked to white people. That's why those catechists believed in the Catholic church. Nobody said: "Oh, you fool you!" No. That's the great Almighty you are respecting and honoring—in a new way. And just as we were brought the sacred pipe, we now had the sacred bread [i.e., the Eucharist] from heaven.

Nick Black Elk used to use that pipe in his wapiya [curing ceremony], and he believed in it. At that time there weren't any doctors, so different ceremonies were used for healing. So I think Black Elk worked according to the Almighty. These old people used this pipe and prayed to one Spirit. That was their foundation. That's what they said.

The catechists would get together, have meetings, encourage each other—show interest in one another. At one such gathering, Nick Black Elk stood up and said: "Yuwipi come from Santee. We have a pipe here. We use that. God gave us that pipe from heaven through a woman. Two young men met her while out hunting. One of them had bad thoughts about her and was punished. But the other one was a good man. She told him, 'I want to explain to the Lakota people how to pray.' She brought that pipe and gave it to an old man—a good man with a good conscience.

"That pipe—it's a road to take—a road of honesty—a road to heaven. It teaches how to lead a good life, like the Ten Commandments. They understood what that woman was saying, and that worship was my formation—my foundation. But my foundation is deepening.

"God made me to know him, love him, serve him. To make sure I do this, God sent us his Son. The old way is good. God prepared us before the missionary came. Our ancestors used the pipe to know God. That's a foundation! But from the old country came Christ from heaven—a wonderful thing—the Son of God. And the Indian cares about this.

"This is not our home. Our home is the new world coming. We come here, lead a good life, and follow the good road. That's the only way to save ourselves and see our relatives again. This body goes, but the spirit keeps on. And if we take the right road, try and lead a good life, be honest, and live as brothers in one relationship, we will see our relatives. We will see God our relative. The evil spirit is against what I say. The evil spirit is like Iktomi, who fools people."[10]

This Nick Black Elk, he was kind of a young fellow. He had catechist instruction. And one brother—his name was Brother Graf—taught him Indian songs like Jesus Cante.[11] So Nick picked up some young fellows and taught them some songs—church songs. And these young fellows learn quickly. They can think without Bible. Word spread that "Black Elk is going to teach the boys church songs, Catholic songs." So while these boys went into the tepee and sang,

Left to right: Catechists Max Bald Eagle, John Kills at Lodge, and Nicholas Black Elk, 1927. (Courtesy of the Buechel Memorial Lakota Museum.)

the people laid on their backs outside just listening. That
was the first time they introduced religious songs.

Lucy also commented on her father's pipe, as well as his
teaching.

He didn't have a pipe until after he was retired from his
missionary work. They used to have a little pipe, which he
and my mother used to smoke, and he was never keeper of
the Sacred Calf Pipe. He used his own when he prayed
to the Great Spirit—nothing else. He never did tell me about
the meaning of the pipe. He'd just say it was something that
was given to them, so it was supposed to be sacred. You
pray with it.

I think it was at the first Sun Dance in 1928 that my
father met Elk Head. He came over to our camp and my
mother told me, "Don't go in front of this man. He's the one
that had the pipe, that sacred pipe." And here my father
said: "Shake hands with him." So I shook hands with him.
And today they keep that pipe up in Green Grass.

I think we accepted that pipe from the Great Spirit
through a sacred lady who brought it to all the human
beings. We say that we Christian women should be like her.
She told the people that a man who has the pipe should
pray with it.

Just like commandments, she told them that men should
be peaceful men, nice men. There should be no quarrels or
arguments, no committing any kind of adultery, and no
feelings to criticize. The Great Spirit created all things
through his power, so man has to love all the creatures—even
the trees. This is what the Pipe Lady instructed. Father
Buechel accepted the Blessed Virgin as the same one who
brought the pipe, and that was what we always thought.

Apart from these references relating to his vision and the
pipe, Black Elk's comments about a sacred tree are per-

haps most familiar to readers of the Neihardt material. At the end of *Black Elk Speaks,* the holy man is pictured looking back on his life and tearfully saying to Wakan Tanka that "the tree has never bloomed" (*BES,* 233). He goes on to plead: "It may be that some little root of the sacred tree still lives. Nourish it then, that it may leaf and bloom and fill with singing birds" (233). Besides this famous passage, the unedited manuscript contains repeated references to the tree.

The account is emotionally powerful, as it depicts Black Elk as a man whose vision would die with him. Readers presume the holy man's references are to the rebirth of a tribal past that is no more and are moved to feel the sadness Black Elk speaks. As DeMallie observes (1984b:56): "With its unrelenting sense of defeat," the book (and especially its conclusion) "became an eloquent literary restatement of the theme of the vanishing American."

However, Lucy was insistent that her father did not speak out of sadness, as these passages implied. Her tone was matter-of-fact as she attempted to communicate the meaning of his references.

The following section also includes Lucy's tradition-based understanding of her Lakota courtship and marriage. (For background, see chapter 1.) On this subject, her comments are typical of the older generation, while seldom, if ever, heard among younger people. Curiously enough, recent evidence suggests that marriage between cousins is on the rise and is no longer associated with a disaster-bearing taboo (DeMallie 1979).

Given the content of the following passage, it should also be noted that, historically, Lakota acceptance of Christianity initially fell within Roman Catholic, Episcopalian, and Presbyterian traditions. These three remain the dominant groups, in spite of subsequent exposure to other denominations. As elsewhere nowadays, and in contrast to the religious sparring of earlier generations, ecumen-

Lucy Black Elk
wearing a woman's
hairpipe breastplate,
1928. (Courtesy of the
Buechel Memorial
Lakota Museum.)

ism has grown over the years, and a spirit of interde-
nominational cooperation for the common good has been
fostered.[12]

In Lucy's words:

*The Great Spirit has promised one day that the tree of my
father's vision was to root, grow, and blossom—to give out its
flourishing sweet scent for everyone, and become a symbol
of life. I know this. He meant it's like the Catholic faith. Our
Lord told St. Peter to establish the religion just like that. The
Great Spirit gave the Sioux people a knowledge of Christianity through the sacred pipe. But this tree would grow and
spread out strong, flowing branches. He had that vision and
learned the tree was to be the Christian life of all people.*

Black Elk, holding prayer book, in right front pew of St. Elizabeth's church, Oglala, South Dakota, 1936. (Courtesy of the Bureau of Catholic Indian Missions.)

At the time before he died, he had a sad tale. He said he didn't do his part in accomplishing this and that the tree was dying. People were not walking the right path. But he still hoped the tree would be able to give forth its branches before it was entirely dead. I know this is what he meant.

The time I got married to Leo was on August 18, 1929, at St. Agnes Chapel—since my father wanted me to be married in the church. I had to marry this man because he did a lot of favors for my folks since they were old. He used to go over there, cut wood, and haul water for them. We had to get water from the creek. My husband had been an Episcopal, so I thought, "If you like him enough, okay, but he has to become a Catholic," so he went and joined the Catholic faith before our wedding. Our celebrating priest was Father Sialm, S.J., and my father was real happy afterward. He honored us by giving a big dinner, or reception.

From this marriage we had ten children, but during the depression we lost six boys.[13] So there are just four surviving now. Leo's grandfather was related to my mother—a cousin—so I'm a first or second cousin to Leo's father. I think that's why we've had tragedy in our family—because we're blood related. A tough life both of us had, but he's now resting in peace.[14] The only disappointing thing is that my father and mother didn't see my grandchildren. My father and mother died before my children grew up. But my father did see my brother Ben's grandchildren. He saw three of them, so I know he was happy to see four generations of Black Elks.

▼

chapter eight

▼

Elder

Following his retirement from church work, Black Elk restricted his activity to more leisurely pursuits during warm weather months. He took particular pleasure in mixing with tourists who flocked to the Rapid City area. His son Ben later assumed such a role and became well known to visitors who toured the Mount Rushmore region.

This summer involvement was a welcome and enjoyable reprieve from the sweltering sameness of summer life on the reservation. Sociable by nature, the old medicine man-turned-catechist was delighted to appear in public with his grandson and to reenact scenes of traditional Lakota life at Duhamel's Sioux Indian Pageant, one of the area's popular tourist attractions. DeMallie speculated that Black Elk's motivation for doing "these sacred rituals appears to have been to teach white audiences that the old-time Lakota religion was a true religion, not devil worship as the missionaries claimed" (1984b:66). If such an underlying reason prompted her father's participation, Lucy was not aware of it. According to her, it "was just a show . . . he never really meant it." The pageant was, rather, an opportunity for her dad to get out in his old age. Furthermore, it was a way for him to "get more side money for the pictures they took of him."

Meanwhile, younger catechists were now undertaking responsibilities formerly handled by Black Elk. They passed on, as best they could, the religious tenets he preached for so many years. Since it was customary for older persons to be guest speakers at special assemblies (still a time-honored practice), Black Elk was now accorded this privilege. He accepted such invitations with enthusiasm.

Elders in fact had few responsibilities, and Neihardt depicted this by saying the holy-man and his friends had little to do "but wait for yesterday." Poetic characterizations aside, the senior generation did have occasion to reminisce nostalgically about their younger days, and Black Elk's granddaughter vividly recalled these gatherings. In his declining years, the holy man was not burdened with household chores and so was free to visit families whose ancestors he had known from another age. A revered catechist and elder, he was welcome wherever he went. He lived through the "old days" and helped forge a new life for others in the reservation era. Nick Black Elk was a special guest at homes, and the people knew he would not be theirs much longer. Lucy recounts:

After he quit being a catechist and had time of his own, he wanted to join in recreational activities. For instance, one time there was a dance being held at the house of one of his older friends. They didn't use to have meeting halls like they do now, so dances were held at homes. Anyway, he wanted to go to that dance real badly. My mother didn't want to go, and I didn't either because I was pregnant at the time. I wouldn't go in that wagon for anything.

Finally, my husband talked about going, and my father said: "We can saddle a horse and we'll ride together. I'll ride on the back." So they both did. It was quite a sight to see because my father wore his Indian costume to that dance. There he was—behind my husband on that horse. As soon as he got on, my father kicked the horse, and it got spooked and started running with my husband and him on it. He let out a whoop like in the old times—hollering out like a cowboy. His little bells were jingling and ringing all the way. My father yelled out: "We're going to fall," but Leo shouted, "Hang on, father-in-law, I don't want you to fall off!" Later on, my mother got after my father and said: "You could have got hurt."[1]

In about 1936, he started working for Alex Duhammel at the Sitting Bull Cave on Highway 16.[2] There was a showplace where they put on a pageant for tourists, and my father had a main part in it—as medicine man. The pageant would show him doctoring a little boy (which was my son Georgie), preparing a death scaffold, and leading the Sun Dance. He would also pray with the pipe and smoke it. But it was just a show, and he never meant it. The women got a dollar and a quarter, and the men got a dollar and a half. It was during depression, but they made quite a bit of money on his performance.

My father was a good friend of Gutzon Borglum, too, and he and Georgie would perform for crowds at Mount Rushmore while it was still not finished.[3] After they finished carving Lincoln, they had a big dedication because Lincoln was the last one. My father went up there in a cable car with my sister-in-law's sister and my boy. They were all dressed in Indian, and my father sang up there on top of Lincoln's head. But by 1947, he was too old to continue doing this work.

My mother died February 19, 1941, and my father took it hard for awhile afterward. They lived northwest of Oglala at the time, so he moved back to Manderson to stay with Ben or my brother Nick's family or myself. On the Decoration Day [i.e., Memorial Day] after she died, my father was

*asked to preach at the cemetery. Of course, he was now
getting old, so he wasn't really strong. Anyway, he spoke
out under the sun for too long a time, because when we
brought him back home he collapsed. But that's the way he
was. Even though he retired, he would still occasionally
give a speech—a good one too.*

Families still assemble in great numbers on Memorial
Day to care for the graves of deceased relatives. Generally,
such a gathering has a priest present who conducts a prayer
service or celebrates a Mass for all in attendance. A "feed"
follows this annual ceremony, so the day is quite a social
occasion. Black Elk was a regular participant in these
activities.

The *Indian Sentinel* reported the death of Black Elk's
wife in a two-page obituary of November 1941. The following excerpts parallel Lucy's recollection of her parents.

*Brings White was a strong and active member of the St.
Mary's Society and set an attractive example of what a
Catholic woman should be. . . . Even during these last few
years, when both Black Elk and Brings White have been
enfeebled by age and illness, their home has been a kind of
mission center where the Sioux in the neighborhood gather
to pray and sing hymns. Whether it was a tent or a cabin, it
has always been a welcome home for the missionary.*

*On one occasion, Father Henry Westropp drove up to the
church at St. Agnes Mission rather late. In those days the
missionaries made their rounds by means of horses and
buggies, often travelling many miles and sometimes reaching their destination after everyone had gone to bed. Father
Westropp stopped his team a few feet from Brings White's
tent and as usual shouted out:* Tunwin, *meaning "Aunt."
This awakened Brings White, who, recognizing the voice,
called back,* Han mitoska, *meaning, "Yes, my nephew."*

Again, Father cheerfully spoke out: Tunwin, wanagi ki

palek cek ama u pelo, *meaning, "Aunt, the ghosts have pushed me here." . . . Father Westropp knew that this expression would amuse his hostess. He always had something clever to say. This is why the Indians called him Little Owl.*

Brings White, of course, was always delighted to receive her "nephew" and, regardless of the hour, would prepare a real Sioux meal for her visitor. All the interesting and amusing stories which had been collected by both since the last visit were told and sometimes all would laugh themselves to sleep.

I am reminded of all this, because just lately good old Brings White passed away peacefully to her reward. Though her death caused great sorrow to Black Elk and her children and many friends, they were consoled by her faith and piety as she received the Holy Food for the last time and the Sacrament of the dying.

The *Sentinel* carried a photograph of Black Elk's wife and family. The reporter was Stephen McNamara, S.J., a priest whose work began at Pine Ridge in 1928.

The catechist's last years left a legacy of impressions. One type of incident was especially recalled by the family and was similar to what is perhaps the most memorable sketch in Neihardt's work. The postscript concluding *Black Elk Speaks* presents a striking example of the holy man's peculiar relationship to nature. He is portrayed as asking for a sign of encouragement, and in the end he receives it. He says it will rain if Wakan Tanka hears his prayer, and it does rain—in a time of drought. Curiously enough, this sort of occurrence is heard in discussions related to the pipe's power in controlling weather.[4] Lucy's account below is representative of the genre.

My daughter Regina always remembers how often my father would go outside and look up at the sky. He would rub his hair backward saying, "Hey, hey, hey, hey," and would know if a storm was coming—even if the sky was all blue. It would come if he said it would.

And that reminds me of the time we were going to have a bad storm—a big thunderstorm. It looked like it was going to have a tornado in it. We didn't have a cellar, only a small grain house to hide in. My father was a pretty old man at the time.

He took his pipe upon a hill and stood facing the west. He then sang this song.

A Thunderbird, that is the nation! (Three times)
The people, you are alive!
A nation that will live well!

After he was finished, you should have seen those clouds. One went off this way, one off that way, and the storm was gone. They must have heard him.

My father must have sung that around my kids because one time we went to town and left my oldest daughter with my in-laws. They put her in the big house and called another uncle of Leo's to go and sit with her. When he arrived, he heard her singing that song. And here the thunder and the wind stopped. We laughed when we heard about that.

My father was a patient man, and sometimes I compare him with my father-in-law, who was just the opposite. He would crab at everything as he got older. But my father never complained. My father was happy all the time. You can see how my father-in-law's son is taking after his father.[5]

My father still liked to visit other people. Even though he retired from his catechist work, he liked to go to sick people and pray for them. If anybody died in a family, he'd visit that family and speak with them and console them. He did a lot of that even though he was retired.

When our family would get together on Thanksgiving Day, my father used to say this prayer. I remember it:

I am talking to you, Grandfather Great Spirit, on this day.
Pitifully, I sit here.
I am speaking for my relatives, my children,
    my grandchildren, and all my
    relatives—wherever they might be.
Hear me, Grandfather, Great Spirit.

With your help, our needs are taken care of.
You have helped us in the time of want during the past.
And on this day we wish to thank you.
Hear me, O Great Spirit.
This day is a day of thanksgiving.
The nations of living things the world
    over—and we the two-leggeds, along with the
    children and the smaller ones with them—come
    to you today to express thanks.

In the future, make us see again a red day of good.
In the past, you have preserved us from evil
    on this red road.
Keep us on this road, and do not let us see anything wrong.

I, my children, and my grandchildren shall
    walk—led like children by your hand.
You have helped us in all things.
And Grandfather, Great Spirit, through your power
    alone we have survived.

Grandfather, Great Spirit, you have come and
    put us down—gathered together on mother
    earth.
And while we continue in this world, you provide food
for all living creatures.
So we give you thanks on this day.
Grandfather,
Take pity on me.

One day, we shall go and arrive at the end of
    the road.

In that future, we shall be without any sin
    at all.
And so it will be in the same manner for my
grandchildren and relatives who will follow as well.
We give you thanks, Grandfather
Great Spirit.
I am sending this prayer to you.[6]

Lucy's daughter Norma recalled these childhood memories of her grandfather.

*After I grew up and went to school, I found out my grand-
father was pretty famous. He was an important person, but
I remember when I was a small girl he had a lot of time for
me. We used to have a real small place, and my parents
made him sleep on a bed while my brother and I slept on the
floor. He'd say to me: "If you want to sleep on this bed,
crawl in." So I always crawled in with him. He always felt
sorry for me.*

*My grandfather always used to babysit for us when my
parents went out, so I'd say to him lots of times: "I want to
ride a horse." So he'd catch our horse named Brownie, put
a halter on it, and set me on top. He'd take me all over these
hills. And while he led the horse, he was either always recit-
ing his prayer book or saying the rosary.*

*Real old men would come to the house and sit on the floor
in a circle telling stories and smoking. They used old Indian words that I couldn't understand, but I would sit with
them all the time next to my grandfather. He might have
been a famous person because of those books he wrote, but I
always remember him being around me and concerned
about me until he died.*

*Georgie [Norma's brother] remembers when my parents
bought him a tricycle, my grandfather would watch over
him as he rode it. My grandfather had a cane, and he'd
watch Georgie to see that he stayed on the road. If he went
off the road, my grandfather would hook the wheel with his*

Black Elk with the Scabby Face family he instructed, 1945.
(Courtesy of the Buechel Memorial Lakota Museum.)

cane and make him go straight. He'd pray as he did that too.[7]

The grandparents of today were young adults toward the end of Black Elk's life, yet old enough to understand why his presence commanded respect. Their religious instruction was administered by younger catechists and priests a generation removed from the holy man, whose boyhood friends were gradually disappearing. One such present-day elder remembers Black Elk as walking from his house to church every Sunday (a distance of two miles), walking stick in hand, and needing help to rise from the Communion rail as infirmity took its toll.

Pat Red Elk, another long-standing member of the community, was a young man during this period, and his account is representative of others from his age group.

Even though they didn't have any formal education, those old converts were really trained to preach. They'd say that Saint John says this here and there, and when I'd get the

The Catholic Sioux Indian Congress, 1946. Black Elk is fourth
from right in top row.

*Bible and read it—they were right! That's what was writ-
ten. I read Scripture, but I can't remember the right words
like they used to be able to do. Yes, those old converts could
really talk—especially about religion. And they'd just
really give you the works! They really knew what to say.*

*Nick was a catechist, and when he got up he really
preached. People sat there and just listened to him. They
could picture what he was talking about. I remember one
time when he was pretty old, he really bore down on them.
He said: "The older people who constructed and kept up
the church are all fading away . . . and the new generation
isn't continuing the work that the people did. When I come to
church in wintertime, there's no firewood in that little box
there [he'd point to the woodbox], and tears come to my
eyes." Nowadays we have education, but we're not that good.*

*On Sunday morning you'd see Nick walking down the
road from where Ben lived—two, three miles outside of Manderson. In wintertime he didn't hardly come—too cold. But*

summertime, spring, and fall, he'd be walking. He was
old, so he got an early start and wouldn't catch a ride. And
every Sunday, he'd join up with John Lone Goose right
around where the store is now, and they'd say the rosary
together. One would begin and say "Hail Mary." The other
would finish the prayer. By the time they got to church,
they had said the whole thing.[8]

Despite ill health, Black Elk lived out his remaining
days in the same contemplative spirit that characterized his
earlier life. Having confronted death in other, more dramatic contexts, the holy man was now resigned to await
patiently its final visit. What restlessness he experienced
came in the form of physical discomfort, in particular, a
stroke that his aged cousin, Little Warrior, was instrumental in relieving.

The Lakota word for stroke is *wanagiktepi*, a literal
translation of which is "killed by ghosts"—an etymology
that conveys the perceived seriousness of the condition.
Little Warrior's skill reflects the rich tradition of healing
ceremonies developed by the Lakota. Home remedies are
still used in modern reservation households (Steltenkamp
1982:129–32; Vogel 1970).

Lucy speaks further of her father's health.

One day, in the spring of 1948, it was really slippery. My
father went outside, lost his footing, fell, and broke his hip.
He was around eighty then, and from that time until his
death he was bedridden. We put him in a wheelchair when
he wanted to sit up or go outside. And after that happened,
he said he was ready to accept his Creator's call any time.
But for me, he said I should try and carry on the works of
the church and go to Mass very often.

When he had that accident, he tried to argue with me,
saying he was alright. But we took him to the hospital any-
way. While he was there his tuberculosis caused him some

*trouble but not serious. He caught that when he was young.
He also had a stroke while there and was given the last rites
for the third time in his life. The second time was when he
was sick.*

*Anyway, he recovered and came to stay here at our house.
Even though he couldn't walk, he still prayed and sang.
There was never a day he complained about his suffering.
He'd sit praying and he'd tell us, "Never fail to miss a day
without your prayers. God will take care of you and reward
you for this. Say the rosary too, because that is one of the
powerful prayers of Our Lord's mother." That's how he was.*

*He was uncomfortable at our house because it was so small
and hot during the summer. So he asked if he could go back
to the hospital, where it was cooler. That's when he moved to
my brother Ben's house, where he stayed until he died.*

*At times, I'd just go over to him and try to make him feel
good. He got to be so blind that he couldn't read his Indian
prayer books, but he had learned them by heart. He seemed
to always have a rosary in his hands, and even though he
was sick, you'd never hear him complain. When he came to
stay at our place, we had to pray. He never forgot.*

Joseph Epes Brown also used to tell of Black Elk's insistence on prayer. While in Denver, the two men stopped at a
diner. In this very nonreligious environment, patrons were
noticeably dumbstruck to witness the aged holy man pray
aloud before eating. The Indian prayer book Lucy recalls
her father memorizing was *Sursum Corda: Lakota Wocekiye na Olowan Wowapi* (Sioux Indian Prayer and Hymn
Book), a compact little book of 386 pages published by the
Central Bureau of the Catholic Central Verein of America,
in St. Louis, Missouri. Lucy continues:

*When my father was released from the sanatorium and was
well enough to stay at our home, he was also partially paralyzed. His mouth was crooked due to the stroke, and he*

had trouble eating. So, as I said, I used to sit down and talk to him to make him feel better, because he was all by himself.

One day I asked him: "Dad, I wonder if this man you call your cousin would be able to bring you out of this stroke?" You see, before my father got crippled, he used to often talk with a man named Little Warrior—and this is who I meant. Little Warrior was a Catholic and did wanagi wapiya [ghost ceremony of healing]. And he was good at that, they told me.

My father didn't really want this, but he had respect for his cousin and myself, so he agreed to go through with it. I called my brother Ben, who was really after this kind of thing—curious about it too—and we arranged to have it at my house. We prepared the sweatlodge, but my father didn't go in—just three older men. He didn't want that doctoring done on him [whereas Ben wanted more exposure to the older tradition].

When we were ready to have that ceremony, Little Warrior said: "You know these other types of medicine men and yuwipi men—they always tell you to close the windows so there will be dark. They tell you to take down from the wall the holy pictures and rosary. I say no. Those are the ones we are going to pray to. Just watch that rosary while this is going on. If you have a rosary, you'd better say it while I'm doctoring your father." That's what Little Warrior said about our picture of the Sacred Heart and this big rosary we had on the wall.[9]

Well, I must have really believed him, because I took my rosary and sat there saying it. Pretty soon, the main time comes for those little spirits to doctor my father. All at once, I'm in the middle of my rosary and I remember what Little Warrior had told me. So I looked up at our rosary on the wall, and you ought to have seen those little things on each bead. Those little lights—there must be a bunch of them— were all glowing on the beads. And that cross, it just glowed.

And the holy picture—the sacred picture—those little things just sat around it. I think they were worshiping the picture.

I noticed after everything was over that my father's mouth had straightened out, so he could eat. Before that, I had a hard time feeding him. My father, after it was all over, said to Little Warrior: "Yes, I'll admit you're good at it. But next time you come to doctor me, don't let those little spirits treat me so roughly. They were really treating me harsh. I'm really tired." Mind you, his mouth was straight and he could eat after that ceremony.

And that's when I got confused. I asked my father: "Why in the world—how is it that you became a Catholic catechist?" Then he told me about his conversion. I had heard the story when I was in the teen age, but I never paid any attention to it. So I was a little older when he explained these things to me. It was after I got married, then I realized and understood these things about my father.

Little Warrior told me: "In my life, there are good spirits and bad spirits. When you pray, the good spirit is always going to help you. In the morning, when you get up, stand in the doorway and pray that the day is a nice quiet day. Give thanks for the day—for coming through the night." I guess he was glad that he slept through the night and woke up again.

He also said: "Don't go out at night too much—that's when the bad spirits are about. If there's anything to eat, like nice fruit or any kind of meat, just put it out there and say, 'That's for you good spirits' and say, 'I want this—a nice day' or make some other request. Break off a chunk of bread and place it out for them. And in the morning take a cup of water. Drink that water—because God has given you that cleansing water for you to drink. Just take a cup and thank the Great Spirit for the day—then pray for the day. And then when you lay down, thank the Great Spirit for the day he has given you." My father did this, so I try to do that too.

Short Bull, or possibly Little Warrior.

One time my husband had to stay home while I took
Georgie and Regina up to the Custer celebration of Gold
Discovery Days.[10] Leo was working then for Albert Yankton, putting up hay. So my husband would stay here at
home all by himself—sleeping here at night and going to
help Albert in the morning. They always helped each other.

Anyway, he came home one evening, and it was still
light outside. It wasn't quite dark. Leo was coming down
the hill toward the house, and he could hear my father singing icilowan [death song] in the house. He tied up his horse,

*walked in, and knew he was present in there. Leo said out
loud: "I hear your voice, but I hope nothing bad happens in
our family." So then he said some prayers and went to bed.*

*Now my father was alive at this time, but he was at the
Sioux San Hospital in Rapid City. Also in that hospital was
my nephew, Benjamin Junior. It was just a short time after
Leo heard my father singing that Benjamin Junior died of
meningitis—so we knew my father was preparing us for it.*

chapter nine
▼

Farewell

Black Elk knew that life's circle was nearly complete, and he calmly awaited his passing. In assuring Lucy that he was prepared, the holy man reported the presence of a phantom visitor that was seen only by him. This claim did not meet with disbelief on the part of his family. Lucy remembered:

One day, my father called my husband and I in and talked to us. He said that his days were coming to an end, and he told my husband, "Take care of my daughter as a father and mother would take care of her." And my husband has done that I guess. My father said, "I am old, so don't take my death too hard. Do not mourn a long time, you know I will be happy. My sufferings will be over, and I will have no hurt. Pray for me as I taught you to pray in your early days. And pray for me. Do not let any single day pass without praying for me." So the last prayer I always say before I go to bed is, "May the souls of all the faithful departed rest in peace." I say that for my father and for all who have died.

As he waited for death, he told me, "Do not worry, there is a man who comes to see me everyday at three o'clock. He is from overseas, and he comes in to pray with me—so I pray with him. He is a sacred man." When he was living, my father always used the phrase wicasa wakan when speaking about a Blackrobe priest. And that's the phrase he used in talking about that visitor—wicasa wakan. So he might have been a Blackrobe who visited him. During this time he received his last rites for the fourth and last time.

He told me: "I know I have a lot of little angels up there in heaven watching over me, and one day I'll see them." He said that during his life as a catechist he baptized a lot of little babies who were dying; since the priest wasn't there, he had to baptize them. Those were the ones he meant. He said that they were his "little helpers" and "guides."

He also said, "It seems like I will go anytime now, so if your car is alright, go after your younger brother. I want to see him." My brother Nick Junior was working way out about fifteen miles from Hay Springs, Nebraska, so we went to get him. He got his pay and came back, but my father died just before he returned. He passed away at my Brother Ben's house on the seventeenth of August, 1950. And he was patient with his suffering right up until the end.

When he was a catechist, he had been given a black shirt, but we couldn't lay him out in that because it was all eaten by mice. So we laid him out in a suit and tie and put his big cross around his neck. The catechists had been given those large crucifixes. He also had his big rosary—one that had big beads and a saint's relic on it. When he was out east, a bishop in New York had given him that rosary and the relic of St. Peter.

According to traditional Lakota belief, one's spirit parted the body at death and, if judged worthy, embarked upon the Milky Way, or "spirit trail," toward the "land of many lodges" (Powers 1975:191). If found wanting for some reason, it became a "wandering spirit" and was sentenced to roaming the earth until deemed fit for entrance to the better life (Hassrick 1964:297). The uncanny luminescence of the sky during Black Elk's wake was an appropriately mysterious occurrence seen as honoring the man whose spiritual vision was now entrusted to those he left behind.

During the night of his wake, natural phenomena conspired to produce images in the sky, which people interpreted as being of supernatural origin. The figures Lucy and others claim to have seen (i.e., the number 8 and a circle) might be construed in various ways. Among the Lakota, the circle was rich in symbolism, and Tyon spelled this out for Walker (1917:160):

The Oglala believe the circle to be sacred because the Great Spirit caused everything in nature to be round except stone. . . . Everything that breathes is round like the body of a man. Everything that grows from the ground is round like the stem of a tree. . . . It is also the symbol of the circle that marks the edge of the world and therefore of the four winds that travel there. . . . it is also the symbol of these divisions of time and hence the symbol of all time.

For these reasons the Oglala make their tipis circular, their camp circle circular, and sit in a circle in all ceremonies. The circle is also the symbol of the tipi and of shelter. If one makes a circle for an ornament and it is not divided in any way, it should be understood as the symbol of the world and of time.

Apropos to the occasion, Westerners might identify the figure 8 as a symbol for infinity. However, such an association is not a traditional one among the Lakota. Nonetheless, apart from being the conjunction of two circles, the figure might also be a kind of celestial marker of the month August, in which Black Elk died (an association perhaps made at the time but now forgotten). Lucy herself was unable to attach a particular meaning to the sight, the details of which are variously reported in the following narratives.[1]

Also contained in these recollections are some clarifications regarding Black Elk's birth. That is, Neihardt reported the holy man to have been born "in the Moon of the Popping Trees (December)" in 1863 (*BES*, 6), while Brown had said Black Elk was born in 1862.[2] Father Lindebner listed 1866 in the Holy Rosary Mission Archives, which was the year in which Lucy understood him to be born. She disputed the month December, saying that July was the real month of his birth and that her father had actually reported to Neihardt the date of his spiritual birth (i.e., his December baptism). Neither Ben nor Neihardt, it seems, were aware of this deeper meaning.

Throughout Black Elk's life, natural phenomena were repeatedly perceived as affirming his prayerful entreaties. Death, it seems, did not curtail this pattern; like a proclamation, a sort of galactic testimony was seen by people at Black Elk's wake. This heavenly display was understood as the sky gleaming bright to light his way to the peaceful land of many lodges.

Black Elk knew the old ways more intimately than most and confronted the transition to twentieth-century life in a manner that helped buoy others who languished. He enjoined his people not to lose their religious integrity and manifested what this responsibility entailed in the face of discouraging trends. Those present at his funeral powerfully felt a cosmic affirmation of the holy man's life and understood this sacred occurrence to be a last blessing bestowed by Wakan Tanka, through Black Elk, upon all in attendance. Lucy recollected:

The night of his wake was one I'll never forget. Others saw it that night, but they don't seem to talk about it. My father said toward the end that "I have a feeling that when I die, some sign will be seen. Maybe God will show something. He will be merciful to me and have something shown which will tell of his mercy."

What we saw that night was the sky in a way we never saw before. The northern lights were brighter than ever, and we saw those figures—the number 8 and a ring, or circle. They were separated by a short distance, but they were there—an 8 and a circle. I always wondered what that meant.

William Siehr, a Jesuit brother at Holy Rosary Mission since 1938, knew Black Elk and had attended the holy man's wake. His recollection of the night was vivid.

Well yes, I remember old Nick, he was the medicine man Neihardt talks about in Black Elk Speaks. He was also a zealous catechist from Manderson. He had quite a bit of influence with the people, old Nick did. He was the old medicine man who, in the old days, was considered something like our priesthood. That is, they respected him for the authority he had, especially in religious matters. He was considered to be quite a noted man among the tribe.

Anyway, I was with Father Zimmerman that night, and we went over to the wake. It was in the old house that's still standing there as you approach Manderson. There were many people sitting nearby the coffin, like they do at all the wakes, but this was a large assembly. There wasn't so much auto traffic in those days, but there were quite a few cars around, and it was impressive to see so many people there. We stayed there and spoke to many of the mourners, and it must have been around 10:30 when we started back up to the old Manderson road.

When we left the place, we noticed that light. The sky was just one bright illumination. I never saw anything so magnificent. I've seen a number of flashes of the northern lights here in the early days, but I never saw anything quite so intense as it was that night.

When we came back from the wake, the sky was lit up, and you could see those flames going into midair. It was something like a light being played on a fountain which sprays up. It seemed like it was rising and moving. There would be some flames going at a great distance way up into the sky above us. And others would be rising and coming into various groups and then, all of a sudden, spurt off on this side and then another side and then off to the center again. It was almost like day when we returned.

Everything was constantly moving. As I said, it was something like a display on a fountain of water where you see light reflecting on the water as it's being sprayed up. That's the way the sky was illumined—something like that— but it was all in every direction. That is, it was all coming up from the east and the south, the north and the west. And they'd all converge up to the top where they'd meet—rising up into the sky, and it was a tremendous sight.

They weren't stars or meteors, but rather, well, they were beams or flashes. And there was a variation of color effect in there—the whole horizon seemed to be ablaze. That's the first time and the only time I ever saw anything like it.

There were different formations in the sky that night which, to me, looked like spires, like tremendous points going up—then flashes. And it seemed like they were almost like fireworks in between. It was something like when a flare goes off in the sky—some sparkle here and there, but spread over such a vast area. And it was not just momentary. We all seemed to wonder at the immensity of it.

I don't recall just what anybody else said, but I know it was something I'll never forget. It was something I rather associated with the old man as he was buried at his funeral. Some sort of heavenly display, a celestial presentation—that's the way I looked at it. It was sort of a celebration. Old Nick had gone to his reward and left some sort of sign to the rest of us. With the Indians here, it seemed like it

John Lone Goose at the Rushville Nursing Home, 1974.

had a real significance. I think it was symbolic. There was something there.[3]

During a 1979 interview, Joseph Epes Brown was asked if he had been present at Black Elk's death (1979:63). Responding that he had been in Europe at the time, Brown did recall what the holy man had foretold, namely, "You will know when I am dying, because there will be a great display of some sort in the sky." Brown said this prophecy was true because, "in talking with people on the Pine Ridge Reservation," he was told that "the sky was filled with falling stars" when Black Elk died—"a very unusual display."

John Lone Goose reflected on that night.

Yes, I remember that night very well, and those bright stars. Everything looked miraclelike. I'm not the only one who saw it. Lots of people did. They were kind of afraid, and I was scared a little bit—but I knew it was God's will. I know

The headstone at Black Elk's grave.

*God sent those beautiful objects to shine on that old mis-
sionary. Maybe the Holy Spirit shined upon him because
he was such a holy man.*

*The night was still and warm with nothing fearsome
about it—just quiet and nice. God was with us that time.
Other people said, "God is sending those lights to shine on
that beautiful man." And that's what I believe.*[4]

According to Lucy, Black Elk "used to say that he was born when the cherries were ripe [July], and the summer before he died he told me he would be eighty-four that year. So, he wasn't over ninety. They never used to celebrate birthdays as we do now, so he used his baptismal date as his birthday—December sixth. He did that because he would say 'I was reborn in baptism.'"

With Black Elk's passing, the reservation knew that a very special member of its community was no longer present. The holy man who had lived so well through so much had been a beacon for others struggling to make their way down the sometimes gloomy corridor of twentieth-century life. But now he was gone, and with his departure, it would seem that part of the reservation conscience had been laid to rest.

Black Elk understood his role as a Catholic catechist to be the desire of Wakan Tanka, "who had chosen him for this work," and he adopted this new form of religious expression with great zeal. The old medicine man-turned-catechist appreciated his earlier tradition but adapted to a historical ethos that made his religious quest a response to Wakan Tanka in the changing circumstances of the here and now. Such was the spiritual impression he tried to etch upon the hearts of his listeners, and Lucy was saddened to think her father's life-message had been lost.

After my father passed away, memories of him stayed with us a long time. Sometimes in church or sometimes at a gathering, somebody would get up and mention his name and speak about him. People would feel he was present in our chapel or meetinghouse. Younger people would even say that we should follow his example, support the church, and pray more often. And some people would say that when they came to church, they thought they saw my father.

Before my brother Nick died, I believe he was trying to follow in my father's footsteps. Sometimes he would pray in times of need, at social gatherings, or at funerals. He also preached and liked to sing in the choir. But his life was cut short, as I have said, when he died in 1959.

Although I don't speak of this, often we still experience my father's help in our lives. If something is going to go bad in our family, or if something is wrong, I know about it. And I think my father is responsible for this.

Just lately, when they took my boy to the hospital, I cried. We had plans for my brother Ben's memorial feast, and here my son was close to death. I asked my husband what we should do and if we should go through with the dinner. He said it was up to me. All of a sudden, something came to me like a flash—like somebody speaking to me clearly. I was told to go through with everything. So I did. What I thought was this. People would come to the memorial for something good. They would pray for the church and express their feelings about our religion—which I'm sure my father enjoyed. That's what he did when he was alive. And he would have thought as I did—to go through with the memorial. What came to mind was the time he had two coffins in church and still preached, even though those two coffins held his own children. I know my father was speaking to me then. We experience things like that.

My son really made a mistake when he went through that sweatlodge ceremony, thinking it was his grandfather's wish. He went and did it, got sick, and almost died. Just before he was flown to the Denver hospital, Georgie was given the last rites and communion. His mouth was dry, so he couldn't swallow the communion and had it on his tongue the entire trip. When he arrived, he got water and could swallow. My son recovered after a long stay there. He said many bad spirits came to fight him, but there was always one good spirit—Jesus. And the bad couldn't do anything to him. That was a miracle.

So when things aren't going right, I remember what my father used to say. "At such times," he would say, "go to church. It is a place of comfort where you will not feel bad.

There's a quiet peace in there. There are no quarrels and nothing is wrong in that church.

"We Indians originally had a wanagi tipi [spirit lodge]. When a family member died, a piece of their hair would be cut off and hung in the back of a tepee. A pipe would be there too.⁵ If it's their child, the father and mother taught the other children not to say anything bad in that tepee— because it was a special place, a sacred place, a place of prayer.

"They'd want their child to have a good life in the other world. They wanted that one to have an easy afterlife, so they prayed for the dead like we do now. The church is wanagi tipi in which Our Lord is present.

"When you go in there, have no feelings of hardship, no wrong feelings, no hatred—nothing like that. Go in there to the Great Spirit. That's the only place where you will be content. If you go to church, worldly things would not disturb you."

So I do as he said and believe what he told me. Sometimes I offer Holy Communion for those who don't do us wrong, and I pray for those who have done us wrong. In that way, I get back on the road again. I know my father led a life like that, and I'm sure he prays for me in the other world. He prays, as do all the poor souls, for us who are living all confused.

A while back, somebody came and reported that certain people were saying bad things about me. When this was told to me I thought, "They hurt me—why don't I hurt them back?" But right away I remembered my father and all that he taught me. When he became a catechist, he had the same kind of trouble. But he was a patient and forgiving man.

When I was tempted to strike back, I thought about my father. I chose instead to follow his way. He practiced a Christian life, and that's the faith I wanted to practice. This younger generation is trying to live without the Christian

*life. They don't seem to be interested and practice the faith.
They've been suffering, I know that. I feel bad about this at
times. So I go to my room, like my father, and pray for
them. I pray that one day they'll return and do as they're
supposed to do—fear God according to the commandments.
I say that prayer for priests, and for unborn children being
killed.*

Like her father, Lucy was discouraged in seeing relatives
and friends become lax in their practice of religion. Such
laxity, she felt, was a major reason why the social conditions of Pine Ridge were not good. In fact, Lucy saw her
own family as a microcosm of the spiritual ferment that
characterized the reservation as a whole. Some people clung
to their religious practice, and some participated halfheart-
edly. Others, meanwhile, simply seemed preoccupied with
material concerns. A sense of personal and communal mission, grounded in religion, had been lost.

This development has been a source of considerable pain
for Black Elk's daughter, and her sadness was particularly
apparent whenever our visiting would be interrupted by
happenings beyond our control. One time, for example, a
distant relative stopped by Lucy's house after a day at the
pub. Unsteady on his feet, the man was distressed to the
point of tears. Unintentionally stepping on my tape re-
corder, he held me and repeatedly implored: "Help me!"
Unmoved herself, but noticing my own uncertainty as to
what exactly I should do, Lucy calmly said, "He wants you
to pray for him."

On another occasion, I spent an afternoon with Lucy in
the presence of a relative who the previous night had been
pushed around and bruised by some neighbors. The relative laid in bed just a few feet away from us during the
course of my visit. With gun in hand, he expressed a hope
that the neighbors would stop by—so that he could shoot
them! Although greatly distracting me, the man's condi-

Ben Marrowbone in front of his house, 1977.

tion moved Lucy to state her convictions with even more force.

Because Pine Ridge was violently polarized during and after the Wounded Knee occupation of 1973, Lucy felt an even more acute need to have her father's life story told completely. A current within the reservation milieu was an invocation of Black Elk's spirit as portrayed in *Black Elk Speaks,* along with an ignoring of the Black Elk of subsequent years, or the person Lucy knew as father. She felt that people, including members of the extended family, were sorely suffering from an ignorance of Black Elk's actual life-style and thinking. Her already long-standing desire to complete his biography was fanned by the flames of a social unrest she wanted to assuage.[6]

As has been clear throughout her narrative, Lucy's devotion to the Catholic tradition of her father was ardent.

Hoping that her father's work for the church would not be forgotten, and revealing a discouragement that was perhaps similar to what he felt in later life, Lucy concluded her recollections:

The past couple of years I've been shocked to hear people say that my father never actually believed in the Catholic religion. I know they're really making a mistake. So please pray that they won't spoil my father's past life and destroy his work for the church. It's really pitiful for our younger people to believe such things and have such misunderstandings about our people. Our older people came to believe in the faith. But these days I'm asked to talk about my father's older practice, and how he rejected Christianity. If I made up stories to please people, I'd be lying. And I don't want to do that. It's not what he would have wanted.

Of historical note in the final narrative below is a reference to Calico, Ben Marrowbone's uncle, who had been a prominent figure in the early reservation community. He had been an *itancan,* or "leader." On the reservation today, a small community north of Holy Rosary Mission is named Calico, after him. Tapisleca (spleen) was its original name. Ben Marrowbone offers these final reflections.

Saving your soul was important to us. That's why the Indian used to keep a relic of someone who died. It would be kept in a tepee maybe two years or four years. This was called a wanagi tipi, *or "spirit lodge." My uncle Calico had a daughter for four years, a nice girl, but she died. He kept some of her hair as a relic.*

People had to show respect for the spirit of the person who died. That relic would be kept in the tepee, and no sharp words were to be spoken in its presence. No quarreling or even loud talk was to be done in that house—because there was a spirit in there. So people respected the dead, and prayed for them. If children forgot and were noisy, or if they went into the tepee before a visitor entered, they would be scolded. Visitors might come and show respect for the relic of the dead. And if little children did not show respect for the visitors, they would afterward be told: "You are impolite . . . you have no manners."

Visiting the church was like visiting the wanagi tipi. Care for the soul and praying for the dead were not new things to us. As I said, when men like Black Elk converted, nobody said, "You fool!" My father's special friend was a screech owl, and he cured people with the screech owl's help. But when my father started to change his ways to church ways, no more screech owl. He changed his practice.

▼

chapter ten

▼

Evaluations

Kiowa scholar N. Scott Momaday has written that in *Black Elk Speaks* "we have access to a principal world view of one of the major tribes of American Indians . . . without knowing precisely where to place [the book] in our traditional categories of learning" (1984:81). Appropriately, he continues, it has been used in such disciplines as literature, anthropology, folklore, religious studies, and Native American studies. Momaday further adds that "we need not concern ourselves with labels here, any more than we need concern ourselves with the question of authorship or the quality of translation or transcription." Rather, Momaday urges us simply to recognize the book as "an extraordinary human document . . . the record of a profoundly spiritual journey, the pilgrimage of a people towards their historical fulfillment and culmination, towards the accomplishment of a worthy destiny" (31).

Momaday could have said more if the preceding chapters had been accessible to analysis. They show that the Lakota own a broader sense of self-definition than what has been popularly portrayed, and that Black Elk's "profoundly spiritual journey" entailed more than was previously revealed. Until now, the people's pilgrimage included paths not clearly charted, and this omission has significantly tailored perceptions concerning Lakota adaptation to change.

In *Black Elk Speaks* and *The Sacred Pipe*, the holy man's life addressed a broad spectrum of human concerns, and many people from around the world paid special attention to what he had to say. This widespread response suggests that his books offered something more than just an interesting study of a man's thought. Black Elk himself alluded to this "more" when he described a sacred ritual to Brown and reflected on the meaning and purpose of life itself. He tearfully observed that "some [were] not even trying to catch it" (1953:138). Momaday said that such a focus was foremost in Black Elk's thought and was essentially what constituted his appeal. Regardless of its philosophical implications, however, his life story has needed a complete telling that might make the previous work more understandable to readers far removed from an earlier Lakota milieu.

In *Black Elk Speaks*, the world received a biography that gave birth to many reprints and innumerable footnotes of opinion and commentary.[1] For the most part, Neihardt's work was read as symbolizing the life journey of the Sioux and, by extension, Native people as a whole. As the preceding chapters have shown, however, more could have been added.

This fuller portrait was sketched by persons who were closest to Black Elk. Their addition provides, as carefully as possible, a better sense of the issues and individuals who composed the cultural horizon of the postreservation period within which Black Elk and his people confronted change. A more holistic portrayal, it lengthens the script of a human drama that initially captured audiences with details that were incomplete.

As shown, Black Elk attained luminary status over the

past several decades among reading audiences as a whole, and among Native people in particular. The general public tended to revere him as an eminently praiseworthy nineteenth-century figure, and social scientists pretty much regarded his life and thought as distillations of a Plains Indian culture that is no more (Hoover 1979). His books were tapped for purposes of cross-cultural comparison and were regarded as a fairly good ethnographic index to Lakota ways of the century past.

Many readers of the Black Elk canon were gripped emotionally. They saw that conquest by whites dealt death to an entire way of life, and the holy man's moving reflections conjured up a powerful vision of those better, yet bygone, days. His compelling observations painted a portrait of extinction for the once-nomadic and proud Lakota people, who now were confined and lifeless. However, his completed biography begs a reexamination of previous material that has figured so prominently within the forging of contemporary Native identity.[2]

Because religion has played an important role within the Indian revitalization movement, Black Elk's vigorous Catholic practice might perhaps stir the most controversy. It runs contrary to what Deloria outlined in *God Is Red,* a text that rode the crest of revivalism largely because of its articulate dismissal of Christianity's relevance for Indian people. A respected social critic and a Lakota himself, Deloria wrote that in Native religion "there is no demand for a personal relationship with a personal savior. Cultural heroes are representative of community experience. They may stand as classic figures, such as Deganiwidah, Sweet Medicine, Black Elk, Smohalla, and even Wovoka" (1973:201). Black Elk's completed biography, however, shows that today's emphasis on "returning to the ways of our grandfathers" can run the risk of replicating moviedom's tendency toward romantic portrayals. A popular sentiment is tapped, but it may be more imaginative than real in reflecting what transpired a century past within the hearts and minds and struggles of the senior generation.[3] Since "grandfather's ways" were more of a search than a well-established discovery, advocates of a "return" might find themselves embracing what their forebears chose to relinquish, modify, or regard as nonessential.

Deloria also stated that "more than one Indian political organization has based its approach to modern problems on *Black Elk Speaks* (1973:51)." He further suggested the book captured what was authentically Indian. Now, however, Black Elk's last sixty years offer a more nuanced perspective on the earlier work, and some may find this later period tainted through "guilt by association" with Western ways (as Brown had said). It was during this "tainted" period, however, that the holy man's inspirational thought was recorded for posterity.

The task then remains to discern what is consistent in Black Elk's life despite the apparently conflicting portrayals. Contemporary social trends might resurrect as sacrosanct a nineteenth-century Indian identity, with the Black Elk model reigning as a favorite, but the biographies should be appraised in their totality. The derivative sketch is far more satisfying, if for no other reason than its completeness.

Framing the problem this way, a significant qualification has been put forth. The man presented here is not a disconsolate elder mourning the loss of a past forever gone. Nor is he a type of Indian "Dick the bootblack," an artificer of some new Native American dream à la Horatio Alger.

Black Elk's adult life has special merit in that it calls for a reevaluation of long-held notions concerning the adaptation of Lakota people to changing times. As indicated, Plains warrior society was itself a relatively short-lived phenomenon. And yet, a static concept of Indianness, wedded only to the nineteenth-century world, has often entrenched itself, for laypeople at least, as the beginning and end of discourse related to Native identity.

Two Leggings of the Crow, interviewed shortly before his death in 1923, epitomizes the orthodoxy that has been too readily accepted as diagnostic of the Indian world at large. Having recounted his life experiences up to 1888, Two Leggings sadly concluded: "Nothing happened after that. We just lived. There were no more war parties, no capturing of horses from the Piegans and the Sioux, no buffalo to hunt. There is nothing more to tell" (Nabokov 1967:197).

Before he died in 1932, Plenty Coups, another Crow leader, reported much the same: "When the buffalo went away the hearts of my people fell to the ground, and they could not lift them up again. After this nothing happened" (Linderman 1962:311).

While Neihardt was interviewing Black Elk, Robert Gessner tapped a similar sentiment within one of his Lakota consultants. "After Wounded Knee all ambition was taken out of us. We have never since been able to regain a foothold" (1931:417).

Such accounts poignantly tell of the cataclysmic social upheaval that Indian groups endured. They report the incalculable toll in lives and lifeways that occurred within Native America and make a euphemism out of academic writings that describe the historic period as simply a "transitional phase of culture." The accent of this literature is grim and compelling, but it errs by being overly retrospective and fatalistic—at least from the updated Black Elk's point of view. Furthermore, defining Indian resilience as little more than a museum piece overlooks the ongoing struggle of Native people in the modern world.

Lucy was largely unaware of the international interest generated by her father's life story, but she was quite attuned to local concerns. She sought to change the image of her father that younger people were beginning to construct, and she wanted known the entirety of what Black Elk spoke. Latter-day revisionists could do what they wanted with her father's books, but Lucy considered herself to be the primary source for defining where further discussion would lead. Lakota sources confirmed the account she gave, so her familial perspective was validated by the community who knew him most intimately.

Traditional Lakota identity had been ascribed to a man who lived most of his life in the twentieth century, but the greater part of his life was never reported. As legitimate as a study of his younger days might have been, it went only so far, and Lucy sought to flesh out a portrait that was heretofore incomplete. As a result, an important by-product of her effort and that of others has been to show how Lakota, before and after their reservation experience, adjusted to changing conditions.

With Black Elk's life bridging significantly distinct periods, a diachronic perspective emerges that few, if any, biographies have provided. It reveals the old culture as an adaptive one, and the holy man as typifying its essence; that is, he was flexible and responsive to the demands of changing conditions. He was neither an artifactual relic of the bison-hunting era, nor was he a prisoner to its substance, even though much literature and opinion suggest this was the case—for him and most others.

DeMallie pointed out that the previous work on Black Elk deserves criticism precisely because of its depiction of him "as more aloof and cut-off from the real world than he actually was" (1984a:124). This is an understatement that has far-reaching implications. Notably, the Black Elk model of Lakota identity has been sustained by both scholarly opinion and Native self-perception to the detriment of, among other things, his people's present-day social adjustment.

Although noted in earlier descriptions of reservation life (MacGregor 1946:26–27), the Lakota desire for a return to what is imagined as a more carefree and pristine condition has emerged with even greater force in recent years. With their sociocultural horizon limited to the more dramatic events of historical times, writers have expended much effort depicting Black Elk's people as a "warrior society" during that zenith period. It is convincingly argued that pursuing military exploits was fundamental to their corporate identity (Hyde 1937; MacGregor 1946; Hassrick 1964; Anderson 1984).

Studies that describe the anomic conditions of twentieth-century reservation life intimate that the Lakota have been disenfranchised from a most important pursuit (i.e., military adventure). Students of Indian culture then perceive the modern era as filled with sad people who mourn their inability to raise war parties or to "count coup" (and wear the associated feathers). Presumably, the social institutions of the past drew their lifeblood from this central activity, and with it gone, the Lakota are reduced to a lingering depression, a grueling and tortuous assimilation, or perhaps (many hope) a new cultural synthesis somehow congruent with a more "glorious" past.

Most of the literature (and folk opinion) has used this terminology either directly or indirectly when referring to Black Elk's people. (It is a warrior astride his mount in the famous *End of the Trail* sculpture.) A review of Lakota culture, however, shows that "warrior society" (and the associations it evokes) is misleading. Now reduced to a commonly shared vernacular, the designation seems explanatory but is not, in fact, as illuminating as it suggests.[4] An undue emphasis has prevailed that the Black Elk biography tempers.

The Lakota ascent to what has been called their Plains dominance was actually a hard-fought and continuous negotiation (Little Thunder n.d.). That is, the Crow, Kiowa, and other groups did not passively submit to being displaced. Rather, they fought to retain their own foothold within a buffalo-bounded ecosystem. During this process, American expansion accentuated militancy and brought prominence to such Lakota leaders as Crazy Horse, Red Cloud, and Sitting Bull. These figures surface as representatives of a long, ongoing struggle for existence that characterized the historical period. The phrase "warrior society" accurately labels an obvious aspect of Plains culture, but it does not reflect the overall systemic adaptation of the people. The economic sphere lends support to this perspective, as the short period of successful, early-reservation pastoralism is a significant indication of the Lakota willingness to forsake a contingency life-style in favor of a more predictable, less-trying mode.

Did Black Elk speak on behalf of a warrior society? Neihardt's interview material contained more militant overtones than appeared in the finished text, but these omissions did not substantially alter a sense of the nineteenth-century milieu that he described. The period was, simply, one of immense struggle marked by the violence of war. Ultimately, then, the explicative value of "warrior society" is minimal, and its relevance to contemporary Lakota can only be metaphoric, as in speaking of the people's "fight" for social justice. Two-thirds of Black Elk's life, like that of many others from his generation, was clearly a decision for alternative routes to survival.

Ethnographic evidence presents a picture quite different from the one so often portrayed by modern media or war buffs. As much as Ruth Hill's best-seller *Hanta Yo* (1979) was criticized, it at least showed how lifeways of the nineteenth-century *gradually* came to be. The Lakota did not just one day decide that social status would be commensurate with coup counts. Sex roles did not become fixed so as to assure success in battle, and nomadism was not imperative because of a newfound equine "technology." Terminology of this nature has tended to distance readers from the actual minds and hearts of Lakota individuals who struggled to survive. The prereservation period was not, in short, free of duress. Maintaining existence via regular war parties was a cultural value that the people would relinquish willingly, should survival be negotiated by other means.

A rereading of the historical period might indeed reveal that war was a way of life, but only because the Lakota were of necessity a defense-minded people (a characteristic noted even in recent years). However, they also occupied themselves with other activities. Their defensiveness was initially not by design but because of pressure exerted upon them by other Native groups. Rather than making a preferential option for war and a military regimen, the people were simply wise enough to protect a long-sought territorial niche.

Far from being a well-oiled military machine, Lakota society maintained a posture sufficient for boundary maintenance. War exploits never required mobilization of very great numbers and in fact seem to have equaled as much or as little time spent on other activities (Two Bulls n.d.). The much-publicized victory of Little Big Horn in 1876 was a grand exception to the rule (over many years) of relatively inconsequential battles. Therefore, instead of considering the warrior element of Lakota society as somehow its essential attribute, it might better be understood as defensive in nature and as but one means of gaining social status—a cultural category subject to fluctuation and variety (One Feather n.d.). Stated in simpler terms, the taking up of arms was a necessity for the protection of kith and kin. Nonetheless, portrayal of the Lakota as an inherently hostile people no doubt lingers because of other reasons only alluded to until now.

Primarily, the United States still fought this "enemy" as recently as 1891. Shortly after this final clash, the advent of the film industry captivated the world and capitalized on America's recently defeated "savage" foes. Ever since, westerns have reinforced the tried-and-true box office draw of Sioux adversaries stalking innocent, yet brave, settlers. Such celluloid fare, and the plethora of Zane Grey or Louis L'Amour-like novels, no doubt greatly influences our national perception. Their repetitive imaging of Native people has created, both inside the classroom and out, a cultural stereotype that Indians themselves find easy to accept.

An example of how perception and reality can conflict in this regard might be seen in the Wounded Knee occupation of 1973. Occurring in the bitter cold of winter, deadly to some of its participants, and divisive of the community, the event was a severely painful experience for the reservation as a whole. Support for the occupation came from an assortment of Native people and sympathetic non-Indians because of anger and frustration arising from grievances that always seemed to go unheeded. What it measurably accomplished is difficult to say, but it has become synonymous with heroic resistance from times past (Akwesasne Notes 1974), and people present at the occupation command a certain reverence for being Wounded Knee "warriors." Fertile imaginations, after the fact, seem to have constructed a reality quite different from the original.[5]

Concurrent with Wounded Knee and its aftermath was the cult-film series featuring Billy Jack, a character who was the quintessential embodiment of an idealized warrior. The series portrayed Billy, who was an Indian, as a former Green Beret with Vietnam experience. He dispatched unfriendly whites with lethal karate kicks (an exotic martial craft apropos of exotic Indian people, so filmmakers would have audiences believe). Lakota youths and others were much entranced by the Billy Jack image; imitations of his black, brimless, beaded hat became the fashion of the day on reservations nationwide. With Billy Jack, the motion picture industry no doubt converted many viewers to the opinion that any other role model connoted a kind of genetic sellout for Indian people.[6]

The deeper truth, however, is that for over two hundred years the Lakota have had to defend themselves. In addition, one hundred years of reservation life have fostered different forms of antisocial behavior that arise largely from the hammerlock of poverty. Such responses have little to do with any kind of earlier ingrained and supposedly warrior tradition.[7]

Erik Erikson worked among the Lakota during the 1930s and addressed some of the issues raised here. He grimly reflected (correctly or not) that even if the Lakota could return to the past, their traumatic defeat and dependence would never be erased. The "psychological effects of unemployment and neurosis . . . tuberculosis, syphilis, and alcoholism" were, among other things, exacerbated when he visited them again in 1950 (1963:163). His prognosis was not very hopeful, and subsequent studies amplified the ominous forecast. They reported that children see their fathers as ineffective models, suffer from family disruption, turn to delinquency, and carry a "generalized rejection of life" (Seward 1956:230). Educational achievement was also found to be radically below that of other groups (Bryde 1966). Despite this bleak pattern, however, the Lakota remain determined to prevent it from continuing. Reservation leadership has not been blind to these issues, which itself is evidence for persons like Black Elk still playing key roles among the people.

A means proposed for the amelioration of Indian cultures in general, and Lakota culture in particular, has been a return to "tradition." Looking back at what was may seem easier to do than solving sociologically what is, but such a focus clearly does not remove all difficulties.[8] As Black Elk's life story has shown, traditions come in different forms, change over time, and compete with one another for ascendancy. His completed biography is thus an important addition to American Indian ethnohistory, since it carries discussion well beyond the staid depiction of stereotypes associated with vanquished, victimized, and "vanishing" peoples.

Langness (1965) has argued that the use of biography has not been plumbed sufficiently by anthropologists, especially since it offers a key to cultural identity that other research fails to articulate. With this comment in mind, the account here can contribute to the development of a more authentic and personalistic understanding of traditional and contemporary culture. Black Elk's completed story challenges the perhaps too facile, even though descriptive, labels and images of Indian people or the Lakota milieu (e.g., warrior society, maladaptive, acculturation, retreatism, anomie). His passage from medicine man to catechist, from horseback to motorcycle and cars, from forager to successful rancher, from buffalo subsistence to sauerkraut, and from buckskin to three-piece suits provides a more accurate picture of what it has meant, and does mean, to be a Lakota. Just as his people owned a broader definition than commonly assumed, so did Black Elk's life include all this, and more.

The special commemorative edition of *Black Elk Speaks* featured an introduction that, because of the omission of this fuller account, reinforced a theoretical misdirection that now might be amended. Namely, the author noted how Neihardt's work had "become a North American bible of all tribes" (Deloria 1979:xiii) and contended that it must be considered an essential canon of Native spirituality from which further theological reflection ought to arise. He said that the book's unanticipated popularity was what Black Elk would have wanted, and that it could serve as an alternative to Western religious thought.

Aware of its authorship problems, Deloria nonetheless gave the work his blessing because of the "transcendent truth" it spoke to all people. Also, a more congenial, culturally rooted religion could be tapped within the life story, since Black Elk represented a kind of lost legacy of religious strength.[9] Culture contact had dispossessed Indian people of everything they had formerly cherished, but Black Elk somehow had stood firm in his beliefs. Despite this popular characterization of the book (and *The Sacred Pipe*), critics have argued that the theology articulated was Neihardt's, not Black Elk's (Holler 1984b:20). When scholars adopt such contrary positions, it is difficult to determine exactly what this holy man of the earlier works actually thought.

The completed biography constitutes an addendum that clarifies these disparate types of observation. Black Elk's life prescription, if it can be so labeled, was not a call for the restoration of traditional Native rites; nor was his Christian practice a signal for renewed evangelistic endeavors among Native peoples for the sake of eradicating an older tradition's religious forms. By the same token, Christianity's importance within the holy man's life cannot be underestimated. His legacy was most succinctly stated in the words of a ninety-year-old relative who appraised her cousin's behavior and thought as follows: "He was a really good fellow. He'd preach about the Gospel. He'd say to 'bring up children according to God's laws. Only Almighty God can change the way things are!' "[10] A witness to what his life had entailed, she distrusted any further reports that time would add to his memory and angrily indicted her people by saying: "Younger ones now don't tell the truth. They never believed. People heard him but did not listen." Her forthright comments were telling. So much was implied in so little.

The Wounded Knee massacre was an event of her early childhood, while her many years were passed in residence near Manderson itself. Matriarch of both the reservation and its Catholic community, this outspoken grandmother knew her cousin to be a man who had lived through many difficult times, a man who had been the district's first and foremost catechist, and one whose "family could have taken better care of him than they did." A woman whose religious instruction was clearly the same as Black Elk's, she shared his lament that the years had devastated the people's behavior. What previously had been a reflexive, spiritual perspective on life was now, in her opinion, not much in evidence among the people.

Black Elk's life clearly encourages a renewed interest in cultural roots that would enliven religious ideology and practice. Ironically, however, when this topic is broached in modern contexts, it is often framed in terms that conflict with the experience of people like Black Elk and his cousin, themselves paragons of tradition. An unidentified speaker at the 1975 Intertribal Conference held in Alberta, Canada, illustrates this paradox. "I'm not condemning that religion that the White man was given to by God. That's *his* religion. It was given to him on another island. Us, too, we was given a way to worship the Creator on this island, but we have lost parts of it, and it's up to us to find it again, and relive it, and be Indian people again." The speaker's position is reminiscent of Brown, who said that Black Elk's Christian years were seen as compromising his Indianness. Hence, Native peoples and others have earnestly struggled to make sense of historical facts (e.g., the conversion experiences), which cannot be dismissed lightly.

Aware that elders have quite openly accommodated non-Native religious traditions, revivalists repudiate the conversion phenomenon in conciliatory terms, along the lines of what another unidentified conference speaker explained: "That's the trouble with our people. When they changed, and they believed, they believed with all their hearts. Then it's hard to bring them back to the right road. But our young people realized that they weren't on the right road. And a few of our elders realized, so they are helping us to come back to the right road."

Black Elk's participation in Christianity, and that of others from his generation, is thus evaluated as sincere, but misguided. A National Geographic film even quoted "the great Oglala Sioux holy-man Black Elk" as prophesying the sentiments expressed above—sentiments that contradict precisely what Black Elk communicated to those who knew him best. Moreover, the film's narrator attributed to Black Elk a prophecy that claimed: "The fifth generation would bring back the old ways. In the fifth generation, Indian people would begin to regain strength and pride. It is now the era of the fifth generation."[11] As authoritative as the educational film may sound, or as persuasive as its arguments ultimately might be, its use of the previous Black Elk material only perpetuates a hermeneutical problem that has been so long-standing. That is, according to the stenographic record, Black Elk actually said, "Perhaps in the sixth generation the tree will bloom as in my vision" (DeMallie 1984b:265).

The interpretation of imagery that appears in this type of literature (and its application to the present) is not, however, the exact science that the film (or other sources) might offer it to be. Contrary to what it might have intended, National Geographic did not provide much clarity as the film equivalently added Black Elk's vision to a lineage of prophetic material that has included such diverse offspring as the Bible, numerology, tarot cards, Nostradamus, and astrology. The symbolic content of these forms and now the vision, the tree, and "six generations" is inherently so diffuse that interpretive difficulties abound. Nonetheless, Black Elk's words can be used to sanction ideologies not easily associated with the person my consultants knew as father and friend.

Black Elk's life and thought can be understood more readily within the context of the religious dynamics of the early reservation. Seen in this light, his portrait of zealous catechist and discouraged elder will not remain the paradoxical profile that bars understanding. That is, much of the discussion spawned by Black Elk has focused on an either-or proposition: he was, at heart, either an old-time medicine man or one who forsook the tradition in favor of something entirely new.[12] What follows will show that neither evaluation is an appropriate framing of the issue.

DeMallie has pointed out that "effective leadership for the Lakotas shifted during the early reservation period from political to religious spheres" (1984b:23).[13] It is not surprising that this change should occur. In his study of Plains Indian religion, Schwarz noted that "the holy man has a 'vision' of the world—its nature, its history and its destiny—and a sense of humanity's place within that scheme. Through that vision, the holy man can hope to solve problems for which the tradition offers no ready-made solutions" (1981:53). It should be clear why such persons were especially prominent during the late nineteenth century. The fluid nature of Plains culture itself made it conducive for religious leadership to emerge even more significantly. As shown, it was Black Elk's abiding sense of religious mission that permitted his own meaningful adaptation to changing circumstances.

A corroborating source for this same theme can be found in the person of George Sword, Walker's multidimensional consultant and man "of marked ability with a philosophical trend far beyond the average Ogalala" (1917:59). In his unfinished autobiography, Sword disclosed that:

When I believed the Oglala Wakan Tanka was right I served him with all my powers. I became a Wicasa Wakan (holy man) . . . a pejuta wicasa (medicine man) . . . a Blotaunka (leader of war parties). . . . I was Wakiconze (civil magistrate). . . . In the war with the white people I found their Wakan Tanka the Superior . . . and have served Wakan Tanka according to the white people's manner and with all my power. . . . I joined the church and am a deacon in it and shall be until I die. I have done all I was able to do to persuade my people to live according to the teachings of the Christian ministers (159).

An Episcopalian, Sword was not unlike Black Elk and many others, who, as MacGregor pointed out, "translated Christianity into the Dakota [sic] way of life"—interpreting it in terms of their previous religious experience (1946:102). Combined with traditions that had evolved earlier, this experi-

ence included (from their most immediate past) the Ghost
Dance, which was itself an import that they received and
accommodated. Here, the religious lens through which the
Lakota viewed existence was circumspect in that an inventory
of things supernatural was open-ended. Maintaining a foothold on the Plains did not allow the luxury of parochial definitions for what was perceived as an omnipresent and awesome
fact of life, the immanence and mystery of Wakan Tanka.

Equally notable at this time was Short Bull. He and
Sword were prominent public figures who came to terms
with both the Ghost Dance and Christianity and who, like
Black Elk, verify the normative role these types of persons
played as religious leaders confronting change.[14] Theirs
was a challenge, as Overholt described, "to put/keep the
world together, and as such was fraught with ambiguity"
(1978:190–91). It should be kept in mind, however, that
survival on the Plains was filled with this ambiguity long
before the reservation period. Hence, the role of the holy
men ought to be seen as long-standing within the tradition
and not just a creation of these more recent times.

Steinmetz classified tradition and innovation as it per-
tained to religion under two labels: Lakota Ecumenist I and
II (1980). The former refers to those who practice the old
and the new traditions separately, while the latter are those
who work to integrate them in some way. Disputing Black
Elk's classification within the second category, Holler argued that the holy man was clearly a traditionalist for
Neihardt and Brown, a dutiful Catholic while employed as
a catechist (1984a:41). Steinmetz's reading of Black Elk's
experience stressed an integration that was largely unconscious (1980:159), while Holler sought to establish the holy
man as a proponent for the practice of traditional rites.
Neither evaluation, however, takes fully into account the
cultural landscape within which Black Elk lived. In this
discussion, it is necessary to realize that life-style and religious practice were not distinct spheres.

The Lakota world of the late nineteenth century was characterized by upheavals that radically altered the people's manner of life. It was during this period that Black Elk was born and raised. Formative in his and the people's experience were such cultural cornerstones as the vision quest, the Sun Dance, nomadism, and the buffalo hunt. Sitting Bull's surrender in 1881, however, marked the end of the nomadic way, sealing once and for all the reservation system still in place today. The last great buffalo hunt was held the following year, and this ushered in a new economy that, ever since, has amounted to some form of subsistence based on government rationing.

Where success, power, and the virtuous life could come from Wakan Tanka through the vision quest, this avenue was gradually sealed off by a variety of measures imposed by the reservation's superintendent. Certain customs were outlawed (notably, the Sun Dance), children were made to leave home and then board at government schools (some, like Ben Black Elk, were taken to Carlisle, Pennsylvania), and sodalities that formerly flourished gradually lost their significance. In fact, reservation-born youth came into a world quite different from that of their parents. Those who rallied around the Ghost Dance of 1890 were, in all probability, the last to have experienced a vision quest that was independent of agency concern, or a Sun Dance that symbolized and reinforced group solidarity.

Witness to and participant in this unfolding drama, Black Elk embodied traditional Lakota ideology as he manifested a resilient willingness to let go of what was and to experiment with what might be the disclosures of Wakan Tanka for his life. Like others similarly situated, he traveled overseas and endured whatever unknowns such a venture entailed. Disillusioned there, he listened to reports of a messiah and, again like others, embraced the new hope offered by ghost dancing.

Where Linton would call participation in the Ghost

Dance an irrational flight from reality (1943), and where Mooney would call it a response to recent and long-standing grievances (1896), persons like Black Elk were willing adherents, owing to a well-conditioned, culturally based disposition toward seeking the power of Wakan Tanka on whatever new horizon it might appear. Earlier in life, while with the Wild West Show in England, Black Elk wrote: "All along I live remembering God. . . . [T]he show runs day and night . . . but all along I live remembering God *so he enables me to do it all*. . . . I know the White man's customs well. One custom is very good. Whoever believes in God will find good ways—that is what I mean" (DeMallie 1984b:8, italics added).

Upon returning to Pine Ridge in 1889, Black Elk again recounted his experiences and once more revealed a religious questing that was thematic to his life. "Of the White man's many customs, only his faith, the White man's beliefs about God's will, and how they act according to it, I wanted to understand. . . . So Lakota people, trust in God! Now all along I trust in God" (DeMallie 1984b:9–10). Nearly twenty years later, now working as a catechist, Black Elk echoed these same sentiments, which had guided him through so much. His letter of October 20, 1907, in *Sinasapa Wocekiye Taeyanpaha* says:

There I met with the White people in a meeting, and I was really glad that I have heard and seen with my own eyes the things they are doing. And we should do the same thing here, but it is very hard for us to do the things that the White people are doing because we have very few things to work with. But again, we must depend on God to help us. My friends and relatives I speak to you from the bottom of my heart. Please try and do the things that we're supposed to do. Let us not forget the main person—that is, Wakan Tanka.

The worldview represented here is a spiritual approach

to life in which religious thought dictates behavior. Lakota holy men like Black Elk were the more visible representatives of this process, but a comparable disposition lay within the population as a whole. Lakota society was not at a loss in surfacing and affirming religious leadership roles, which proliferated within the emerging denominations.

Linton stated that movements such as the Ghost Dance arose during the acculturative process, when exploitation and frustration are experienced by a dominated people (1943). According to Mooney's thesis, the Ghost Dance was only a symptom and expression of the real causes of dissatisfaction that had been growing among the Lakota (1896). Valid as these observations might be, they simply represent a phenomenological description of the more apparent conditions of the early reservation social milieu. Black Elk's completed biography, however, illuminates the "cognitive map" that guided people like himself *past* the Ghost Dance and into still another mode of adaptation, namely, active participation within an organized denomination of Christianity, along with the acculturation such participation included.

Like others of his generation, Black Elk had been a respected religious practitioner, and when such persons affiliated with Christian sects, their following did not turn a deaf ear on this already-established leadership. As Lucy herself stated, the missionaries seemed to look for such persons. People received the assuring presence of their own religious specialists—many of whom, it appeared, were successfully discerning a new course that seemed to have the blessing of Wakan Tanka. Regardless of affiliation, the holy men were bridges of adaptation who strove to lead the people into new regions of experience. Their fundamental role was to preserve and foster a religious consciousness that had so long enabled the people to confront whatever challenged them.[15]

Essentially, when people like Black Elk or Sword, Fills

the Pipe, or Black Fox strove to lead their people into the twentieth century, their role as new-order holy men served the people well, providing a self-direction that was elsewhere very difficult to experience. This self-direction, a kind of vision quest gone communal, explains in large part why denominational affiliations became so widespread and important during the early reservation period. External conditions could drastically change and be controlled or manipulated by non-Lakota agents, but the people's internal environment was theirs to determine.[16] Missionaries seem to have spoken a religious language that was comprehensible to the holy men. The latter, in turn, translated the new revelation to a following who trusted their discernment.

Discussion of such a process becomes fruitless when attempts are made to quantify Christian accretions or Lakota residues, and conscious or unconscious reconstructions. Theological speculation, if it can be called that, has been shown in Black Elk's life to happen as instinctive, or as a matter of course, when he spoke with priests or other catechists, or with anyone who broached the topic. Neihardt and Brown were simply the first to report, in print, the thoughts of a man whose life had long been given to such reflection. Among the more recent examples, Fools Crow's biography is additional evidence of this same pattern at work.[17]

A case has been made for viewing *The Sacred Pipe* as Black Elk's Lakota counterpoint to Catholic sacraments—a kind of compromising syncretism being the result. However, the holy man's disposition was not so narrow.[18] He did not seem to have felt "the need of coordinating and systematizing . . . beliefs as strongly as we do" (Durkheim 1965:193). The early Black Elk material might suggest this kind of analysis, but his more comprehensive portrait advises analytical restraint. That is, the holy man did not embrace Christian practices only insofar as they matched traditional constructs. Nor did his Christian perspective divorce him from the essentials of Lakota spirituality for in fact there was only one essential to maintain: namely, searching for and reliance upon Wakan Tanka in the everyday course of events.

MacGregor's sociological study of Pine Ridge provides a fruitful perspective on issues that bore upon Black Elk toward the end of his life. Importantly, his work illuminates the social context within which Neihardt and Brown found the holy man; that is, his research was undertaken during the years *between* visitations by the authors. Most pertinent is MacGregor's comment on religious practice. "Christian Churches too appear to be losing some of their former hold as . . . many Indians are now following the trend of the local white population away from control by the Church" (1940:103).

Residents of Pine Ridge, although removed from mainstream America, were not insulated from the secularizing forces of the dominant society. World War II contributed to this trend by drawing large numbers into the armed forces, while relocation programs similarly expanded Lakota experience. Such in outline was the unfolding social scene that Black Elk witnessed. Not only did many people have a loose hold on traditional religious forms, but they were also showing laxity in their practice of the Christian or, indeed, any way.

Black Elk's reprimand in later life of the Manderson Catholic community reveals the kind of discouragement he endured as an elder. Far from being an acknowledgment of his erroneous Catholic practice, *The Sacred Pipe* was simply another attempt to rally his people's religious fervor by whatever means were at his disposal. Earlier in life he respected the Thin Elk decision to resume traditional participation and to discontinue Christian practice—not because he felt their choice was theologically more sound or because he was indifferent to their concerns or because he was vacillating in his own commitment. Important to Black

Elk was the quest itself. Whereas his destiny was that of a
Catholic catechist, others might pursue alternate paths.
The Thin Elk decision, because it was apparently rooted in
sincerity, was a journey upon which he could bestow his
blessing. By contrast, the elder Black Elk seems to have
been discouraged by so many people abandoning a trek in
any direction.

Evaluations of what actually transpired when Christianity encountered Native religious practice are sometimes
puzzling, as in the case of Grobsmith's ethnography on the
Rosebud Lakota. She cites, for example, the "popular notion . . . that Catholic missionaries were cruel and patronizing to the Indians" (1981:83) and suggests, via MacGregor
(1946:92), that the early reservation period can be sum-
marily regarded as a time when "missionaries created resistance by trying to eradicate the native religion instead of
using it as a frame of reference in which to introduce Christianity. They attempted to impose Christian morality by
suppressing Indian custom. . . . They tried to drive out in-
discriminately Indian ways which had no relation to religion
in the Indian mind." She admits, however, that "there is
also clear evidence that the church in general and the clergy
in particular devoted great efforts toward assisting the
Sioux during the most harrowing period in their history."
Her conclusion is that "succeeding generations made . . .
their peace with Christianity" and that it is surprising "the
high degree to which Christianity has been assimilated into
native life . . . considering its low acceptance initially"
(1981:83).

Such interpretations are difficult to understand. Maybe
the abundance of catechists disproves what is assumed to
be a "low acceptance" of Christianity among the people.
Perhaps the popular notion about "cruel and patronizing"
Catholic missionaries is mistaken, for why did succeeding
generations bother to "make peace" in light of such a history?

Representatives of the different denominations no doubt

had many varied encounters with many varied individuals within diverse contexts. As Prucha has pointed out: "A variety of white settlers, agents, soldiers, and missionaries created a complex web of relationships that is almost impossible, in this latter day, to disentangle. All that one person can reasonably be expected to do is to investigate particular groups, aspects, or activities, a few at a time, with the hope that each study will contribute to a better understanding of the whole." (1988:130). This complexity is perhaps why Grobsmith cautions those who might rely too heavily on one evaluation of so complex an interaction:

History . . . will reveal the very deep if ambivalent relationship between the Indians and the church and the secure place the church occupies in most people's lives. . . . Although missionaries may have capitalized on a situation ideal for introducing a new religion, the Indian people recognized that those missionaries were not themselves to blame for the changes; on the contrary, their sympathetic assistance was deeply appreciated and still is to this day. . . . It is common for the non-Indian outsider to regard Christianity as alien to the Indian. But, in fact, nearly all Lakota are Christians, even those who are also active in native ritual. For the Indian people themselves, the church is an integral and important institution in Lakota society. (1981:82, 86)[19]

The content of the above citation is reflected in Black Elk's life. Given the paucity of such encompassing biographies as his, the non-Indian outsider, some Native people themselves, and knowledgeable others may not be aware of this broader perspective.

The previous focus on Black Elk's early Lakota formation deserves qualification because it does not adequately reflect the social system that now has been long in place among his people—a social system with which he was quite familiar. As a result, the holy man of Neihardt and Brown cannot enlighten cultural discourse in quite the same way as before. During my relationship with Lucy, however, a series of incidents occurred that tended only to reinforce the earlier, incomplete portrayal of Black Elk's life.

I was invited to attend a special picnic the family had planned. Christopher Sergel, a New York playwright, had composed a work based on *Black Elk Speaks,* and he thought it important that his lead (actor David Carradine) and entourage visit Black Elk's surviving relatives. Included with the group was John Neihardt's daughter, Hilda, who served as the expedition's photographer.

Familiar with Carradine's popular television series "Kung Fu," the younger members of the family were quite excited to be hosting such a celebrity. Their enthusiasm was contagious, since the older folk decided to slaughter a cow for this special occasion (no small thing for people who were quite destitute). Ironically, this special gesture of Lakota hospitality was not mentioned by anyone, and so their sacrifice went unnoticed by the featured guest, who, it turned out, was a practicing vegetarian.

The playwright and his wife comported themselves as grateful guests, amicably chatting with everyone they met. They seemed to relish the contrast of this occasion with what they probably knew back home in an urban environment. Hilda, meanwhile, moved about getting photographs of the visitors mixing with Lucy's family. The actor's three-year old son, Free, played with other children who also were present. Except for a brief demonstration of his skill in the martial arts, Carradine kept a low profile and responded to the occasional question directed his way. He did so, that is, until deciding to take a swim in the swollen creek nearby.

Perhaps assuming his hosts customarily disrobed for such purposes with little attention to anyone present, Carradine casually stripped and strode into the water for a swim. At Lucy's request, the older children hurriedly rounded up the young ones and, eyes averted, provided the actor with the privacy ordinarily expected for swimming of this nature.

The romantic literature often leads readers to believe that this was the way "natural" people go about swimming, so I could appreciate how people of goodwill might unwittingly violate custom. But all this transpired quickly, and everyone's attention was diverted to something new that unfolded.

One of the visitors suggested that Lucy be pictured presenting a pipe to the actor. Directed to an open space, Lucy was positioned upright as Carradine (now clothed) fell to his knees, arms outstretched, in front of her. Repeatedly corrected by younger family members as to how one should hold the pipe for such a pose, Lucy was finally photographed. A kind of dramatic passing on of her father's spiritual legacy was thus staged, the photos of which perhaps were used later on for advertising purposes in cities far away. Immediately following Lucy's debut as pipe-holder, the guests bade farewell and drove to Rapid City in order to connect with their respective flights home.

The fruits of this encounter between Hollywood and Lucy's family ripened shortly after, and the play *Black Elk Speaks* was performed in a number of cities. *Tulsa World* columnist Danna Sue Walker reported the following on November 18, 1983:

Carradine visited the Black Elk wilderness in South Dakota with Chris Sergel, who authored the play, and with Neihardt's daughter, Hilda. . . . Carradine said the group met with Black Elk's granddaughter, Lisa Long Hill, and Lucy Looks Twice. Lisa performed the peace pipe ceremony with the three, and Carradine was made to promise he would play the part of Black Elk. The two women thought Carradine sounded much like Black Elk. [Actually, Lisa's name was Lone Hill, and she was Black Elk's great-granddaughter.]

A brochure put out by the American Indian Theatre Company also reported that "Carradine discussed *Black Elk Speaks* with Lucy Looks Twice, daughter of the holy man. She gladly gave Carradine permission to play her father in the play." Both the columnist and the brochure mentioned that plans were underway to film the production.

As early as the fall of 1976, the play had been performed, with Lisa having a small part. Lucy herself had even been flown to Washington, D.C., as an honored guest of the production. When I inquired as to how she felt about the course of events, Lucy expressed ambivalence. Extended family members were excited about involvement with the play, and Lucy too was provided with travel opportunities and attention that previously had not been part of her life. Accepting the script as simply a work based on her father's early life, she saw its importance in terms of calling attention to her people's history. She said that there was interest in the play, "since [my father] was a witness to the Wounded Knee massacre." In her opinion, the twentieth-century part of her father's life was on another level entirely and was pretty much disconnected from concerns addressed by the play. In this sense, she walked a path already pioneered by her father.

Resurrection of the nineteenth-century image of Black Elk relies heavily on its romantic appeal, and bolstering this appeal is a portrayal of the holy man as a resolute traditionalist who repudiates the alienating, technological world so foreign to his youth. Ethnic resurgence, literature, and drama provide staying power for such a characterization, and as shown, the human appetite for this type of representation seems to persist. The effort in this book, however, has been to reach a deeper understanding of how persons like Black Elk came to terms with conflict generated by the clashing of cultures.

Most of Black Elk's life was occupied with issues of the twentieth-century reservation era, and his energies were directed at concerns that still prevail today. His grieving later in life was not nativistic retreatism, for he had confronted as much as anybody and still retained "the power to live" meaningfully in a world far different from the one of his youth. The sadness he experienced was because "some [were] not even trying to catch it."

Words attributed to the holy man have been invoked to rally his people from social torpor, and application of his thought in this regard is legitimate. Black Elk was not reluctant to verbalize strongly felt sentiments, and his strategy for renewal was framed within the religious perspective. That is, challenging his people was well within his sense of mission. His prescription for adjustment was religious, with social or political agendas flowing from what he deemed foremost—a spiritual base.

Neither Brown nor Neihardt addressed the social milieu of the aging holy man. Instead, readers were presented the timeless portrait of an elder, suspended in nostalgia and melancholy, hermetically insulated from his people's twentieth-century plight. Readers were left to imagine what this social disenfranchisement entailed, as specific issues were nowhere reported. Thematic to both works is an image of nineteenth-century Sioux imprisoned within their reservation borders, waiting for, as Neihardt said, yesterday. Much more, however, needed to be stated if Black Elk's life was to be fully understood.

According to Fools Crow, the 1930s were: "the worst ten years I know of . . . because of problems caused by intoxicated people. . . . [S]uch shameful behavior. . . . [At a gathering of holy-men] we discussed many things, but in the end concluded that the solution was not in our hands, that all we could do for the moment was to fall back on our prayers" (Mails and Chief Eagle 1979:148–49). This meeting of native holy men, which included Black Elk, is central to understanding what undergirded their worldview. Strategies for social change came after, or flowed from, a religious foundation.

A Sioux social worker commented upon the high alcoholism rate at Pine Ridge (80–95 percent), and her discouragement is a kind of updated Black Elk, who, during his own life, witnessed the problem arise.[20] The social worker's observation is cited merely for the purpose of conveying a sense of the holy man in practical terms—minus the generalized symbols and images of his persona in *Black Elk Speaks* and *The Sacred Pipe*. The issue addressed here is one that he knew well, and the holy men tried to avert its spread by resolutely steering their energy in the direction they considered to be of foremost importance. The social worker commented that:

People still sit around crying about how it's all the white man's fault for bringing us firewater. Well, five generations later, we better start taking some responsibility ourselves— because we are committing self-genocide, breeding a new generation of idiots. If it keeps up at this rate, 50 years from now there won't be a Sioux on the reservation who can think straight even if he is sober. (Talbert 1986:9B).[21]

Nothing as pointed as the above appears in Black Elk quotations, and as a result, room has been left for interpreting him in broad, humanistic or nativistic terms. Such were, however, the kinds of concerns that confronted and discouraged him in later life, to which he applied his religious solution. Essentially, Black Elk was a social critic who derived his own strength and inspiration from the Lakota-Catholic religious sphere and who, in turn, used that framework to challenge his people unto renewal. As early as 1907, he was aware that his task of fostering and maintaining this religious consciousness would not be easy. A March 15 letter of his reads in part: "I spoke mainly on Jesus—when he was on earth, the teachings and his sufferings. I, myself, do a lot of these things. I suffer, and I try to teach my people the things that I wanted them to learn, but it's never done. . . . [Y]ou know when one sheep is surrounded with wolves, it has no place to go. That's how we are. We are ready to be eaten up" *(Sinasapa Wocekiye Taeyanpaha)*. Black Elk's life and thought were indeed consistent with the leitmotif of Lakota culture and the basic spiritual posture its holy men tried to preserve.

Religious practice played an important, perhaps underestimated role within the strategies of adaptation to life on the Plains.[22] It had served the people well. With multifaceted changes accosting Pine Ridge, Black Elk had little else to offer as a life-giving alternative.

With the gradual loss of this reflexive religious disposition, Lakota culture was truly undergoing a major modification. As Mekeel's study noted after the Neihardt visit, "oriented by the particular times of their childhood and early youth, people born in different eras of Pine Ridge history [held] widely differing attitudes" (1935:5). Primary among these differences were religious practice and the Lakota religious perspective toward life itself. Religion had been something far more than just an aspect of culture for this people. It was instrumental in nurturing their ability to confront change. Black Elk's life clearly demonstrates this, as he represented a senior generation for whom "the Sacred [was] not an epiphenomenon, or secondary expression of reality; it [was] the deepest aspect of reality" (Grim 1983:4).

Given this new understanding of Black Elk, further inquiry can be carried forth in many directions. How, for example, did denominations within Christianity effectively communicate their doctrines to the Lakota (and other groups)?[23] To what extent were Native practitioners at odds with, or compliant to, the teachings administered by different denominations? In what specific ways did governmental agencies impede or promote the varying denominational agendas? What was the recidivism rate of medicine men who became church leaders, and why did this occur? What social factors challenged, as never before, the long-standing Lakota reliance on the sacred (however defined)? And how is this reliance, or basic approach to life, evident today, despite pressures that militate against it? Such are the types of questions embedded within the completed portrait of Black Elk. Nonetheless, as important and intriguing as such considerations might be, the over-riding concern here has been to set forth an examination of Black Elk's life that is empirically verifiable.

Readers of the earlier Black Elk material were left to ponder the complexity of the holy man. In the end, however, his life and thought are fairly straightforward. Those who have chosen instead to hunt for something more sublime will, as before, never catch it.

Lucy (Black Elk) Looks Twice modeling Lakota
powwow shawl, moccasins, beaded earrings, and
medallion, 1975.

▼

▼

Epilogue

Lucy Looks Twice, the last surviving child of Black Elk, died on April 23, 1978. She was consoled to know that the content of her father's thought had been captured in these pages.

Lucy was ill for a long time before she died, and on several occasions I confided that her passing would leave a void in my life. I encouraged her to hold out against the ravages of infirmity. So much had been exchanged during our visits. Many persons, places, and thoughts were raised in conversation by me, an inquisitive grandchild from a far different background, with her, a reassuring grandmother who tempered my emotion and concerns with a wisdom that conveyed solace.

To a great extent, the accounts here have filled that anticipated void, for they are a legacy telling of the infinite woven within the finite concerns of everyday Lakota, and indeed all, human life. As such, Lucy, her father, and his friends still speak. They do so to readers still en route to the land of many lodges.

▼

▼

Notes

Preface

1. "Lakota," the preferred term today, is linguistically more precise than the word "Sioux," but the latter is still used. See chapter 1 for a full discussion of this nomenclature.

2. Although its pagination differs from that of the two earlier editions, the Pocket Book reprint of *Black Elk Speaks* (1972) is cited in this text because for some time it has been commonly available to readers. References to this edition are abbreviated as *BES*.

3. Although translations of Wakan Tanka vary, "Great Spirit" is the one most commonly heard (today interchangeable with "God"), a supernatural creator-figure perceived as the source of all power.

4. The charge has been made that Neihardt, a nationally acclaimed poet, embellished Black Elk's observations—as Sally McClusky (1972), among others, has indicated. DeMallie's publication of Neihardt's field notes (1984b) helped clarify this issue, but *Black Elk Speaks* still remains a classic description of the Oglala worldview.

5. Powers appropriately titled an article "When Black Elk Speaks, Everybody Listens" (1990), as the following citations suggest. Norman Perrin, a biblical scholar at the University of Chicago, drew upon Black Elk for purposes of cross-cultural comparison vis-à-vis New Testament writers (1974). Willoya and Brown invoked the holy-man to support their doc-

trine of a universal religion (1962). Steinmetz (1980), after Duratschek (1974), argued that the holy-man exemplifies a phase in the evolution of theological reflection. Vine Deloria, Jr. argued that "God is Red" (1969), Black Elk articulating a pan-Indian spirituality quite distinct from notions associated with "white" religion. Sculptor Marshall M. Fredericks honored Black Elk with a bronze monument, and F. W. Thomsen depicted the holy man's vision on a memorial tower overlooking Dana College in Blair, Nebraska. Poet Donna Duesel de la Torriente produced *Bay Is The Land (To Black Elk)* (1982), a work claiming to be "an astounding proclamation made by a white American about the long-awaited dream of Black Elk." Leanin' Tree and Sunrise Publications (who accent their work with a "back-to-nature" motif) likewise peppered their products with quotations from the holy man. Where psychologist Carl Jung theorized about and directly referred to Black Elk (1970:206), novelist Thomas Berger was more covert. Readers of his *Little Big Man* (1964) (and viewers of the subsequent motion picture) were entranced by the story's pivotal character, Old Lodge Skins—a pseudonym, it seems, for Black Elk à la Neihardt. Such gnosticism was not required in 1979 when actor David Carradine was cast in the lead role of a largely fictionalized Black Elk. David Humphreys Miller produced two books (1957, 1959) that describe the Ghost Dance and Custer's fate from the viewpoint of Indian witnesses, the holy man being one of his key consultants. Hassrick's standard ethnography of the Sioux (1964) notes Brown and Neihardt as basic resources, while a contemporary analysis of Oglála religion (Powers 1974) cites the Black Elk material as authoritative. Moon's 1982 best-seller *Blue Highways*, a first-person account of traveling across modern America, noted *Black Elk Speaks* as a kind of intimate, literary traveling companion. Kehoe's study of the Ghost Dance (1989) devoted an entire chapter to the holy man's key role within contemporary revitalization efforts. Although not related to the patriarch, Wallace Black Elk no doubt caught the reading public's eye in 1990 with his handsome volume, ambiguously entitled *Black Elk*, which contained the religious perspective of this modern-day "shaman." Anthropologist William Lyon suggested (incorrectly, as later will be shown) that readers could regard Wallace as representing his namesake's spiritual legacy. Other books and articles (e.g., Capps 1976; Tedlock & Tedlock 1975), too numerous to list here, simply echo what this summary suggests. Finally, *Black Elk Speaks* has been published in German, Flemish, Dutch, Italian, Danish, Serbo-Croatian, Swedish, and Spanish.

6. For years, Ben was known as the "other face" on Mount Rushmore because of his popularity there with tourists. Ben had also appeared in motion pictures. This Black Elk, the media favorite, was the man some associated with books. *Healing of Memories* by Dennis and Matthew

Lynn (1974) quotes *The Sacred Pipe* and in a footnote does, in fact, erroneously attribute authorship to Ben.

7. Gretchen Bataille's article "Black Elk—New World Prophet" quotes Neihardt saying the holy man was "kind of a preacher"—an ambiguous rendering of what Neihardt meant and of Black Elk's style (1984:139). He was not "preachy," as such a reference might imply.

8. The title of *Black Elk's Story* (Rice 1991) probably captivates readers like the aforementioned (and equally misleading) *Black Elk* (Lyon and Black Elk 1990), this "armchair ethnology" being an example of just such speculation.

9. Holy Rosary Mission, founded by the Jesuits in 1888, continues today as a major educational institution of the Pine Ridge Reservation. Calling an older person grandmother or grandfather is a respectful gesture in Lakota tradition. This practice will surface again in a consideration of Lakota prayer that begins "Tunkashila Wakan Tanka," or "Grandfather Great Spirit." Similarly, in treaty gatherings, the president of the United States was referred to as grandfather. Chapter 1 discusses the importance of kin term usage among the Lakota.

10. Over the course of time, smaller grandchildren repeatedly—and delightfully—interrupted my visits, despite the seclusion of the pine bough shade.

11. Wallace Black Elk (cited earlier in reference to his book) was active with the American Indian Movement's occupation of Wounded Knee in 1973, and I assumed he was related in some way to Lucy's father. I inquired about his identity and was emphatically told that Wallace was no relation. The Black Elk name was regularly in the news during this very difficult time, and so Lucy was all the more anxious to have her father's life reported in its entirety (and not have his name confused with anyone else's). Curiously, William Lyon refers to the senior holy-man as Nick and to his contemporary coauthor as Black Elk—a form of address not employed by Lakota of the modern era (even though stereotypes would suggest otherwise).

12. Lucy's bias, if it could be called that, was simply to tell what she knew about her father's life. Whatever she reported (apart from family matters) was corroborated by Black Elk's former acquaintances.

chapter one
▼
Lakota Culture

1. The Algonquian word may have carried the more generic meaning "enemy" (Gallatin 1836). Others, meanwhile, have proposed that the word was derived from the French *sou* (or *sous*), a coin of minimal worth (again, a caricature of the people).

2. While practicing my Lakota vocabulary, I was corrected by a young person who said I was mispronouncing certain words—whereupon I was introduced to the Dakota dialect with my *l*'s replaced by the person's *d*'s. I was reminded of Lucy's experience as a child when she returned from Marty, South Dakota, and was teased for speaking with a slightly different accent. (See chapter 5, in which Lucy says: "I talked like a Yankton.")

3. Prairie/woodland people also refer to "council fires," so the metaphor may date back to when the ancestors of the Lakota lived in the eastern forests. The Assiniboine formerly were associated with the Nakota but split from this group during the early historical period. Henceforward they were referred to as rebels.

4. Although Plains cultures are frequently referred to as buffalo cultures, many non-Indian (and even Indian) peoples would be hard-pressed to elaborate the specifics listed here. Clearly, more than a source of food was lost with the disappearance of this animal (Dary 1974; *Wind River Rendezvous* 1983).

5. Later religious practice often aligned itself with the different camp memberships.

6. Lucy did not know these people, who were friends of her brother, Ben.

7. Place-names in Ontario, Canada, include the word "Sioux" (e.g., Sioux Lookout, Sioux Narrows) and are associated with this more eastern origin. Apart from the "emergence myth" origin story, one (perhaps of less antiquity) tells of a long journey from the banks of an eastern body of salt water (presumably the Atlantic Ocean) to a region with large bodies of fresh water (the Great Lakes) where bark lodges were erected (the early historical, woodland period).

8. Lucy's courtship and marriage in the 1920s still generally reflected the traditions reported here (see chapter 7).

9. In light of this cultural vocabulary, Catholic references to Fathers, Sisters, Brothers, and God's children resonated well with Lakota listeners (see chapter 4). This cornerstone of the Lakota worldview is detailed here because of implications related to "belonging" within the new world of twentieth-century reservation life. "Making relatives" (i.e., creating "fictive" kin) was too important to be restricted by skin color, and so this "familializing" of others accompanied the people into the contact period (and beyond).

10. Throughout the chapters that follow, individuals are periodically referred to by kin terms on the basis of the system described here and not necessarily, as one might assume, on bloodline (i.e., consanguinity).

11. In the midst of a face-off between Crazy Horse's people and the army, one of the former confronted the latter by riding up, warbonnet in place, and stopping the column. In what would appear to be a very tense moment, the rider said: "Let's dismount and have a smoke. Even a man about to die

takes time to smoke" (i.e., partakes in a religious observance). Cf. Clark 1976:63.

chapter two
▼
Genealogy

1. Lucy's account might be regarded as an early twentieth-century experience of traditional Lakota "camp life" described in chapter 1.

2. This same information is given in *Black Elk Speaks* (53); page 199, however, mentions only one brother and one sister. "Give me eighty men and I would ride through the whole Sioux nation" was the boast of Captain William J. Fetterman before his command's annihilation on December 21, 1866, near Fort Phil Kearny in Montana. This so-called Fetterman Massacre is what Lucy refers to as the "battle of the one hundred slain"—the old Lakota way of describing this incident of Red Cloud's War (1866–68). The now-controversial Fort Laramie Treaty ended this conflict, as the United States was forced to accede to Lakota demands and withdraw from the Powder River country (Hebard and Brininstool 1922; Howard 1968; Hyde 1937; Olson 1965; Vestal 1932). For the past hundred years, a claim to the Black Hills was pressed by different Lakota groups, and a judgment was finally rendered on their behalf. Instead of the monetary settlement offered, some of the people insist upon a return of the land itself, which has prompted further litigation.

3. E.g., Black Elk's father (DeMallie 1984b:102), Lucy's half-brothers (13), and Black Elk's second wife (23). William and John were given the birth names of Never Showed Off and Good Voice Star, respectively; cf. Pine Ridge census rolls, 1893, 1896, and 1901 (National Archives and Records Service, Record Group 75, Microcopy M595, rolls 365, 367, and 368). The baptismal records of Holy Rosary Mission also contain such information along with occasional comments inscribed by the priests.

4. Mainline Christian denominations today, especially Roman Catholicism after Vatican II, express orthodoxy in ways different than in Black Elk's time. Curiously, the institutional model of Black Elk's Catholicism, which was more formalist than personalistic in its ritual and teachings, seems to have had a persuasive appeal that many adherents of later years did not appreciate as readily as Black Elk did.

5. The addition Lucy might be referring to is discussed in chapter 6.

6. Neihardt's terminology is at variance with this usage in the sense that Black Elk's designation as *pejuta wicasa* was more apt for the period covered in *Black Elk Speaks*. That is, the subtitle should have referred to Black Elk as a medicine man, not a holy man.

7. *The Sixth Grandfather* reports Black Elk saying that Kills the Enemy

was named One Side because of "his hair being cut on one side," and that ever since appearing this way in Black Elk's vision, he has been "One Side" (235). DeMallie mentions that Neihardt minimized "the imagery of warfare and killing" in the finished text (1984b:53), which could be another reason for avoiding the name "Kills the Enemy." Warrior hairstyles of the historic period could be the inspiration of such a name, but a more likely explanation might be found in Riggs's mention of an "antinatural" force or entity behind the *heyoka* practice. According to Riggs, "He is represented as a little old man with a cocked hat on his head"—a description exactly matching how Kills Enemy comported himself (quoted in Buechel 1970:174), a behavior quite consistent with Kills Enemy's long-standing *heyoka* identity.

8. Black Elk may have chosen his daughter's name as a devotion to Saint Lucy, whose name means "light." Within Catholic tradition, her assistance is sought by those having eye trouble.

9. In a 1991 interview, medicine man Pete Catches said, "There are a lot of fake medicine men . . . they have no power, no sacred reason, no spiritual contact" (Jeltz 1991). See chapter 4 for a discussion of Pete's religious practice.

10. See also Del Barton's novel *A Good Day to Die* (1980). The 1990 motion picture *Flatliners,* a film dealing with life-after-death experiences, begins with one of its characters saying, "Today is a good day to die," which further illustrates the continued currency of Black Elk material.

chapter three
▼
Conversion

1. Visiting Black Elk's coworker stirred sadness within me, and I felt a great deal of sympathy for the old man. As with Lucy, for example, a kind of kinship developed when, over time, she addressed me as *takoja* (grandchild). Similarly, with John, calling him "grandfather" seemed very natural soon after our visit began.

2. Jesuit history attributes the Lakota invitation to Pine Ridge and Rosebud as part of a tradition related to DeSmet's revered stature among the people. Critics of this interpretation argue that the Lakota request had nothing to do with religion but was actually a political ploy. That is, since the government had given jurisdiction of Pine Ridge to the Episcopalian church, the insistence upon Jesuit presence was simply a form of Lakota resistance in the guise of religion. Lucy mentioned that her father respected Red Cloud because of his decision to request Jesuits, and for his "choosing the 'Blackrobes' to teach the children of his people."

3. These archives will hereafter be noted as MACIM. They contain the

diaries cited, the Sialm citations, the *Indian Sentinel,* and the missionary newspaper *Sinasapa Wocekiye Taeyanpaha.*

4. According to Holy Rosary Mission's baptismal records, the famous Chief Red Cloud was christened "Peter," since he was, as Christianity says of the apostle Peter, first in rank among his people.

5. C. M. Weisenhorn wrote an obituary for Lindebner (on file at the Marquette Archives) that reported the following: "Towards the very end, he seemed to have forgotten every language but that of his apostolic labors and he spoke and prayed only in Lakota Sioux. 'Maria omakigago! Wakantanka imacuwo!' "Mary help! Lord take me!"

6. Forty-one band-derived communities were located on the Pine Ridge Reservation in 1935.

7. Given Lindebner's fluency in Lakota, it is questionable whether he addressed Black Elk in English on this occasion.

8. DeMallie (1984b:10) mentioned that Black Elk was baptized Episcopalian (at least nominally) as early as 1886, a requirement for participation in Buffalo Bill Cody's traveling show.

9. William Lyon, coauthor of *Black Elk,* states he has reason to believe otherwise (1990:xiii), though gives no evidence. Exegesis of the earlier Black Elk material has been open-ended and thus has permitted assertions such as these.

10. Raised within the Catholic tradition, I was not inspired when I heard the story and was perplexed by information that seemed contradictory. That is, I knew of the high regard bestowed by older Lakota upon many of the first-generation Jesuits, and yet this type of confrontational interaction did not seem very endearing.

11. Sialm's diary (no. 54) reported an experience Black Elk had with Lindebner that captured both the priest's style and one of the reasons why the catechist held him in such high regard. Black Elk said: "We were three men at the little church at Potato Creek. Father Lindebner cooked for us three with his little stove. He could cook for only one man at a time. First he cooked and gave it to me. Then he cooked for the second man. And lastly he cooked for himself."

12. Father Zimmerman's obituary for Black Elk in the October 1950 issue of the *Indian Sentinel* recounted his understanding of the holy-man's conversion in the following fashion: "Finally, the ice was broken. [He] became curious about the new religion, then interested, and at length professed his willingness to . . . be baptized" (102). A similarly unextraordinary course of events was reported by John Lone Goose, who said that Sam Kills Brave's entreaty simply led Black Elk to receive instruction from Father Aloysius Bosch, S.J., and that his lessons occurred at Manderson during the priest's frequent visits.

Certain persons, events, and interpretations within *The Sixth Grand-*

father do not match the accounts provided here. Where DeMallie reports that Black Elk's medicine practice "quickly brought him into conflict with the missionaries," Lucy said her father did not meet any Jesuits until his conversion. DeMallie also relates that Black Elk told Neihardt "that once, when he was performing a ceremony, a Jesuit priest arrived and destroyed the sacred objects he used in his curing. The patient recovered, but the priest was killed soon after by falling from a horse" (1984b:12). Ironically, the only priest on record to have died at Holy Rosary after falling from a horse was Father Bosch, the priest to whom John Lone Goose attributed much of Black Elk's instruction. Furthermore, Father Bosch died five months after the injury was sustained (although dying five months after the alleged incident perhaps may be considered "soon" when dealing with retributive religious justice). Disparate recollections of people and events possibly became misconstrued or reinterpreted either by Lucy or John or were somewhere mangled within the flow from the holy man, through his interpreter-son Ben, to Neihardt's notes many decades after the fact.

13. *IS* is the abbreviation for the *Indian Sentinel,* the "Official Organ of the Catholic Indian Missions," published out of Washington, D.C., and now no longer produced.

chapter four
▼
Catechist

1. DeMallie states that Black Elk missed the annual congress in 1931 because it coincided with the last two days of Neihardt's visit; the senior catechist's absence from the event was "no doubt conspicuous" (1984b:46). With the rest of his family at the congress, Black Elk probably attended the final day, once Ben bid farewell to the Neihardts (48). Whether he did or not, one's absence on such occasions was, in fact, not out of the ordinary.

2. Chapter 1 noted the importance among the Lakota of establishing kin. The Catholic terminology here represents a convergence of cultural systems that aided rapport. Lucy mentioned that her father called Lindebner not only "short Father" but also "little brother," an affective term for the man with whom he worked so closely.

3. I did hear about Black Fox later on from one elderly Manderson resident who claimed Black Fox was gifted in (among other things) telling the exact age of any stranger.

4. References to "prayer" by Lakota speakers can be ambiguous, since the same word refers both to an individual's prayers and to one's denominational affiliation.

5. A distant, aged relative of Black Elk's recalled that at one time "Nick

had fifty head of cattle." In fact, before the First World War, Lakota cattle-raising was quite successful, making the allotment of rations almost unnecessary.

6. The early Jesuits of both missions were predominantly German born, as reflected in this regular menu item. Black Elk's receptivity of the German Jesuits may very well have been aided by his familiarity with Germany itself, a country he visited while in Buffalo Bill's Wild West Show.

7. Bible passages and hymns were translated into Lakota by early missionaries, and Lucy's reference is to such a collection. Stephen R. Riggs of the Congregational church was a missionary of forty-two years among the Lakota who compiled a text of the Bible, hymns, and other literature in the Lakota dialect before his death in 1882. Further linguistic work was done by Franz Boas and Ella Deloria. Before these labors, Lakota had been an unwritten language.

8. The papal letter of May 15, 1956, "Haurietis Aquas," encouraged Catholics to maintain the traditional devotion to the "Sacred Heart of Jesus," and Lucy had been trained from early childhood to recite certain prayers associated with what this was intended to symbolize, namely, Christian love. Theresa Martin (1873–97), known to Catholics as "the Little Flower of Jesus," was a Carmelite nun recognized by the church as a saint in 1925. Devotion to her was particularly strong in Catholic circles during the time Nick Jr. was ill.

9. Waking up his wife in the middle of the night by pretending to look blindly in another direction might have been Black Elk's way of encouraging her to leave a light on.

chapter five
▼
Missionary

1. Lucy's reference is to the Native American Church; cf. La Barre 1969.

2. Black Elk's children Agatha and Mary died at the same time.

3. DeMallie (1984b:38) notes that Father Buechel denounced the Rabbit Dance at the 1929 Congress (the priest reportedly said it was one of the "chief evils threatening the family"). Not to be construed as caricature, Buechel's comments were part of a larger address entitled "What Must Be Done to Preserve the Indian Race?" The breakup of family life was the theme of his presentation, and among the chief evils contributing to this were the dance, "hasty marriages and the spirit of idleness among the young people" (*IS* 1929:151–52). Father Buechel left "the solution of the problem . . . entirely to the Indians." DeMallie noted that the Oglalas seemed to have agreed with Buechel, as they pledged to abstain from the

dance (Black Elk was one of the delegates). Interestingly, DeMallie's report on the Neihardt visit cites the occurrence of a Rabbit Dance! The catechist was a kind of cohost for the poet's entourage, but his precise role in orchestrating the visit is not clear. Neihardt's correspondence with government officials suggests, however, that this particular celebration was not Black Elk's idea (DeMallie 1984b:38–39).

4. The customary procedure at funerals is to wake the deceased at a meeting hall or a church for at least a night, with mourners present throughout the time until after burial, whereupon a "feed" is held for all present.

5. This type of exchange was perhaps cited in the pamphlet because of its apologetic content, as it shows Black Elk refuting the Protestant fundamentalist critique of Marian devotions among Catholics. This type of doctrinal conflict accompanied denominational presence among Indian peoples, who in turn were schooled to defend their new affiliation.

6. Father Perrig's diary entry of December 15, 1908, also notes that "James Grass and Nick Black Elk, who had gone to convert the Winnebagoes, returned after having achieved nothing."

7. In the Neihardt transcripts, Black Elk claims to have started the wearing of ghost shirts, but this practice is not confirmed in other documents of the period (DeMallie 1984b:262).

8. St. Peter's Church is thirteen miles north of present-day Manderson.

chapter six
▼
Life Story

1. The priest's diary reports the following curious exchange: "Black Elk asked F. Sialm: 'Do you understand the Indians?' Father answered with the question 'Do you, being an Indian yourself, do you understand them?' He said: 'No.'"

2. Forty years after Sialm stated this objection, McCluskey reported Neihardt as saying that the final three paragraphs of the book were what Black Elk "would have said if he had been able" (1979:232). Holler disagrees with Neihardt's opinion that these most-quoted passages of the work reflected the holy-man's thought (1984:36–37).

3. This letter may be the addition Lucy said her father gave Neihardt (see chapter 2).

4. Personal communication from both Brown and Catches.

5. An oblique reference to his children's discord is made when recounting his involvement in the Ghost Dance and in Wounded Knee: "At this time I had no children and maybe if I had been killed then I would have been better off" (DeMallie 1984b:275). Without the background provided here, readers would not understand why Black Elk offered this reflection.

6. See "Re: Nick Black Elk as 'veteran catechist'; 'Feast of Christ the King,' 1937, (appeal letters written by Joseph A. Zimmerman, S.J.)." In this same material, Zimmerman reports Black Elk's writing letters in 1934 that were related to the Neihardt material: "after the book was published he made in English and in Sioux formal statements of his Catholic faith signing them before witnesses" (MACIM).

7. Bones figure prominently in Lakota mythology, particularly within the story that relates the coming of the Sacred Pipe, wherein a character is reduced to skeletal remains for pursuing a self-centered course of action (Brown 1953:3–4). Melody suggests the meaning here is that "the life of [egocentric] gratification is itself that of bones" (1980:12). It is not surprising that Black Elk drew upon this conventional metaphor to illustrate a morality that was thematic in his life both before and after his conversion.

chapter seven
▼
Sacred Visions

1. Joining the litany of works related to the vision are *Keepers of the Fire: Journey to the Tree of Life, Based on Black Elk's Vision* (Eagle Walking Turtle 1989) and Time-Life Books, which featured the vision in a special series of works dealing with mysticism and the occult (1989).

2. Goll's black road ending in hell is green on some maps. John Lone Goose refers, like Goll, to a black road, whereas Lucy reported the map as having red and yellow roads. Different versions existed (the one pictured here, printed in India, was one of the standards employed at Pine Ridge).

3. These catechetical instruments are, in the literature, sometimes called ladders (Hanley 1965; Pipes 1936:237–40; Prucha 1988:130–37). Some were more crudely drawn than the ones used at Pine Ridge, and some were decidedly sectarian in their portrayal of Christian history.

4. Although colors carried conventional associations, latitude did exist for individual usage (i.e., colors could be multivocal). What they denoted often depended upon context—and the practitioner's inspiration. Additionally, it is not uncommon to hear Indian religious leaders today refer to the colors yellow, black, red, and white as representing the four "races" of humanity, which is often said to be a traditional association.

5. In an interview shortly before his death, Neihardt was asked if Black Elk's Catholicism "colored his thinking." His response: "It might have, here and there in spots, but fundamentally no" (taped interview of F. W. Thomsen with John Neihardt, Dana College, Blair, Nebraska).

6. This quotation may have been composed entirely by Neihardt, as it does not appear in the stenographic record. However, DeMallie mentions that some material is simply unable to be located (1984b:346n). Within

the fieldwork setting, one often learns about matters in casual conversations, or through offhand remarks, and must rely on memory of the details discussed when sitting down to write. Because of the correspondence of the above quotation with Black Elk's experience, something of this nature may well have transpired.

7. For Black Elk's description of the Sun Dance, see Brown (1953:67–100). See also Leslie Spier (1921:451–527) for a cross-cultural analysis of this ritual. Until his death, Lucy's husband was one of the men responsible for finding and setting up a cottonwood tree for use in the yearly Sun Dance at Pine Ridge.

8. Before her death in 1936, Martha Bad Warrior, a ninety-nine-year-old keeper of the pipe and relative of Elk Head's, provided privileged information to Wilbur Riegert concerning the pipe. His account of this meeting was published posthumously in 1975 in Rapid City, South Dakota.

9. Green Grass, South Dakota, is a secluded community on the Cheyenne River Reservation, home of the Miniconju branch of western Lakota and the place where the original sacred pipe is kept (Steltenkamp 1982:38–49).

10. Iktomi is the spider, the trickster character of the Lakota.

11. Sung to the tune of the more traditional Christian hymn "Praise God from Whom All Blessings Flow," *Jesus Cante* (Heart of Jesus) is still popular among older Lakota Catholics.

12. Pine Ridge became a reservation in 1878 and was administered by the Episcopalian church, who established its mission in 1875 through the Grant administration's "Peace Policy." Lakota requests for "Blackrobes" were finally approved, and so the Jesuits arrived in 1888.

13. Regarding the loss of these children, Lucy said: "I felt bad for a long time, but Father Zimmerman was right there to comfort me. I always thought, 'God wants them. God took them.' He loved them so much that he didn't want them to go through what's coming in the future."

14. Leo died on November 21, 1974.

chapter eight
▼
Elder

1. Lucy also mentioned that her father "even owned a race horse at one time called 'Button.' He ran quarter mile. Later, he used him [as] a workhorse."

2. DeMallie says Black Elk started work for the pageant (begun in 1927) in 1935 or earlier (1984b:63).

3. John Gutzon de la Mothe Borglum (1867–1941) was the chief sculptor at Mount Rushmore.

4. Although Lucy said that the prayer he used for averting bad weather

was in his prayer book ("it means the same thing . . . that prayer is in the prayer book"), she may have meant the "sacramentary" text used at Catholic liturgies (which contains prayers for favorable weather). Weather control is reported elsewhere in North America as part of the shamanic vocation. See Landes 1971:134.

5. Leo was still alive at the time this interview took place, and Lucy's reference is to him. His mood was not pleasant that particular day.

6. This is a translation of the prayer Lucy uttered from memory in Lakota.

7. Norma Regina Looks Twice, granddaughter of Black Elk, died in the fall of 1978.

8. The store referred to here is just a short distance from the church—an indication of how slowly the two men must have walked (since the rosary prayers take some time to recite).

9. Powers stated in his study of *yuwipi* that "no one wearing a [Catholic] medal would be permitted to stay in the meeting. One man had a rosary in his pocket but was afraid to say so. Soon something in the darkness picked him up and threw him out the window" (1982:54). Ben Marrowbone said that *yuwipi* practitioners did not want "holy pictures" around because they were afraid of them. Different approaches to these types of ceremony seem to exist, given Little Warrior's use of such objects. The argument could be made that Little Warrior did not, strictly speaking, conduct a *yuwipi* practice. Steinmetz, however, classifies him as *yuwipi* (1990:26).

10. An annual tourist event held in the Black Hills town of Custer, South Dakota.

chapter nine
▼
Farewell

1. This celestial occurrence might have been the Perseid meteor shower, the most active and most visible of such phenomena in recent history.

2. Miller suggested that Black Elk's birth was even earlier than 1862 (1957:185), while his tombstone reads 1858.

3. Brother Siehr died in the spring of 1990 at Holy Rosary Mission.

4. John died November 23, 1975, and was buried at Manderson.

5. Cf. Brown 1953:10-30.

6. The Catholic church at Wounded Knee was one of the buildings occupied and considerably damaged, along with its contents. Occupation supporters regarded its ruin as legitimate symbolic protest, while Lucy regarded it as desecration, both of a religious place and of her father's memory.

chapter ten
▼
Evaluations

1. Ironically, when first published, neither *Black Elk Speaks* nor *The Sacred Pipe* attracted much attention.

2. Other Native groups also grapple with this issue, and Black Elk's image often has been enlisted to aid their effort. For example, Omaha spiritual leader Joe Kemp said that "Black Elk was a sacred man to whom *Indians* turned in time of need" (italics added). He offered this reflection to an audience at the ground-breaking ceremony for a Black Elk monument in Blair, Nebraska.

3. This sentimentality may be comparable to political rhetoric that invokes an idealized "spirit of democracy" existing among the nation's Founding Fathers.

4. One shortcoming with this approach is pointed out by Beatrice Medicine (1983:267–77). At Wounded Knee, a spokesman for the American Indian Movement said AIM was "a new warrior society," and this label was destined to capture imaginations. In rhetoric still fashionable among some Indian groups, he said that "white persons" conceive of warriors as the "armed forces . . . hired killers," but Indian people have "men and women of the nation who have dedicated themselves to give everything that they have to the people. A warrior should be the first one to go hungry or the last one to eat . . . the first one to give away his moccasins and the last one to get new ones. That type of feeling among Indian people is what a warrior society is all about. He is ready to defend his family in time of war—to hold off any enemy, and is perfectly willing to sacrifice himself to the good of his tribe and his people. That's what a warrior society is to Indian people." (*Akwesasne Notes* 1974:61–62).

5. The Mohawk occupation of Oka, Quebec, in 1990 revealed a willingness to continue to employ the militant strategy born at Wounded Knee. One of the keynote speakers at Lake Superior University's Conference on Indian Affairs (1991) proudly reported that fifteen-year-olds also manned the barricades at Oka and were willing to die for the principles championed by some of their elders. The speaker's position was not espoused by all Oka participants, who, as in the case of Wounded Knee, differed on which principles to champion.

Lucy drew upon the warrior metaphor, too, but in a way that conflicts with the earlier stereotype of her father. She said his contemporary message would be "to call the people to religion . . . 'teach your children prayers, see that they go to church; that's the only way—the church and the family . . . to be children of God and soldiers for Christ. You must stand the ground and make the fight.'"

6. Although *The Trial of Billy Jack* carried a disclaimer that its similarity to persons living or dead was purely coincidental, the film did in fact dramatize (with names and places changed) a major incident that led to the occupation of Wounded Knee, namely, the killing of Raymond Yellow Thunder at an American Legion Hall in Gordon, Nebraska. More recent films such as *War Party,* released in 1989, continue this type of characterization with a decidedly militant theme. The youthful protagonists of this modern-day story are encouraged by a religious elder to charge their horses at the trigger-ready National Guard (equivalently to commit suicide). The movie thus concludes with the youths reenacting a Blackfeet attack, in which they died. (Such an attack was perceived as the sole option for Blackfeet, and for like-minded "warriors" of today.) Interestingly, Dennis Banks, a leader of the Wounded Knee occupation, appeared as a character in the film.

7. Social protest in the style of Martin Luther King or Gandhi has not elicited the widespread response that these armed confrontations have garnered, perhaps because of the entrenched warrior stereotyping described here. The "new Indian wars" of recent years, however, have been "fought" by Native people in the courtroom and by those who have assumed decision-making roles in religious, educational, health, and human service fields.

8. Both Indian and African American groups have experienced a loss of ethnic identity, which the "pride in heritage" trend has sought to redress.

9. Deloria's work challenged Christian churches to "inculturate" their religious practices even further. As a result of his critique and that of others, some denominations have been more sensitive to not confusing theological dogma with ascetic and cultural observances from the older tradition.

10. This relative did not wish to be identified in this text for fear of reprisal arising from her comments. A "woman of few words," rugged, and forceful in tone, she digressed little and did not mince her words.

11. *The New Indians,* produced in 1987 by the National Geographic Society. Conference quotations are from this film.

12. DeMallie notes that discussions of this topic usually dissolve "into political rhetoric rather than objective assessment" (1984b:80).

13. The government's 1894 survey of Indians stated that medicine men wielded much influence at Pine Ridge especially.

14. Short Bull was a leading proponent of the Ghost Dance, along with Kicking Bear, his brother-in-law. According to Jesuit tradition, Sword would visit with Father Digmann and discuss theological matters at great length.

15. Sectarian affiliation was not unlike sodality memberships within the older tradition (see chapter 1). In fact, a certain competitiveness, exclu-

sivity, or special identity seems to have been associated with such participation in both the old and the new orders.

16. This same theme is apparent in a study among the modern Tswana of Southern Africa. See Alverson 1978.

17. Bucko indicated that Black Elk's extended reflections on the meanings and symbols of the sweatlodge ritual are the first of any length within the literature. Previous material had "focused on the many pragmatic uses of the sweat lodge." However, after this initial theologizing, subsequent writings have expanded the interpretive script articulated by practitioners and investigators (Bucko 1992:85). Lucy mentioned that Buechel's long-standing relationship with Black Elk included many hours of theological discussion, interaction that perhaps moved Black Elk to emphasize symbolic meanings that earlier accounts did not contain. Codification, or standardization, was more the tradition of his Catholic practice than that of his Lakota heritage (134). Steinmetz mentions that Fools Crow, a practicing Catholic, "formed many of his Lakota Christian beliefs on his own, without the assistance of a Catholic priest" (1990:8). This observation is consistent with information Lucy provided regarding her father's and her own experience.

18. Hultkrantz considers *The Sacred Pipe* "the most widely read work on Plains Indian religion" (Capps 1976:91). As such, it especially needs the caution offered here. An attempt to make Black Elk's thought in *The Sacred Pipe* something that it is not indicts researchers who "treat rites rather like a set of clues or a test to be solved by finding answers that all fit together. . . . as though the cry 'It fits' would convincingly repay the effort and ingenuity" (Lewis 1980:186).

19. MacGregor's reading of the early period would lead one to believe that all missionaries represented a ghoulish presence that attracted no one. (But then we would have to question why so many Lakota were devout participants within the different denominations.) In contrast, Duratschek's work tends to highlight the success of Catholic missionary efforts. One account offsets the other, but the social equation was more complicated than simply an interplay of missionaries and Indians. The reservation system included persons whose interests had nothing to do with, or were at cross-purposes to, the work undertaken by different denominations. The array of profiteers, bootleggers, transient government personnel, and other passersby lent a certain credibility to missionaries who remained over time. That is, their altruistic presence (or just their willingness to live in simplicity among the people), however appreciated, was not so ambiguous.

20. Black Elk himself did not consume alcohol.

21. Fetal alcohol syndrome is referred to here, as it has become a severe problem at Pine Ridge.

22. A similar argument is made for explaining the emergence of the Midé

Society among the Ojibway as a "tool" of adaptation during the historical period (Grim 1983:72–73).

23. Scholarly assessments of, polemics against, and apologias for Christian missionary efforts within Native North America are extensive. For a sampling, see Berkhofer 1965; Bowden 1981; Deloria 1973; Harrod 1971; and Moore 1982.

Bibliography

Akwesasne Notes (Mohawk Nation). 1974. *Voices from Wounded Knee: The People Are Standing Up*. Rooseveltown, N.Y.

Alverson, Hoyt. 1978. *Mind in the Heart of Darkness*. New Haven: Yale University Press.

Anderson, Gary Clayton. 1984. *Kinsmen of Another Kind: Dakota-White Relations in the Upper Mississippi Valley, 1650-1862*. Lincoln: University of Nebraska Press.

Baraga, R. R. 1973. *A Dictionary of the Otchipwe Language*. Minneapolis: Ross & Haines.

Barrett, Richard A. 1984. *Culture and Conduct: An Excursion in Anthropology*. Belmont, Calif.: Wadsworth Publishing.

Barton, Del. 1980. *A Good Day to Die*. New York: Doubleday.

Bataille, Gretchen M. 1984. "Black Elk—New World Prophet." In *A Sender of Words: Essays in Memory of John G. Neihardt*, ed. Vine Deloria, Jr. Salt Lake City: Howe Brothers.

Berger, Thomas. 1964. *Little Big Man*. New York: Dial Press.

Berkhofer, Robert F. 1965. *Salvation and the Savage: An Analysis of Protestant Missions and American Indian Response, 1787-1862*. Lexington: University of Kentucky Press.

———. 1978. *The White Man's Indian: Images of the American Indian from Columbus to the Present*. New York: Alfred A. Knopf.

Bogoras, Waldemar. 1965. "Shamanistic Performance in the Inner

Room." In *Reader in Comparative Religion: An Anthropological Approach*, ed. William A. Lessa and Evon Z. Vogt, 454–60. 2d ed. New York: Harper & Row.

Bourguignon, Erika. 1979. *Psychological Anthropology: An Introduction to Human Nature and Cultural Differences*. New York: Holt, Rinehart & Winston.

Bowden, Henry Warner. 1981. *American Indians and Christian Missions: Studies in Cultural Conflict*. Chicago: University of Chicago Press.

Brown, Dee. 1970. *Bury My Heart at Wounded Knee: An Indian History of the American West*. New York: Holt, Rinehart & Winston.

Brown, Joseph Epes. 1953. *The Sacred Pipe: Black Elk's Account of the Seven Rites of the Oglala Sioux*. Norman: University of Oklahoma Press.

———. 1979. "The Wisdom of the Contrary." *Parabola* 4 (no. 1): 54–65.

Brumble, H. David, III. 1981. *An Annotated Bibliography of American Indian and Eskimo Autobiographies*. Lincoln: University of Nebraska Press.

Bryde, John F. 1966. *The Sioux Indian Student: A Study of Scholastic Failure and Personality Conflict*. Vermillion: University of South Dakota.

Bucko, Raymond A. 1992. "Inipi: Historical Transformation and Contemporary Significance of the Sweat Lodge in Lakota Religious Practice." Ph.D. diss., University of Chicago, Department of Anthropology.

Buechel, Eugene. 1970. *A Dictionary of the Teton Dakota Sioux Language*. Edited by Paul Manhart. Pine Ridge, S.D.: Red Cloud Indian School.

———. 1978. *Lakota Tales and Texts*. Edited by Paul Manhart. Pine Ridge, S.D.: Red Cloud Indian School.

Capps, Walter Holden, ed. 1976. *Seeing with a Native Eye: Essays on Native American Religion*. New York: Harper Forum Books.

Castaneda, Carlos. 1968. *The Teachings of Don Juan: A Yaqui Way of Knowledge*. New York: Ballantine Books.

Catlin, George. 1844. *Letters and Notes on Manners, Customs, and Conditions of the North American Indian*. 4 vols. London: The Author. Reprint. New York: Dover Publications, 1973.

Chittenden, Hiram M., and Alfred T. Richardson. 1905. *Life, Letters, and Travels of Father Pierre Jean De Smet*, S.J. 4 vols. New York.

Clark, R. A. 1976. *The Killing of Chief Crazy Horse*. Lincoln: University of Nebraska Press.

Crapanzano, Vincent. 1977. "On the Writing of Ethnography." *Dialectical Anthropology* 2:69–73.

Dary, David A. 1974. *The Buffalo Book*. New York: Avon Books.

Deloria, Ella. 1944. *Speaking of Indians*. New York: Friendship Press.

―――. N.d. "Teton Myths." American Philosophical Society MS. Franz Boas Collection.

Deloria, Vine, Jr. 1969. *Custer Died for Your Sins*. New York: Macmillan.

―――. 1973. *God Is Red*. New York: Grosset & Dunlap.

―――. 1979. "Introduction," *Black Elk Speaks*. Lincoln: University of Nebraska Press.

DeMallie, Raymond J. 1978. "Pine Ridge Economy: Cultural and Historical Perspectives." In *American Indian Economic Development*, ed. Sam Stanley, 237–312. The Hague: Mouton.

―――. 1979. "Change in American Indian Kinship Systems, the Dakota." In *Currents in Anthropology: Essays in Honor of Sol Tax*, ed. Robert Hinshaw. The Hague: Mouton.

―――. 1984a. "John G. Neihardt's Lakota Legacy." In *A Sender of Words: Essays in Memory of John G. Neihardt*, ed. Vine Deloria, Jr. Salt Lake City: Howe Brothers.

―――. 1984b. *The Sixth Grandfather: Black Elk's Teachings Given to John G. Neihardt*. Lincoln: University of Nebraska Press.

Densmore, Frances. 1970. *Chippewa Customs*. Minneapolis: Ross & Haines.

DeVoto, Bernard, ed. 1953. *The Journals of Lewis and Clark*. Boston: Houghton Mifflin.

Dollard, John. 1935. *Criteria for the Life History*. New Haven: Yale University Press.

Dorsey, James Owen. 1894. *A Study of Siouan Cults*. Eleventh Annual Report of the Bureau of American Ethnology, pp. 351–544.

―――. 1897. *Siouan Sociology*. Fifteenth Annual Report of the Bureau of American Ethnology, pp. 205–44.

Driver, Harold E. 1969. *Indians of North America*. Chicago: University of Chicago Press.

Duesel de la Torriente, Donna. 1982. *Bay Is the Land (to Black Elk)*. Reseda, Calif.: Mojave Books.

Dunsmore, Roger. 1977. "Nickolaus Black Elk: Holy Man in History." *Kuksu: Journal of Backcountry Writing*, no. 6:4–29.

Duratschek, Sister Mary Claudia. 1947. *Crusading along Sioux Trails: A History of the Catholic Indian Missions of South Dakota*. Yankton, S.D.: Grail.

Durkheim, Emile. 1965. *The Elementary Forms of the Religious Life*. New York: Free Press.

Eagle Walking Turtle. 1989. *Keepers of the Fire: Journey to the Tree of Life, Based on Black Elk's Vision*. Santa Fe: Bear & Company Publishing.

Eggan, Fred R. 1966. *The American Indian: Perspectives for the Study of Social Change*. Chicago: Aldine Press.

Erdoes, Richard, and John (Fire) Lame Deer. 1972. *Lame Deer: Seeker of Visions: The Life of a Sioux Medicine Man*. New York: Simon & Schuster.

Erikson, Erik. 1963. *Childhood and Society*. 2d ed. New York: W. W. Norton.

Faulkner, Virginia, and Frederick C. Luebke, eds. 1982. *Vision and Refuge: Essays on the Literature of the Great Plains*. Lincoln: University of Nebraska Press.

Feraca, Stephen E. 1961. "The Yuwipi Cult of the Oglala and Sicangu Teton Sioux." *Plains Anthropologist* 6:155-63.

———. 1962. "The Teton Sioux Eagle Medicine Cult." *American Indian Tradition* 8 (no. 5): 195-96.

Furlong, Jay. 1980. "The Occupation of Wounded Knee, 1973." Master's thesis, University of Oklahoma, Norman.

Gallatin, Albert S. 1836. *A Synopsis of the Indian Tribes within the United States East of the Rocky Mountains, and in the British and Russian Possessions in North America*. Transactions and Collections of the American Antiquarian Society, vol. 2.

Gearing, Fred. 1970. *The Face of the Fox*. Chicago: Aldine Publishing.

Geertz, Clifford. 1968. "Religion as a Cultural System." In *Anthropological Approaches to the Study of Religion*, ed. Michael Banton, 1-46. London: Tavistock.

———. 1973. *The Interpretation of Cultures*. New York: Basic Books.

Gessner, Robert. 1931. *Massacre*. New York: Cape & Smith.

Gill, Sam D. 1982. *Native American Religions: An Introduction*. Belmont, Calif.: Wadsworth Publishing.

Goddard, Ives. 1984. "The Study of Native North American Ethnonymy." In *Native American Naming Systems*, ed. Elizabeth Tooker. American Ethnological Society Proceedings 1980. New York.

Goll, Louis J. 1940. *Jesuit Missions among the Sioux*. St. Francis, S.D.: St. Francis Mission.

Grim, John A. 1983. *The Shaman*. Norman: University of Oklahoma Press.

Grobsmith, Elizabeth S. 1981. *Lakota of the Rosebud: A Contemporary Ethnography*. New York: Holt, Rinehart & Winston.

Hanley, Philip M. 1965. The Catholic Ladder and Missionary Activity in the Pacific Northwest. Master's thesis, University of Ottawa, faculty of Theology.

Harrod, Howard. 1971. *Mission among the Blackfeet*. Norman: University of Oklahoma Press.

Hassrick, Royal B. 1964. *The Sioux: Life and Customs of a Warrior Society*. Norman: University of Oklahoma Press.

Hebard, Grace Raymond, and E. A. Brininstool. 1922. *The Bozeman Trail: Historical Accounts of the Blazing of the Overland Route into the Northwest, and the Fights with Red Cloud's Warriors*. 2 vols. Cleveland: Arthur H. Clark.

Hill, Ruth Beebe. 1979. *Hanta Yo*. New York: Warren Books.

Holler, Clyde. 1984a. "Black Elk's Relationship to Christianity." *American Indian Quarterly*, Winter, 37–49.

————. 1984b. "Lakota Religion and Tragedy: The Theology of *Black Elk Speaks*." *Journal of the American Academy of Religion* 52 (no. 1): 19–45.

Hoover, Herbert T. 1979 *The Sioux: A Critical Bibliography*. Bloomington and London: Indiana University Press.

Howard, James H. 1968. *The Warrior Who Killed Custer: The Personal Narrative of Chief Joseph White Bull*. Lincoln: University of Nebraska Press.

Hunt, George T. 1967. *The Wars of the Iroquois: A Study in Intertribal Trade Relations*. Madison: University of Wisconsin Press.

Hyde, George E. 1937. *Red Cloud's Folk: A History of the Oglala Sioux Indians*. Norman: University of Oklahoma Press.

————. 1961. *Spotted Tail's Folk: A History of the Brulé Sioux*. Norman: University of Oklahoma Press.

Hyers, M. Conrad. 1969. *Holy Laughter: Essays on Religion in the Comic Perspective*. New York: Seabury Press.

James, William. 1961. *The Varieties of Religious Experience: A Study in Human Nature*. New York: Macmillian.

Jeltz, Patsy. 1991. "Elder Pete Catches Shares Wisdom." *Lakota Times*, July 24, B1.

Jung, C. G. 1970. *Mysterium Conjunctionis*. Princeton, N.J.: Princeton University Press.

Kardiner, Abram. 1945. *The Psychological Frontiers of Society*. New York: Columbia University Press.

Kehoe, Alice Beck. 1989. *The Ghost Dance, Ethnohistory and Revitalization*. New York: Holt, Rinehart & Winston.

Kemnitzer, Luis. 1969. "Yuwipi." *Pine Ridge Research Bulletin*, no. 10:26–33.

————. 1970. "Cultural Provenience of Objects Used in Yuwipi: A Modern Teton Dakota Healing Ritual." *Ethnos* 35:40–75.

Kenton, Edna. 1954. *The Jesuit Relations and Allied Documents*. New York: Vanguard Press.

Kluckhohn, Clyde. 1945. "The Personal Document in Anthropological Science." In *The Use of Personal Documents in History, Anthropology, and Sociology,* p. 29. Social Science Research Council, Bulletin 53. New York.

Kroeber, Karl. 1983. "Reasoning Together." In *Smoothing the Ground: Essays on Native American Oral Literature,* ed. Brian Swann, 347–64. Berkeley: University of California Press.

Krupat, Arnold. 1981. "The Indian Autobiography: Origins, Type, and Function." *American Literature* 53 (no. 1): 22–42.

La Barre, Weston. 1969. *The Peyote Cult.* New York: Schocken Books.

Lame Deer, John. 1972. *Lame Deer, Seeker of Visions.* New York: Simon & Schuster.

Landes, Ruth. 1971. *The Ojibwa Woman.* W. W. Norton.

Langness, L. L. 1965. *The Life History in Anthropological Science.* New York: Holt.

Langness, L. L., and Gelya Frank. 1981. *Lives: An Anthropological Approach to Biography.* Novato, Calif.: Chandler & Sharp, Publishers.

Lehmer, Donald J. 1977. "Selected Writings of Donald J. Lehmer." In *Reprints in Anthropology,* vol. 3. Lincoln, Nebr.

Lévi-Strauss, Claude. 1969. *The Elementary Structures of Kinship.* Boston: Beacon Press.

Lewis, Gilbert. 1980. *Day of Shining Red.* New York: Cambridge University Press.

Lewis, Thomas. 1970. "Notes on the Heyoka: The Teton Dakota 'Contrary' Cult." *Pine Ridge Research Bulletin,* no. 11:7–19.

Lincoln, Kenneth. 1983. "Native American Literatures," In *Smoothing the Ground: Essays on Native American Oral Literature,* ed. Brian Swann. Berkeley: University of California Press.

Linden, George W. 1983. "Black Elk Speaks as a Failure Narrative." Dakota History Conference.

Linden, George W., and Fred W. Robbins. 1982. "Mystic Medicine: Black Elk's First Cure." Dakota History Conference.

Linderman, Frank B. 1962. *Plenty-Coups: Chief of the Crows.* Lincoln: University of Nebraska Press.

Linton, Ralph. 1943. "Nativistic Movements." *American Anthropologist* 45:230–40.

Little Thunder, Jake. N.d. *Tiospaye.* Curriculum Materials Resource Unit, Oglala Sioux Culture Center, Red Cloud Indian School, Pine Ridge, S.D., in cooperation with Black Hills State College, Spearfish, S.D.

Lowie, Robert. 1948. *Social Organization.* New York: Rinehart.

———. 1963. *Indians of the Plains.* American Museum of Natural History. Garden City, N.Y.: Natural History Press.

Lynn, Dennis, and Matthew Lynn. 1974. *Healing of Memories.* Ramsey, N.J.: Paulist Press.

Lyon, William, and Wallace Black Elk. 1990. *Black Elk*. New York: Harper & Row.

McClusky, Sally. 1979. "Black Elk Speaks and So Does John Neihardt." *Western American Literature* 6:231–42.

MacGregor, Gordon. 1946. *Warriors without Weapons*. Chicago: University of Chicago Press.

McGregor, James H. 1940. *The Wounded Knee Massacre from the Viewpoint of the Sioux*. Baltimore: Wirth Brothers.

Mails, Thomas E., and Dallas Chief Eagle. 1979. *Fools Crow*. Garden City, N.Y.: Doubleday.

Marty, Martin. 1970. *Righteous Empire: The Protestant Experience in America*. New York: Dial Press.

Maynard, Eileen, and Gayla Twiss. 1969. *That These People May Live: Conditions among the Oglala Sioux of the Pine Ridge Reservation*. Community Mental Health Program, Pine Ridge Service Unit, Aberdeen Area, Indian Health Service, Pine Ridge, S.D.

Medicine, Bea[trice]. 1969. "The Changing Dakota Family." *Pine Ridge Research Bulletin*, no. 9 (June): 1–20.

———. 1983. "Warrior Women: Sex Role Alternatives for Plains Indian Women." In *The Hidden Half: Studies of Plains Indian Women*, ed. Patricia Albers and Beatrice Medicine, 267–77. Lanham, Md.: University Press of America.

Mekeel, Scudder. 1935. *The Economy of a Modern Teton Dakota Community*. New Haven: Yale University Press.

Melody, Michael E. 1980. "Lakota Myth and Government: The Cosmos as the State." *American Indian Culture and Research Journal* 4 (no.3 3): 1–19.

Miller, David Humphreys. 1957. *Custer's Fall*. New York: Bantam Book.

———. 1959. *Ghost Dance*. New York: Duell, Sloan, & Pearce.

Milligan, Edward A. 1973. *Wounded Knee 1973 and the Fort Laramie Treaty of 1868*. Bottineau, N.D.: Bottineau Courant Print.

Mirsky, Jeannette. 1966. "The Dakota." In *Cooperation and Competition among Primitive Peoples*, ed. Margaret Mead, 382–427, rev. ed. Boston: Beacon.

Momaday, N. Scott. 1984. "To Save a Great Vision." In *A Sender of Words: Essays in Memory of John G. Neihardt*, ed. Vine Deloria, Jr., 30–38, Salt Lake City: Howe Brothers.

Moon, William Least Heat. 1982. *Blue Highways: A Journey into America*. New York: Fawcett Crest.

Mooney, James. 1896. *The Ghost-Dance Religion and the Sioux Outbreak of 1890*. Smithsonian Institution, Bureau of American Ethnology, Annual Report, 14, pt. 2. Washington, D.C.

————. 1907. *The Cheyenne Indians*. Memoirs of the American Anthropological Association, vol. 1, pt. 6, pp. 357–442.

Moore, James T. 1982. *Indian and Jesuit: A Seventeenth-Century Encounter*. Chicago: Loyola University Press.

Morgan, Lewis Henry. 1962. *League of the Iroquois*. Secaucus, N.J.: Citadel Press.

Nabokov, Peter. 1967. *Two Leggings: The Making of a Crow Warrior*. New York: Thomas Y. Crowell.

Neihardt, John G. 1972. *Black Elk Speaks: Being the Life Story of a Holy Man of the Oglala Sioux*. New York: Pocket Book Edition.

————. N.d. Ms. fieldnotes for *Black Elk Speaks*. Columbia: University of Missouri Library.

Newcomb, W. W. 1950. "A Re-Examination of the Causes of Plains Warfare." *American Anthropologist* 52 (July–September): 317–30.

Nichols, William. 1983. "Black Elk's Truth." In *Smoothing the Ground: Essays on Native American Oral Literature*, ed. Brian Swann, 334–43. Berkeley: University of California Press.

Nurge, Ethel, ed. 1970. *The Modern Sioux: Social Systems and Reservation Culture*. Lincoln: University of Nebraska Press.

Obrian, Lynn Woods. 1973. *Plains Indian Autobiographies*. Boise State College Western Writers Series, 10. Boise, Idaho: Boise State College.

Oliver, Symmes C. 1962. *Ecology and Cultural Continuity as Contributing Factors in the Social Organization of the Plains Indians*. University of California Publications in American Archeology and Ethnology, vol. 48, no. 1.

Olson, James C. 1965. *Red Cloud and the Sioux Problem*. Lincoln: University of Nebraska Press. See pp. 71–87.

One Feather, Gerald. N.d. *Lakota Wohilikeequapi*. Curriculum Materials Resource Unit, Oglala Sioux Culture Center, Red Cloud Indian School, Pine Ridge, S.D., in cooperation with Black Hills State College, Spearfish, S.D.

Overholt, Thomas W. 1978. "Short Bull, Black Elk, Sword, and the 'Meaning' of the Ghost Dance." In *Religion*, 171–95. Lancaster, Pa.

Parkman, Francis. 1950. *The Oregon Trail*. New York: Signet Classic.

Parssinen, Carol Ann. 1974. "In Pursuit of Ethnography: The Seduction of Science by Art." University of Pennsylvania, Center for Urban Ethnography, Manuscript.

————. 1975. "Paradigms of Ethnographic Realism." Selected Proceedings of the 1975 Conference on Culture and Communication, Working Papers in Culture and Communication, 1:1. Philadelphia: Temple University.

Pearce, Roy Harvey. 1965. *Savagism and Civilization: A Study of the*

Indian and the American Mind. Baltimore: Johns Hopkins University Press.

Perrin, Norman. 1974. *The New Testament: An Introduction*. New York: Harcourt Brace Jovanovich.

Pipes, Nellie B. 1936. "The Protestant Ladder." In *Oregon Historical Quarterly* 37 (September): 237–40.

Powers, William K. 1975. *Oglala Religion*. Lincoln: University of Nebraska Press.

———. 1982. *Yuwipi: Vision and Experience in Oglala Ritual*. Lincoln: University of Nebraska Press.

———. 1990. "When Black Elk Speaks, Everybody Listens." In *Religion in Native North America*, ed. Christopher Vecsey, 135–51. Moscow: University of Idaho Press.

Powers, William K., and Marla N. Powers, 1986. "Putting on the Dog." *Natural History* 95 (no. 2): 6–16.

Proudfoot, Wayne. 1985. *Religious Experience*. Berkeley: University of California Press.

Prucha, Francis Paul. 1988. "Two Roads to Conversion: Protestant and Catholic Missionaries in the Pacific Northwest." *Pacific Northwest Quarterly* 79 (no. 4): 130–37.

Puhl, Louis J. 1963. *The Spiritual Exercises of St. Ignatius*. Westminster, Md.: Newman Press.

Radin, Paul. 1971. *The Trickster: A Study in American Indian Mythology*. New York: Schocken Books.

Rice, Julian. 1991. *Black Elk's Story*. Albuquerque: University of New Mexico Press.

Riegert, Wilbur A. 1975. *Quest for the Pipe of the Sioux*. Rapid City, S.D.

Riggs, Stephen. 1977. *Dakota Grammar, Texts, and Ethnography*. Dept. of the Interior, U.S. Geographical Survey of the Rocky Mountain Region. Reprint. Marvin, S.D.: Blue Cloud Abbey.

Rousseau, Jean-Jacques. 1964. *The First and Second Discourses*. New York: St. Martins Press.

Ruby, Robert H. 1955. *Oglala Sioux*. New York: Vantage Press.

———. 1970. "Yuwipi, Ancient Rite of the Sioux." *Pine Ridge Research Bulletin*, no. 11:20–30.

Sandoz, Mari. 1942. *Crazy Horse: The Strange Man of the Oglalas. A Biography*. Lincoln: University of Nebraska Press.

———. 1961. *These Were the Sioux*. New York: Dell.

Schwarz, O. Douglas. 1981. *Plains Indian Theology: As Expressed in Myth and Ritual and in the Ethics of the Culture*. Ann Arbor, Mich.: University Microfilms International.

Seward, G. 1956. *Psychotherapy and Culture Conflict*. New York: Ronald Press.

Sialm, Placidus. N.d. "Diary." Bureau of Catholic Indian Mission Archives at Marquette University, Milwaukee.

Spier, Leslie. 1921. "The Sun Dance of the Plains Indians: Its Development and Diffusion." *Anthropological Papers of the American Museum of Natural History*, pp. 451–527.

Starkloff, Carl. 1974. *The People of the Center: American Indian Religion and Christianity*. New York: Seabury Press.

Stauffer, Helen. 1981. "Two Authors and a Hero: Neihardt, Sandoz, and Crazy Horse," *Great Plains Quarterly*, Winter, 34–66.

Stedman, Raymond William. 1982. *Shadows of the Indian: Stereotypes in American Culture*. Norman: University of Oklahoma Press.

Steinmetz, Paul B. 1980. *Pipe, Bible, and Peyote among the Oglala Lakota*. Stockholm Studies in Comparative Religion 19. Sweden: Motala. Reprint. Knoxville: University of Tennessee Press, 1990.

Steltenkamp, Michael F. 1982. *The Sacred Vision: Native American Religion and Its Practice Today*. Ramsey, N.J.: Paulist Press.

Stolzman, William. 1974. *Cannunpa Kin: The Pipe, a Position Paper for Common Understanding of Medicine Men and Catholic Pastors*. 3d rev. St. Francis, S.D.

———. 1986. *The Pipe and Christ*. Pine Ridge, S.D.: Red Cloud Indian School.

Talbert, Bob. 1986. "Quotebag." *Detroit Free Press*, June 28.

Taylor, Allan R. 1975. "The Colorado University System for Writing the Lakhota Language." *American Indian Culture and Research Journal* 1:3–12.

Tedlock, Dennis, and Barbara Tedlock. 1975. *Teachings from the American Earth: Indian Religion and Philosophy*. New York: Liveright.

Terrell, John Upton. 1979. *The Arrow and the Cross: A History of the American Indian and the Missionaries*. Santa Barbara, Calif.: Capra Press.

Thwaites, Reuben Gold, ed. 1896. *The Jesuit Relations and Allied Documents: Travels and Exploration of the Jesuit Missionaries in New France, 1610–1791*. 73 vols. Cleveland: Burrows Brs.

Twiss, Gayla, and Eileen Maynard. 1969. *That These People May Live: Conditions among the Oglala Sioux of the Pine Ridge Reservation*. Community Mental Health Program, U.S. Public Health Services, Pine Ridge, S.D.

Two Bulls, Moses. N.d. *Itancan*. Curriculum Materials Resource Unit, Oglala Sioux Culture Center, Red Cloud Indian School, Pine Ridge, S.D. in cooperation with Black Hills State College, Spearfish, S.D.

Utley, Robert M. 1963. *The Last Days of the Sioux Nation*. New Haven: Yale University Press.

Vestal, Stanley. 1932. *Sitting Bull: Champion of the Sioux*. Boston: Houghton Mifflin.

Vogel, Virgil J. 1970. *American Indian Medicine*. Norman: University of Oklahoma Press.

Walker, James R. 1917. "The Sun Dance and Other Ceremonies of the Oglala Division of the Teton Dakota." In American Museum of Natural History, *Anthropological Papers* 16, pt. 2, pp. 50–221. New York.

———. 1980. *Lakota Belief and Ritual*. Edited by Raymond J. DeMallie and Elaine A. Jahner. Lincoln: University of Nebraska Press.

———. 1982. *Lakota Society*. Edited by Raymond J. DeMallie. Lincoln: University of Nebraska Press.

———. 1983. *Lakota Myth*. Edited by Elaine A. Jahner. Lincoln: University of Nebraska Press.

Wallace, Anthony F. C. 1966. *Religion: An Anthropological View*. New York: Random House.

———. 1969. *The Death and Rebirth of the Seneca*. New York: Vantage Books.

Wallis, Wilson D. 1919. *Sun Dance of the Canadian Dakota*. Anthropological Papers of the American Museum of Natural History, vol. 16, Personal Narratives, pp. 317–81. New York: The Trustees.

Waters, Frank. 1984. "Neihardt and the Vision of Black Elk." In *A Sender of Words: Essays in Memory of John G. Neihardt,* ed. Vine Deloria, Jr. Salt Lake City: Howe Brothers.

Willoya, William, and Vinson Brown. 1962. *Warriors of the Rainbow: Strange and Prophetic Dreams of the Indian Peoples*. Healdsburg, Calif.: Naturegraph.

Wind River Rendezvous. 1983. "The Buffalo Culture of the Plains Indians." vol. 13, (April–June) St. Stephens, Wyo.: St. Stephen's Indian Mission Foundation.

Wissler, Clark. 1912. "Societies and Ceremonial Associations in the Oglala Division of the Teton-Dakota." American Museum of Natural History, *Anthropological Papers* 2, pt. 1, pp. 1–99. New York.

Zimmerly, David. 1969. "On Being an Ascetic: Personal Document of a Sioux Medicine Man." *Pine Ridge Research Bulletin*, no. 10:46–69.

Zimmerman, Bill. 1975. *Airlift to Wounded Knee*. Chicago: Swallow Press.

▼

▼

Index